Organization Behaviour for Leisure Services

Organization Behaviour for Leisure Services

Conrad Lashley and Darren Lee-Ross

ELSEVIER
BUTTERWORTH
HEINEMANN

AMSTERDAM BOSTON HEIDELBERG LONDON NEW YORK OXFORD
PARIS   SAN DIEGO SAN FRANCISCO SINGAPORE SYDNEY TOKYO

Elsevier Butterworth-Heinemann
Linacre House, Jordan Hill. Oxford OX2 8DP
200 Wheeler Road, Burlington MA 01803

First published 2003
Reprinted 2003

British Library Cataloguing in Publication Data
A catalogue record for this book is available from the British Library

Library of Congress Cataloguing in Publication Data
A catalogue record for this book is available from the Library of Congress

ISBN 0 7506 5782 0

For information on all Butterworth-Heinemann publications visit our website
at www.bh.com

Printed and bound in Great Britain by Martins the Printers

Contents

List of figures

List of tables

Acknowledgements

Our attempts to produce a text that addresses the study needs of potential readers have been greatly helped by a number of volunteers who have taken the time to read sample chapters and provide feedback. Their suggestions, comments and encouragement were very welcome and much appreciated. The individuals are Natalie Toms, Ruby Kitchen and Paul Hardy in the School of Tourism and Hospitality Management at Leeds Metropolitan University, and Craig West, Fiona Shaw and Alison Carisbrook in the Nottingham Business School at Nottingham Trent University.

Introduction

- understand hospitality, leisure and tourism services
- recognize the similarities and differences faced by leisure service providers
- show how the study of organizational behaviour (OB) is shaped by the nature of leisure services
- understand the structure of this book and the approach taken to the study of organizational behaviour in leisure services.

Understanding leisure

Leisure is an increasingly important economic activity in mature service economies. Leisure, is described by the *Collins English Dictionary* as, 'an opportunity for ease and relaxation', and therefore implies non-work time. The *Oxford English Dictionary* defines leisure as 'The state of having time at one's disposal, free unoccupied time'. Indeed, the origin of the word is rooted in the Latin word *licere*, 'to be allowed'. In its broadest sense leisure encompasses all those waking activities that are not work activities. Leisure services, however, describe services provided by various organizations to occupy leisure time. For the purposes of this book these leisure services are usually experienced out of the home, though there are some overlaps. Typically we include:

- eating and drinking out
- staying away from home
- travel involving visits to leisure locations
- visiting places involving travel from home
- participating in and watching sporting activities
- attending theatrical and other cultural occasions
- shopping as a leisure activity.

These activities are a major aspect of the global economy. The International Labour Organization's (ILO's) report for 2001 in its survey of global provision, referred collectively to some of these sectors as 'Hotel, Catering and Tourism Sector'. It defined the sector as incorporating a full array of establishments providing food, drink and accommodation, at work and in an array of institutions, travel and tourism, as well as conference and exhibition activities (ILO, 2001: 5). The report estimated the world value of these industries to be US$3.575 billion, and employment internationally to be over 100 million people. Though it varies between countries and regions, the overall picture is one of 2–3 per cent annual growth across the globe. This text recognizes the key similarity and differences between the organizations supplying leisure services and will provide insights into some problems specific to the sector.

Leisure services are difficult to define because of the overlapping nature of the activities under discussion. There are many disagreements about how leisure, hospitality and tourism activities relate to each other. Nationally and internationally there is evidence of academics, industrialists and policy-makers using the same terms to describe these activities in ways that lack precision and often contradict each other. This text provides a working model that assists understanding of how the activities relate to each other, though the authors do recognize that there are some difficulties and problems. Figure I1.1 suggests that one way of bringing them together through leisure services as a starting point.

If leisure time is defined as non-work time spent following an interest or activity, then we describe *leisure services* as 'services provided by leisure service organizations to occupy leisure time'. We do, however, recognize that hospitality, leisure and tourism services describe slightly different uses of leisure time and organizations providing these services display both similarities and differences. The following will attempt to draw on these similarities where appropriate. It is also important to recognize that, although our text is chiefly concerned with *leisure service organizations*, leisure activities also take place in the home.

LEISURE SERVICE ORGANIZATIONS		
Hospitality	**Recreational leisure**	**Tourism**
Hotels, timeshare, serviced and non-serviced accommodation Restaurants and cafés Bars, pubs and nightclubs	Museums, theatre, cinema, family entertainment centre, and concert activities Gaming, bingo, tenpin bowling, sports, recreational, golf, spas and health activities Arcades and retail shopping	Travel agencies and tour operators Airlines, bus companies and train companies Attractions and theme parks, resorts Conference and event venues

Figure I1.1 Leisure retail services

Customers' expectations of leisure service organizations are frequently shaped by their experiences in the home. Expectations of host and guest relationships in restaurants, bars and hotels are an example here.

Figure I1.1 suggests that hospitality activities – eating and/or drinking and/or staying away from home are a significant element of leisure activities. That said, hospitality is not tourism. People who go out to drink in bars and eat in restaurants are not all tourists. Yet travel away from home, and tourism, will frequently involve eating and drinking and staying away from home; tourism involves more activities than eating away from home. Similarly, tourists often travel for leisure and recreational purposes to visit museums, sports venues or shopping venues. Organizations in the sector are increasingly overlapping in the service they offer customers. Many hotels now offer health and leisure facilities. Pubs and bars offer increasingly sophisticated food menus. Most leisure facilities and museums have restaurants and bars, and tour operators package hotel accommodation with visits to museums, galleries and other recreational interests.

In this book we therefore define leisure services as services associated with provision that is linked with leisure time activity and recreation. However, some of the activities that involve hospitality and tourism overlap with work-motivated activities. Business lunches, business trips and conference attendance all may involve organizations providing food and/or drink and/or accommodation away from the workplace, but are associated with work activities. They also use these leisure venues as a recreational device for improving work effectiveness and business relationships.

To some extent these tensions and inconsistencies in our definition are explained through the recognition that the organizations concerned are largely providing services with some common features that give them a coherence of similarity. In particular we can say that:

- these are all service organizations
- frequently these organizations are managing tensions between different stake-holders
- frontline staff play a key role in delivering the service to customers
- customers receive the service by attending the service provider's premises
- frequently production and consumption of service occur on the provider's premises
- premises mostly are located close to customers or where customers want to be
- a growing number of these service organizations supply services through many hundreds or thousands of premises.

Services and service organizations

Leisure service organization are those organizations providing hospitality, leisure and tourism services as outlined above. They face some difficulties and problems that make the study of organization behaviour a key requirement. Services in general are said to involve four distinctive features that distinguish them from manufacturing, mining or farming. These are defined as follows:

1 *Intangibility* Successful service encounters will be based on employee performance and abilities to generate an emotional response in customers; for example, hotel, restaurant and bar customers want to feel welcome and wanted. Often the impacts cannot be defined and measured in material terms.
2 *Heterogeneity* Every service encounter is produced by the personal behaviour of the service provider and meets unique responses from the customer. In these circumstances services are said to be heterogeneous. Each service encounter is said to be a unique encounter. A receptionist in a leisure club, or a cast in a theatre, may appear to give the same performance each time. It is, in fact, different each time because they themselves enter each new encounter informed by the experience of previous encounters. Customers, also, are different from each other, as they too are shaped by past experiences.
3 *Perishability* Service encounters occur once and are time specific. Thus it may be possible to replace a physical drink in a bar if the customer is not satisfied, but the smile and greeting cannot be reworked if the customer feels unwelcome. As service interactions are mostly time specific, it is not possible to rework service defects, and in leisure service organizations service has to be 'right first time'.
4 *Inseparability* The service worker producing, and the service customer consuming, the service have to be present. This inseparability means that leisure service organizations need to be located where customers want to receive the service, and there are limits to the amount of centralization of service production.

These features present customers with some real dilemmas when faced with decisions to purchase a service. The significance of the intangibles, the potential uniqueness of each service encounter and the perishability of the service, in particular, make it difficult for customers to predict what they are going to get. A response to these problems of prediction has been the growing reliance on 'branded' leisure services. Here the leisure service organization claims to produce a particular service experience. Hotel, bar, restaurant, leisure club and tour operating chains are, in one way or another, making attempts to provide predictability to the customer. Customers have responded by using branded leisure service organizations. In most mature service economies big multi-unit service organizations dominate the leisure service market. Firms like McDonald's Restaurants, Marriott Hotels, Thomson Travel and David Lloyd Leisure communicate clear messages to customers about the service they will provide.

This book focuses on the organizational experiences, particularly the difficulties and dilemmas these leisure organizations face when attempting to provide reliable services across hundreds or thousands of units. The performance of unit managers and staff has an immediate impact on each customer's experience. If customers experience service that does not match their expectations, or if staff do not respond favourably to their requests, customers become dissatisfied and may decide not to use that organization again. In fact, service organizations reflect a number of tensions between the three key stakeholders – customers as recipients, and managers as agents of owners and employees, both of whom are both service providers. Figure I1.2 reproduces Bateson's representation of these tensions.

The centrality of the control issue in the successful management of services should not be underestimated and has been well documented by Bateson (1985). He suggests that the successful delivery of most services requires that both the customers and employees surrender some control to comply with management's chosen service delivery system. Thus it is likely that customer satisfaction (both internal and external) will be influenced by the extent to which each party perceives that they maintain some control over the service encounter. This makes leisure organizations interesting to study because relations between customers, owners/managers and staff will always be based on tensions and conflicting needs that can never be completely reconciled, only recognized and negotiated.

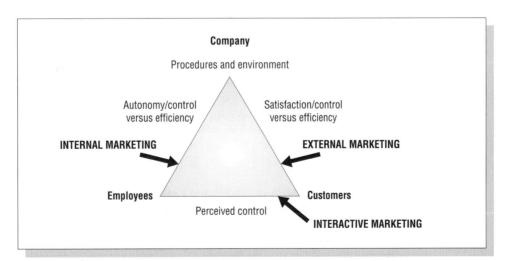

Figure I1.2 The perceived behavioural control conflicts in the service encounter
Source: Bateson (1985).

Organizational behaviour

The term 'organizational behaviour' is a convenient way of referring to the multiplicity of interrelated influences on, and patterns of, behaviour of people within organizations. This book is an advanced introduction to the fundamental issues involved and relies on the interdisciplinary perspectives of psychology, sociology and anthropology.

A central aim of this book is to provide the reader with the conceptual tools necessary for analysing organizational behaviour in the context of hospitality, leisure and tourism provision, and understanding events in order to take appropriate management action. Although many more issues are worthy of inclusion, the framework adopted discusses and questions a number of key elements including:

- organizational structures and behaviour
- commercial hospitality, leisure and tourism in a service context
- the individual and the organization
- groups in the organization
- management within the organization.

Chapters 1 to 3 of the book deal with the characteristics of leisure service organizations and the impact that these have on organizational behaviour, organizational management and organizational design. The high significance of employee performance in matching customer expectations in organizations operating in many sites has driven many leisure service organization managers to explore forms of organization structure that move away from the traditional command and control structures developed for armies and the 'warfare' of capitalism.

Delayered structures and learning organizations are some of the metaphors used to describe organizations designs needed in multi-unit, branded leisure service organizations. These structural metaphors are often shaped by the recognition that individual performance at a micro level may make or break the service event. The reaction of organization members to customer complaints and 'out of brand' unusual requests depend on individuals being able to provide both the physical behaviour and emotional responses required of the 'brand'. Hence individual commitment, motivation, reward and performance have a key significance.

Chapters 4 to 8 explore issues related to the individual and some of the social and psychological impacts of organizations on individual behaviour and performance. The impact of other individuals is dealt with on two levels. The first explores the social psychology of group membership on individual performance, and shows how work groups and teams are used as management techniques within organizations. The second level explores organizational culture as a form of macro group culture that again shapes the organizational context in which individual organization members operate.

Chapters 9 to 12 deal with issues related to the management of people in a leisure services context. Empowerment has been a recent metaphor advocated as a way of creating the flexibility and responsiveness needed in leisure service organizations. Empowerment, when thoughtfully applied, can represent techniques for managing both frontline staff and managers in a way that replaces external control of behaviour with internal forms, whereby individuals are encouraged to control themselves within set limits. Following from this, Chapter 10 deals with communication issues

– a particular problem when dealing with multi-unit organizations operating across international boundaries. Leisure service organization members frequently represent diversity in terms of gender, ethnicity, culture and religions, and the management of diversity requires some special attention. Finally the role of managers, management and managerialism requires discussion as one, albeit a dominant one, of a number of metaphors of leisure service organizations.

Reflective practitioners

Throughout the book we invite you to reflect and consider issues that have been discussed earlier. This process of reflection is designed to aid your understanding and to help you remember the concepts under discussion. In addition, the book aims to help develop 'reflective practitioners', that is, people who are able to think and do. The concepts being developed throughout the book are not included merely as an intellectual exercise; they assist those interested in leisure organizations to better understand the behaviour of organization members. Reflective practice represents a process of thinking that is helpful both for the study of organizations and for those for those who will manage them.

The text is also informed by recent research on learning styles preferences of students on programmes aimed at the study of leisure services (Lashley, 1999; Lashley, 2001; Lashley and Shaw, 2002). The research uses an adapted version of Honey and Mumford's eighty-questions instrument based on the original by Kolb (1985). Kolb's work originally developed four-quadrant learning styles based on two continuua. Honey and Mumford relabelled these as learning by experience and learning by conceptualization; and learning by experimentation and learning by reflection. Figure I1.3 reproduces these two quadrants and the four learning styles positions that they produce.

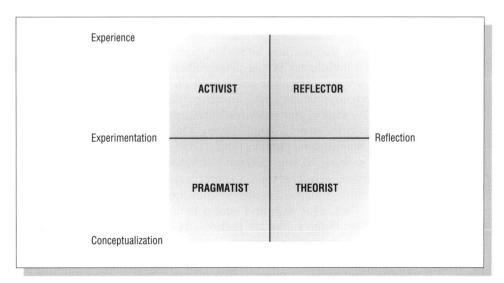

Figure I1.3 Honey and Mumford's four learning styles
Source: Honey and Mumford (1986).

Hospitality, Leisure & Tourism Series

In each case the learning style inclines the student to learn with certain preferences. Going back to Kolb's original work (1985) each of these preferences is formed by personality and brain side preference. Figure I1.4 reproduces the basis of the Kolb approach. Again there are two continuua on relates to introversion and extroversion, and the other on the proneness to use either left or right hand side of the brain.

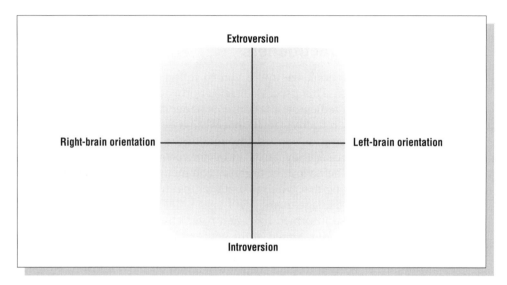

Figure I1.4 Kolb's model underlying learning style preferences
Source: Kolb (1983).

Hence, these personality factors create an approach to learning that may or not be compatible with the way that teaching and learning are organized. The results suggest that most of our students enter leisure service programmes with a strong learning style preference that needs to be understood and addressed.

The results highlight a strong preference for Activist learning styles across most programmes. Given the nature of the research instrument, a student could potentially register strong preferences for all learning styles. In the sample, few students register strong or very strong preference for learning in other styles. More importantly, substantial minorities register low or very low preference for learning in Reflector, Theorist or Pragmatist styles.

Without wishing to run through the whole model, it is worth reiterating that Activist learners learn best by doing and feeling, and talking with others. They rely more on intuition than on analysis. They need to see the practical application of knowledge. They enjoy here and now activities, such as business games, teamwork tasks and role-playing. They are particularly keen to learn by 'doing', and typically find theoretical approaches difficult. They are attracted to 'people' industries and like active involvement. They work well with others. They will try new ideas. They like variety and excitement. However, they experience difficulties that many experienced educators will recognize. They rarely plan their actions. They rush into answers, and in examination situations may run out of time because they spend too much time on the early questions. They tend not to put effort into topics that are not of interest and they often leave things to the last minute.

Kolb states that the most effective learning involves all aspects of the learning styles. They must reflect on actions undertaken – seeing how these reflections fit with theories – consider how they might need to alter future actions, and then act. Figure I1.5 reproduces these stages involving both collective and individual reflection.

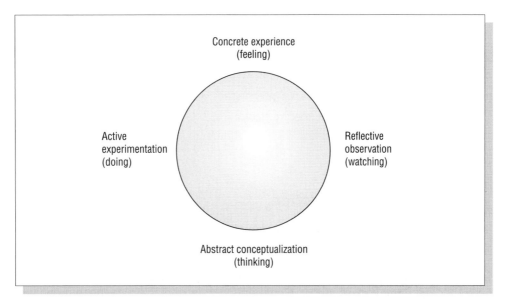

Figure I1.5   Kolb's learning cycle (1985)
Source: Lashley (1995).

For the purposes of this book, and for future activities, we suggest that the process of learning needs to move through the stages outlined on Kolb's model. Active experience need to be followed by reflection, including the critical evaluation of the experience, and consideration of how these experiences inform or adapt theoretical understanding and how this might inform future actions. Traditionally this is shown as a cycle, as in Figure I1.5; however, it is more accurately a series of spirals where the process of acting, reflecting, theorizing and deciding on future actions leads from the past to new learning situations. Figure I1.6, in our view, expresses this process more accurately.

So what does all this mean for the book? Well, if we are dealing with readers who are mostly reflective practitioners, we will set learning in practical and active situations. Case studies and active learning exercises are designed to engage the activist learner, but in a way that demonstrates the importance of theories and concepts. At various points in the text and at the end of each chapter you will be invited to reflect on issues that have been discussed earlier. We urge you to undertake these exercises because they are an important part of the process of developing reflective practitioners.

We hope you enjoy the book. Good luck!

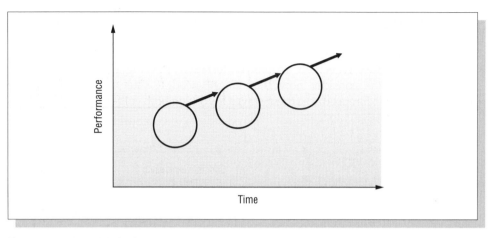

Figure I1.6   A model of reflective practice

Reflective practice

1 Define hospitality, recreational leisure and tourism services. Critically discuss these definitions in a way that shows how there are ambiguities in many current definitions.
2 Analyse the similarities and differences of organizations that make up the leisure service sector. Comment on the extent to which these organizations have similar tensions and inconsistencies to manage.
3 Evaluate the importance of the behaviour of people who make up leisure service organizations. Discuss the importance and conflicting needs of the key stakeholders in hospitality organizations.
4 Discuss the reflective practitioner and the approach needed to get the most out of this text.

CHAPTER 1

Hospitality, leisure and tourism services and organizational behaviour

After working through this chapter you should be able to:

- define organization behaviour and contributing disciplines
- critically discuss different ways of describing organizations
- discuss the service context in which leisure service organizations operate
- identify and critically discuss different strategies engaged.

All organizations are by definition organizations of people, but leisure service organizations require intensified focus on members' behaviour, because members' behaviour has a key significance for the delivery of customer satisfaction and customer perceptions of service quality. The organizational processes whereby managers manage frontline staff in particular and all staff in general are a central concern. Both those interested in the study *of* leisure service organizations as major employers and those studying these organizations in preparation *for* work in the sector need to develop a critical understanding of the relationship between leisure service organizations and the different people who make up the membership.

Case study 1.1

Fred Brown is a regular customer of a major chain store. He is a fan of the store and uses the firm on at least a weekly basis, usually charging purchases on his store card. On average he spends £1000–2000 with the firm per annum.

One day in the run-up to Christmas, Fred found that his wristwatch battery had stopped working and he returned the watch to a chain store for repair. He knew that the watch would need to be sent away to the manufacturer because the waterproofing could not be repaired in-house. When he presented the watch to the appropriate counter he was told, 'We are not accepting any watches for repair until after Christmas'. Fred explained that he had made a special journey to the store and would prefer to leave it with them. A senior assistant said, 'We are not accepting repairs until the New Year, because our draws are full of stock'. Fred said, 'Look I am a regular customer and it is inconvenient to return again to the store, please let me leave it with you, it is only one small watch'.

The senior assistant said, 'I am not accepting this watch for repair, that is our policy and we are not going to change it just for you'. Fred became very angry and left the store. He had the watch repaired at a competitor store and has vowed not to return to the original store. He now tells his story to all his friends and contacts insisting the store has 'gone down the pan recently'. 'In the past the service was great, they would have just accepted it and explained that it might not be sent away until the new year.'

Reflective practice

1 Reflect on Case study 1.1. Did the counter assistants meet Fred's customer service expectation?
2 Why did the staff react the way they did?
3 Was Fred to blame?

Clearly the perception of poor service experienced in a shop, hotel, restaurant, travel agency or any other leisure service can be down to the inappropriate behaviour of rogue individuals, but there are other explanations that reflect the organizational context in which she or he works:

- high levels of staff turnover result in staff shortages
- a lack of training
- staff absences put individuals under added pressure
- having to work long hours
- autocratic and bullying supervision
- low motivation due to poor pay and conditions
- concern over organization-threatened organization changes.

Most of these issues influence the behaviour of individuals and originate in the way organizations employ and manage the individuals in that organization. This chapter will discuss the need to study organizations and why organization behaviour studies provide valuable insights into leisure service organizations. The chapter also considers different ways of thinking about organizations and the relationships between organization members. These different perceptions of organizations fundamentally shape the way that people within the organization, and external to it, see an organization in very different ways. Flowing from this it is important to understand the nature of the service context in which leisure service organizations exist. The role of organization members and the design of their job roles may vary considerably between different leisure service organizations. Certainly the roles of managers and the way they devise organization policies towards other organization members are considered as a way of encouraging critical thought and insights into policies that may reflect just one of a number of actions.

Understanding organization behaviour

The distinction made earlier between the study *of* leisure service organizations and the study *for* leisure service organizations is an important one. Most of those who read this book are likely to be studying courses that prepare them for careers in hospitality, leisure or tourism occupations. In many cases these programmes develop an awareness of how to manage the activity concerned and are, rightly, concerned with developing concepts and skills needed for effective performance in these sectors (Doherty *et al.*, 2001). That said, the study of leisure service organizations invites a more critical perspective that is required in the development of the 'reflective practitioner'. Organization behaviour as an interdisciplinary topic allows a more analytical stance than a simple managerialist perspective might consider.

Huczynski and Buchanan (2001: 3) suggest that, 'Organizational behaviour has a controversial relationship with management practice' and they criticize many US and British texts for being overly managerialist (Mullins, 1999) for several reasons. They suggest that these more managerial texts that are overly focused on the study for organization performance fail to deal with the 'political' dimensions of organizations:

- *Power inequalities* in organizations are often ignored in the study from this uncritical perspective. Power in organizations is unevenly distributed and management represents an elite group that has access to information and resources that are not available to employees. How this uneven power is exercised is an interesting topic that reflects on the decision-making process and reward structures.
- The *subject agenda* is narrowed to issues of practical management applications under this managerialist approach. Subjects that are not of an immediate practical

application may get squeezed out. This may reduce understanding of issues that have long-term interest, and those that are more critical of management practice.

- Organizations comprise *multiple stakeholders*, of which managers are just one group who have a stake in understanding behaviour in organizations. The subject will also be of interest to other stakeholders such as employees, trade unions, customers, suppliers and the communities in which organizations are located.
- Managers are often prone to be *fashion victims* in their search for methods and techniques with which to manage. The more managerialist approaches tend to view these management fads uncritically and encourage managers to consider 'quick fixes' to long-term and complex problems. The chapter on employee empowerment and discussion of emotion intelligence later in the text provide examples.

Key point 1.1

The study of organizational behaviour encourages a critical perspective that challenges the view of the management of leisure service organizations as being unproblematic and simple.

This book assumes that leisure service organizations are best understood as a collective of interest groups and that effective management of these organizations needs to be aware of the full array of interests involved. Indeed, many leisure service organizations can be criticized for operating with only shareholder interests in mind (Lashley, Thomas and Rowson, 2002). The dominance of concern for building shareholder value, almost without thought for other interests, is ultimately counterproductive and an issue to which this chapter returns later.

Leisure service organizations are focused on the provision of services that occupy people's non-work time. They share some features that are common to all organizations in that they represent social arrangements involving collective goals and controlled performance (Huczynski and Buchanan, 2001). This latter feature is important because organizations are different to, say, football supporters or regular drinkers at the same pub. They are, therefore, more than social arrangements with collective goals.

- Organizations are concerned with performance to achieve goals.
- They involve choices about best use of resources to achieve goals.
- They monitor performance of individuals in pursuit of the goals.
- They control performance and take corrective action where needed.
- Controls only work when individuals comply with instructions.
- Organizations often involve specialization of tasks and the division of labour.
- Admission to membership of an organization is normally controlled.
- Loss of membership can occur.

The study of organizations involves a number of themes that cover the scope of this book:

- *Individual factors* are concerned with personality and perceptions that may influence how the individual performs in the organization. Many leisure service organizations attempt to recruit people who are people orientated and who have good social skills (Lashley, Thomas and Rowson, 2002). In Case study 1.1 it may be that the shop assistants were not suitable for frontline customer contact.
- *Group factors* include the study of the way groups are formed, and the way that groups provide a sense of identity to individuals and influence the way individuals behave. In addition the study of intergroup relationships within organizations can be useful for understanding both relationships between managers and other organization members in industrial relations and in diversity management. The two assistants in Case study 1.1 may feel angry with managers because of recent changes and this has influenced their approach to customers.
- *Structural factors* influence the design of the organization and the contexts in which individuals work. The number of employees responsible to a supervisors, or the number of levels between the frontline staff and the senior management have an impact on the levels and types of contact between staff and the management hierarchy. Many leisure retail organizations have been attracted to employee empowerment as a way of managing staff because it is believed empowerment will improve service quality through improved employee commitment. In Case study 1.1 it may be that the shop assistants feel disempowered and fixed on one instruction at the expense of good service.
- *Process factors* determine how the organization deals with organization members as employees and the systems in place which are designed to enhance and deliver service quality. The approach taken to the recruitment and selection of new recruits, the induction and training, management processes and reward systems can influence the behaviour of individuals. The shop assistants could be poorly rewarded, and untrained in good customer care.
- *Management factors* involve consideration of how managers operate within the organization, their chosen style as leaders or the culture they are creating. Over-controlling management can produce frustration and lead to disempowerment. The action of the shop assistants might be a response to the way they are being managed.

Key point 1.2

The study of organizational behaviour involves a multidisciplinary approach that includes individual, group, structural, process and management factors.

Case study 1.2

Like many of its competitors, the Friendly Pub Company has high levels of staff turnover. Current rates average 220 per cent for the group of 90 pubs across the Midlands and North of England. But rates in individual pubs range from 10 per cent to 450 per cent.

Sam Brown calls a meeting of senior colleagues to discuss the causes of staff turnover and how to remedy it. Several managers make a contribution but all seem to suggest different causes.

Ted Brown, Operations Manager, said, 'It's the people around today, they don't want to stay long, people today aren't committed'.

Sally North, Training Manager, disagreed, 'It's not them, it's the way we treat them; our managers do not carry out proper induction programmes and many of them bully staff once they've started'.

Jane Fallon, a senior pub manager, said, 'We just had six staff all leave at once, it's like when one goes they all go'.

Reflective practice

1 Using Case study 1.2, identify the different sources of organization behaviour being used by the three managers?
2 Suggest what is needed in any policy designed to reduce staff turnover.

Describing organizations

Organizations are described in different ways by different commentators. To some extent these differences reflect political and philosophical perspectives and abilities to be analytical rather than descriptive. There are several ways of structuring these differences in approach; this chapter introduces two models. The first model refers to the way different commentators consider organizational conflict (Fox, 1973). Is conflict unhealthy, healthy or inevitable? The second explores metaphors used to describe organizations: are they like orchestras, like prisons or like machines (Morgan, 1997)?

Organizational conflict

Many leisure service organizations have been criticized for having high levels of staff turnover, high levels of staff absenteeism, poor quality, low productivity and poor wages (DfEE, 1999; HtF, 2002; Lashley and Rowson, 2000). In some cases strikes by organization members occur, though this varies among sectors and countries.

In the UK for example, strikes in hotels are infrequent and usually confined to one hotel, while in New York hotel workers are more likely to take strike action more frequently and across several hotels.

All these situations reflect conflicts within leisure retail organizations. When a person leaves an organization or takes a day off, they are frequently doing so because they are dissatisfied at work but do not have the chance to take collective action with their work colleagues, which strike actions involves.

Commentators respond to conflict in organizations in different ways. The model developed by Fox (1973) is useful. Even though it was primarily developed to inform the understanding of industrial relations in the UK, it is helpful because it can be adapted to reflect different 'philosophies' of organizations and relationships within them.

Each uses a frame of reference that makes assumptions about the organization and its members. It is a means whereby people make sense of events and actions through the expression of accepted norms within a social domain such as, group, occupation, subject discipline or political allegiance. Group influences on behaviour are discussed further in Chapter 7.

- *Unitarists* perceive the organization as harmonious and conflict as bad. The frame of reference views the organization as a seamless whole, with harmony between organization members, structures that are co-operative and with committed organization members and loyal teams. Where problems and conflicts occur they are seen as due to some unusual effect like communications breakdowns. Reasons are likened to an illness where consultants are needed to sort out the malady, or due to 'troublemakers' such as trade unions or 'militants'. This view is held by many managers and assumes that organizations are they way they are for 'technical' reasons because that is the way they have to be in a 'free market' context. At root the approach fails to recognize the political nature of organizations and power relationships within them. Problems occur because this somewhat naive view fails to recognize the complexity and conflicts inherent in organizations.
- *Pluralists* see organizations as collections of groups with different interests, goals and objectives. These groups have overlapping and differing goals for the organization, which sometimes result in conflict with other groups. In particular, managers in the organization hierarchy are unlikely to have the same goals as employees in the lower levels of the organization. In some cases conflicts occur between departments, say between kitchen and restaurant, or between accountings and marketing departments. Approaches to organization with this pluralist perspective suggest that conflict regulation is needed; ways of managing the conflict that is bound to occur and resolving differences before they become harmful.
- *Interactionist* perspectives flow from the pluralist view. Here conflict is recognized as both inevitable and potentially beneficial, because it results in change. Organizations therefore require a means not only to allow conflict to be brought to the surface, but also to be dealt with it in a positive manner. The key for these commentators is that there is an optimum level of conflict – too little and the organization is stale, too much and it distracts efforts.
- The *radical pluralist* perspective recognizes that organizations will largely involve conflict because under a capitalist system of organization the interests of shareholders, managers and employees differ. Indeed, the differences are not just accidents of organization structures; as with the pluralist, radical pluralists see differences rooted in conflict over resources. Wage levels are important for employees, but represent costs for the organization's shareholders. Managers largely work in the interests of the shareholders, although they are also employees like other organization members. These radical pluralists are interested in the causes of non-conflict as well as in the causes of organizational conflict. Given these inevitable conflicts within organizations, why is there so little open conflict?

Most industrial practitioners, academics and organization members will hold one or other of these four frames of reference when they comment on organizations. In some cases individuals may recognize and apply different frames of reference in different circumstances.

Key point 1.3

Individuals hold different frames of reference and this will influence what they notice in their environment, and they interpret the events noticed differently. These will, in turn, influence how they expect others to behave and how they themselves behave.

Case study 1.3

At the same meeting of managers at the Friendly Pub Company, other managers expressed their views about what could be done about the high levels of staff turnover in the pub estate.

Ted Baker, a regional manager, said, 'We aren't getting our message across. We are a great company to work for, but these people just don't stay with us long enough to find our'.

Helen Ramasay, the Personnel Manager, said, 'We need to go and study the pubs where staff turnover is low. The managers in those pubs are doing something right. We can learn from them how best to retain staff'.

Dave Bassett, a consultant, said, 'Staff turnover is a sign of conflict, it is inevitable but we need to manage it; let's find out what is causing dissatisfaction'.

Reflective practice

1 Using Case study 1.3, identify the different views of organization conflict being used by the three managers?
2 Suggest what is needed in any policy designed to reduce staff turnover.

Metaphors of organizations

Morgan (1997) presents a number of metaphors of organizations that help to frame the assumptions and priorities that individuals use when discussing organizations. The various organization theorist approaches from different social science perspectives lead to different metaphors implicit in the analysis of organizations. The following nine metaphors are suggested by Morgan (1997):

1 Organizations as *machines* metaphor considers the component elements and the way they work together.
2 Organizations as *biological organisms* metaphor suggests that key focus of the organization is of a living entity and the way that body is healthy or unhealthy.
3 The *human brain* metaphor considers the organization as a learning organization and considers the way that knowledge is being shared.

4 The *cultures and subcultures* metaphor considers organizations as cultural contexts that involve the formation of a culture and the integration of management of subcultures flowing from departments to occupational groups.

5 The *political systems* metaphor is concerned with power and politics in organizations as exercised by individuals and groups.

6 The *psychic prison* metaphor considers the way that organizations constrain and shape the individual's beliefs, attitudes, values and behaviour.

7 The *systems of change and transformation* metaphor tends to focus on process of development and change within organizations.

8 The *instruments of domination* metaphor stresses the role of organizations in dominating the majority of organization members for the benefits of the few.

9 The *orchestra* metaphor is used to emphasize the idea that individual organization members bring their own skills, but ultimately play as a team.

All these metaphors are useful in giving insights into aspects of organizations and organizational life. Like the frames of reference discussed earlier, the metaphor approach helps to explain differences in ways of looking at organizations and the differences that may occur between people looking at the same thing.

Key point 1.4

Metaphors are used to describe organizations as objects, and these metaphors are different and focus on different aspects of organizations.

The service context

The preceding sections have shown that different insights into organizational behaviour and comments about the nature of organizations themselves stem from different academic disciplines, different philosophical and political perspectives and, ultimately, different values, attitudes and beliefs and about people and behaviour in organizations. Similarly, leisure service organizations are not all the same, in that they are often providing different types of services and require different service performance from service employees. This section explores some of the features of services to establish some of the variations.

The literature on the distinctiveness of services when compared with manufacturing makes play of four features of services: intangibility, heterogeneity, perishability and inseparability (Cowell, 1984). The provision of intangibles is said to be a defining feature of service industries (Cowell, 1984). Some services, such as consultancy or legal advice, may have no tangible output. However, many firms provide a combination of tangible outputs in the form of meals and drinks plus intangibles in the nature of the service – how a customer is treated during the service encounter. Thus, service deliverers will be in different positions in relation to their customers and the sources of customer satisfaction. Figure 1.1 typifies the relationship between tangibles and intangibles among different leisure service deliverers.

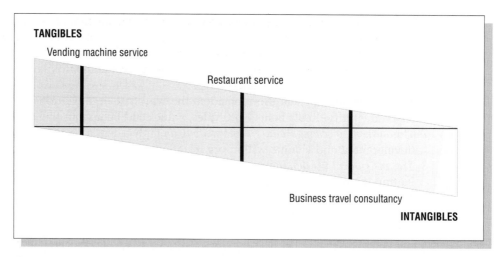

Figure 1.1 Continuum of tangibles and intangible services

The relationship between tangibles and intangibles as sources of customer satisfaction is an influential factor in determining the employment strategies that an organization uses and the means by which service jobs are defined.

As the significance of the *intangible element increases*, there needs to be more commitment to 'delight the customer'. The service customer's experience is the service provided by staff members.

In Figure 1.1, business travel consultants have a one-to-one relationship with clients, their ability to develop good relationships with clients is key to building repeat business.

Service delivery is variable and difficult to standardize because of the personal nature of the contact between the customer and the service deliverer. Thus, individuals may well vary in their interpretation of customer needs. Elements of human 'chemistry' may affect performance; some individuals may be more personally committed to successful service encounters. Customer expectations of satisfactory service vary and are difficult to predict. Hence, it is difficult to say the service delivery is homogeneous, even where the service is relatively simple.

Having made this general point there is variety between different types of services and the degree of standardization (homogeneous) and within services provided. Some leisure service organizations are able to standardize the tangible elements of the service encounter. For example, many tour operators, travel firms, health and fitness clubs, fast-food deliverers, branded restaurants, budget hotels and others operate standardized products and services to customers who demand the predictability and the security of the brand.

Reflective practice

1 Consider the list of leisure sectors provided above and suggest examples of branded leisure service organizations operating in the sector.

Many of these firms have also attempted to standardize the intangible elements of the service encounter by *scripting employees*, whereby training includes phrases and words to use during service. McDonald's Restaurants and Disney World are well-known examples of organizations that have tried to standardize the service encounter in this way. Figure 1.2 provides a model of differences between leisure service organizations.

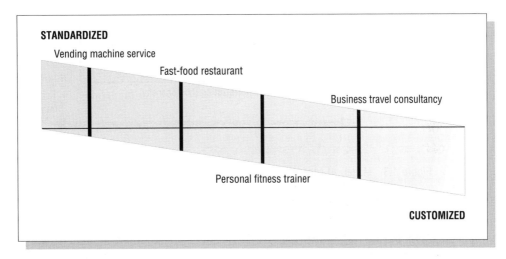

Figure 1.2 Continuum of standardized and customized services

Other service organizations are in positions where the encounters with customers are more individualized (customized and heterogeneous) and difficult to predict. Obviously, the pure intangible interactions within professional services are individualized and thereby customized.

Successful encounters will depend on the individual service deliverer being able to interpret the requirements of customers and adapt the service delivered to their wants. Consultancy firms can be said to offer these services.

Other organizations may well require that frontline staff deliver a standardized product in the tangibles but then require a more individualized service in the intangibles. Harvester Restaurants provides a good example here. Menus, prices, decor, premises and so on are highly standardized but require staff to be sensitive to the service needs of individual customers – for example, families, older customers, office parties.

Inseparability and perishability are also important features of service provision that have an impact on the management of human resources. For example, the perishability factor has influenced many service organizations' anti-trade union policies.

However tangibility/intangibility and customization/standardization are the most influential features in determining people management practices. The interplay between these two continua sets up four types of service offer to customers that, in turn, requires different contributions from employees. Figure 1.3 brings together the two continua to produce a four-quadrant matrix through which to establish different ideal types of service offer (Heskett, Sasser and Hart, 1990; Schmenner, 1995; Lashley, 2001).

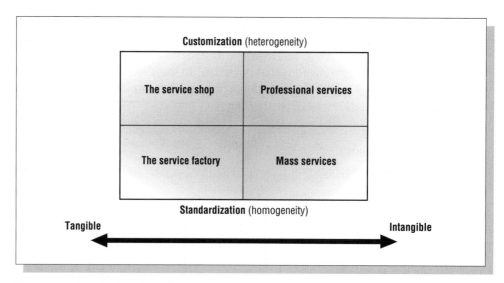

Figure 1.3 Models of service offer

In Figure 1.3, *professional services* cover those services which are provided in-dividually, where few clients have exactly the same requirements or needs. They are intangible dominant; thus the service delivery is highly dependent on the skills of 'frontline' personnel. *The service shop* involves the delivery of services that are customized round a fairly predictable set of variations. They are more tangible dominant; customers may need to be advised and counselled about the best package of service for them, but the range of skills needed by the service employee is narrower. *The service factory* covers those services in which the service is standardized and tangible dominant. Customers are buying into the predictability and standardization of the service encounter. *Mass services* are those where the range of service is stand-ardized, but the source of satisfaction is more intangible dominant. Again the 'front line' is important but the range of skills required is limited.

These models are helpful in establishing types of service operational types that are likely to impact on the best fit with the management of organization members. They also establish a means by which leisure services might be graphically located at points within the quadrants.

Employment strategy in leisure service organizations is concerned with *both* control and commitment. Given the nature of most service encounters within leisure service organizations, employee commitment to successful encounters *should* be of vital importance. Even greater emphasis would be given in situations where organizations are adopting a business strategy based on service quality.

Given the sometimes contradictory nature of business objectives that stress the importance of 'delighting the customer' and maintaining the integrity of a branded concept, frontline staff need to provide customer service within controls set by the organization. In these circumstances control and commitment are of equal impor-tance, not two ends of a dichotomous scale.

Figure 1.4 suggests that a range of control techniques are available to leisure service organizations, and these techniques range along a continuum between exercising

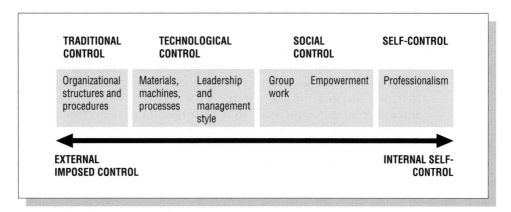

Figure 1.4 Variations in the locus of control of employee performance
Source: Lashley (2001).

externally imposed managerial control over the employee and that which encourages employees to control their own behaviour by internalizing the objectives of the organization.

The importance of employee discretion as an element of job design is crucial to understanding organization behaviour in leisure services. As stated earlier, employee commitment to organizational objectives for service quality, fault detection, operational improvements and so on, are as important to service operators as these are to their manufacturing counterparts, but in many operations employees have to be given discretion to make decisions about the service interaction. Frontline personnel in luxury hotels or in operations like TGI Friday, have tended to 'make it up as they go along'.

The amount of discretion to be exercised by employees in leisure service organizations will be determined by the nature of the service type that is being offered by the leisure service organization. Each service type requires different service performance from those organization members providing immediate service contact. The employment strategies that 'fit' with these models of service type are discussed more fully in Lashley (2001).

- *The service factory* represents service processes where there is low labour intensity and low customization (and, thereby, high standardization) of the service for customers. Fast-food operations are typical of this operational type. McDonald's Restaurants is an example of this service type. Employee performance has been 'routinized' and jobs are designed to be done in 'one best way' designed by the organization. Service deliverers typically are not required to exercise a high degree of discretion because the use of technology and production process limits the need for personal judgement.
- *The service shop* involves a service delivery that requires more customization, but relatively low labour intensity. In other words, it may be difficult to predict individual customer needs, but when they are identified they involve relatively low labour intensity, or the application of one of a prearranged repertoire of actions by frontline staff. TGI Fridays represents an example of this type of operation. Here service deliverers need to adapt their performance to meet the needs of predictable

but different customer service types. This type of service involves 'mass customiza-tion' similar to manufacturing industry.

- *Mass service* represents service processes which involve a relatively high degree of labour intensity, but with a limited amount of customization. The Marriott Hotel brand provides an example of a mass service organization. It is possible to predict customer services, but the nature of the service being delivered requires a fair amount of contact with staff. Here staff need to develop relationships with cus-tomers and make them feel special. Discretion may be needed when dealing with customer complaints and unusual requests.
- *Professional services* are those in which there is a high degree of customization of the service to individual customer needs and a high degree of labour intensity. Customer needs are hard to predict, so service deliverers have to exercise a high degree of discretion. Business travel consultants require skills that can be applied to the needs of individual clients.

Key point 1.5

Leisure services vary in the offer made to customers and the discretion to be exercised by employees. These differences have an impact on organization behaviour in leisure service organizations.

Case study 1.4

Harvester Restaurants

All staff in Harvester Restaurant units are organized into three autonomous teams which reflect the key operational areas – bars, restaurant, kitchen. Each team has its 'team responsibilities', that is, those aspects of business performance for which it will be accountable. In the restaurant, for example, the team will be responsible for guest service, guest complaints, sales targets, ordering cutlery and glassware, cashing up after service and team member training. In the more advanced cases, teams take part in the selection and recruitment of new team members.

A shift co-ordinator helps co-ordinate the activities of the team. This person is a team member, serving on table, cooking the grills or serving in the bar, but assumes additional responsibilities during the shift. In the restaurant the shift co-ordinator would take on the team responsibility for cashing up at the end of service and ensuring table layout was compatible with prior bookings. Several different team members would take on the role of shift co-ordinator during the week.

In addition to these roles, one of the staff members operates as the appointed person during each shift. This person would again be a member of one of the teams working in the restaurant, bar or kitchen during the shift, but would accept responsibility for securing the building, putting the shift's takings in the safe and handing over keys to the next appointed person. As with the shift co-ordinator, appointed persons receive no extra responsibility allowances, though in practice they get more pay by being on duty for longer hours. Given that these are often seen as core tasks in a traditional manager's job, it is interesting to note that there were no increases in security problems as a result of this initiative.

Restaurant management consists of just two roles – team manager and coach. In this organization the team manager and team coach were no longer 'managing' the staff but were responsible for enabling and facilitating staff to be more self-managing and empowered.

The most effective autonomous groups were based on fairly stable groups within the workforce. In some cases, employees had been working in the establishment for five or six years and, in some, over ten years. Strong group bonds and stability had been established before the introduction of work groups. Senior executives reported difficulties in establishing groups where there was a stubborn labour turnover problem, or where key members of the work team left and 'pulse turnover' resulted. Some unit managers and coaches also found difficulty in adjusting to the different approach needed.

Senior managers were convinced that the approach had been a success. They reported improved levels of sales, reduced stock holding, reduced labour costs and improved labour retention. Customer complaints were dramatically reduced and some restaurants registered no customer complaints for over several months.

Reflective practice

1 Using the case study above, identify the form of control being used by organization managers.
2 What appear to be the key benefits for organization members and customers?
3 Suggest the potential difficulties for organization managers.
4 What service type appears to fit with this approach?

Employment practice

Thus far the chapter has explored differences in perspectives that social scientists may bring to bear on leisure service organization through both the study of organizational behaviour and the study of organizations. It has also considered the nature of the service context that impacts on the services provided by leisure service organizations. In all cases, the chapter attempts to convey differences and complexity. There is no single type of leisure service organization, as there is no one way of commenting on the behaviour of leisure service organization members or the nature of organizations. Similarly, employment practices found within leisure service organizations vary.

Johnston (1989) a range of service strategies that could be used by service organizations. Two in particular seem relevant to studying leisure service organizations. The dominant style identified by a number of research projects is a *cost-focused* strategy (DfEE, 1999; DfEE, 2000; Lashley, Thomas and Rowson, 2002). The other strategy is *quality focused*.

The cost employment practice

In essence this involves a cost-focused approach by managers that aims to create competitive advantage by cost management and low selling prices. Labour costs in particular are seen as a key issue to be controlled and minimized.

Labour costs represent a key aspect of operating cost that organization managers perceive to be most available to control. They define labour costs as the rate paid per hour multiplied by the number of hours bought, plus on costs, and are expressed as a percentage of operating costs.

Many leisure service organizations appear to work to this cost competitive strategy. The concern for pay rates often locates wages at legal minimal levels. In the UK for example, the legal minimum wage legislation offers minimum protection for young people.

A recent research project for the North West Tourism Network suggested that the 'hospitality sectors' in Greater Manchester were prone to pay low wages, and employed large numbers of young people whereby rates could be further reduced (Lashley, Thomas and Rowson, 2002). Employees often complained that they were not being paid for the hours worked. These findings are consistent with national studies that conclude that, 'Government statistics still show the industry hosts four of the ten lowest paid jobs in Great Britain – kitchen porters, bar staff, catering assistants and waiting staff' (HtF, 2002: 1)

The problem with this low-cost strategy is that it yields additional costs that are rarely considered; for example:

- high levels of staff turnover
- recruitment difficulties
- skills shortages
- low productivity
- absenteeism
- lost customers
- added costs of attracting new customers
- deliberate acts of sabotage by frontline organization members.

Recruitment problems and difficulties occur largely in the hotel, restaurant and bar sectors of tourism in Manchester. With a few exceptions, low pay rates that do not compete with firms in other sectors leads to recruitment difficulties. These firms frequently pay at the national minimum rate, or few pence above it. Some employers target young people under the age of eighteen so they can pay even below this rate.

The report shows that many of the key competitors for these same staff are paying above these rates as a deliberate policy of attracting staff. The Benefits Agency suggests that an employee needs to be paid at least £5.00 per hour for the job to be sufficiently rewarding to outweigh the loss of unemployment benefit. Few of these firms had any understanding of the labour market in Manchester and the pay rates needed to retain staff once recruited.

Organizations following these low-cost strategies in fact have low skill expectations, jobs frequently have been deskilled and employers are merely recruiting people with social skills and the ability to perform basic tasks. Potentially there are plenty of recruits, but there are reported difficulties of retaining staff when they have been recruited. These high levels of staff turnover increase the demand for staff because employers are permanently attempting to refill vacant posts.

The problem is compounded by these organizations' approach to accounting for business performance. They frequently use simple costing systems and crude financial measures. Sales levels, profit levels and shareholder value are important measures, but these can be misleading if not used with a more *balanced score card* approach.

Quality employment practice

The second strategy attempts to gain competitive advantage in the marketplace by building and consistently delivering service quality. It is claimed, on the one hand, that a service quality strategy is difficult to reproduce because it cannot be copied, as it builds a loyal base of customers. The cost strategy, on the other hand, can be copied and results in fickle customers anxious to chase the lowest cost for services provided.

Quality is not used as an absolute term, service quality relates to customer expectations and is best understood as 'fitness for purpose'. The approach recognizes that people are the key asset of the organization and adopt employment practices that are consistently applied and compatible with the customer service offer.

Labour service quality management recognizes frontline staff skills and commitment as fundamental. Staff training is delivered to all organizations. Frontline staff are empowered to 'delight' customers. Rewards are above average for the sector or competitor firms. Promotion and development policies aim to retain staff and develop them through a planned programme.

The leisure service providers are moving to becoming 'learning organizations'. Most will use balanced score card approaches to evaluate organization performance. Measures typically include:

- staff retention and staff turnover rates
- staff training activity
- competitive base rates of pay
- bonuses rewards systems
- employee satisfaction measures
- service quality audits
- customer complaints audits
- mystery customer scores
- sales growth
- profit growth
- cost reduction.

The balance score card allows an organization to recognize that different stakeholder interests may exist and that these are likely to influence perceptions of organization performance.

The balanced score card enables organizations to consider the range of factors that are likely to contribute to organization success. In the long run, shareholder value will be improved if staff and customers are satisfied.

These measures are then used by organizations following the quality strategy to evaluate performance at every level of the organization and its management. These frequently are linked to performance bonuses. In other words, the processes of management accountabilities must also reflect the balanced score card priorities.

Key point 1.6

Employment practice in leisure service organizations varies, and shapes much of the management practice and priorities within these organizations.

Conclusion

This chapter has discussed a number of dimensions that assist in developing an understanding of variation in organizational behaviour studies applied to leisure service organizations. At a fundamental level, the need to engage in the study *of* leisure service organizations as well as in the study *for* leisure service organizations is essential. Without denying the importance of studying for occupation in leisure services, the study of these organizations encourages a reflective approach that is essential for both pure academic study and for those who will ultimately be reflective practitioners in the sector.

The study of organization behaviour encourages this reflective approach through consideration of the totality of the organization and the impact of organization membership on individuals. The multidisciplinary approach to organizations also encourages the development of a multifaceted understanding of the complexity of organizational life, and the subtleties required of organizational commentators and practitioners. The fact that individuals perceive organizational behaviour and organizations from different starting points and perspectives means that it is unwise to assume that all organization members see things in the same way. They are unlikely, therefore, to identify the same issues as problems; nor are they likely to have the same solutions to problems once agreed upon.

Within the context of leisure service organizations, service offers to customers differ and the work required of organizational members will differ accordingly. In particular, the discretion required of an organization member will vary in different organizations. In part these are a by-product of the nature of the service being offered, but they are also an outcome of assumptions made by organization managers. Employment practice is ultimately a result of managerial choices, practices and processes used to implement and evaluate these employment practices.

Reflective practice

1 Define organization behaviour and contributing disciplines.
2 Critically discuss different ways of describing organizations.
3 Discuss the service context in which leisure service organizations operate.
4 Critically discuss organization managers and identify different strategies engaged.

Organizational structure and design

- identify and explain key contingencies affecting the structure and design of leisure service organizations

- identify basic organizational structures in leisure services

- understand the principles of organizational structure and design

- discuss how structure and design impact on members and performance of leisure service organizations.

Prior to discussing structure and design, it is worth reminding ourselves what organizations are and what they do. Beardshaw and Palfreman (1991: 25) view organizations as entities which exist principally by selling goods and services. They also classify them using typical organizational objectives; for example, in the case of trading organizations: 'profit maximization . . . brand leadership, market domination, and corporate growth' (ibid.: 28).

These perspectives alert us to basic issues of organizational function (selling), product (goods and services) and strategy (brand leadership and so on). However, in terms of organizational behaviour, these notions are less useful due to their narrowness of scope. Organizational behaviour focuses on people within firms and how they perceive the world. Robbins (1998: 2) provides a succinct and more appropriate definition: '[An organization is a] consciously co-ordinated social unit, composed of two or more people, that functions on a relatively continuous basis to achieve a common goal or set of goals.'

For our purpose, we can take Robbins's 'social unit' and 'to achieve a common goal' as people working together in the organization to produce and provide a 'composite product'. This is simple enough but gives the false and somewhat old-fashioned impression that managing the process is straightforward. It ignores the fact that employee attitudes and behaviour are unpredictable and based on individual emotions, belief systems, personalities and backgrounds. Furthermore, from a 'pluralist' perspective it is now known that individuals have a variety of needs and goals in addition to those of the organization.

Similar to that of the early classicists, contemporary management thinking shares the belief that structure and design influence members' attitudes and behaviour. In contrast, the modern approach acknowledges the pluralist perspective and advocates more fluid, dynamic and hybrid organizational structures. Thus, attempts are now being made to incorporate the aspirations of workers into overall strategic plans such that employee wellbeing and productivity are maximized simultaneously.

However, structuring organizations is not a haphazard affair (although sometimes it might feel that way). To be effective, firms must first contemplate:

- where they are
- where they want to be

In other words, they must formulate strategic plans based on a vision, their environment and other contingencies. Once a strategy is in place, the organizational structure and design can be planned, implemented and revisited depending on prevailing environmental factors.

Reflective practice

1 Identify the formal structure and design of an organization of which you are a member or familiar with.
2 Do you believe the above structure explains all of the tasks and processes encountered in your job?
3 How do you think people react to jobs that are highly structured?
4 Give some examples of how your attitudes and behaviour were affected by structures present in your employing organization.

5 Do you believe that every individual member of an organization can be motivated by its structure all of the time?

6 List four examples of leisure service jobs and whether you think they are best undertaken by individuals or groups.

Organizational structure: what does it mean?

In a generic sense, the *Collins Oxford English Dictionary and Thesaurus* defines structure as: 'arrangement of parts in construction and buildings'. Hatch (1997) similarly comments that structure can relate to physical configurations existing within organizations, including buildings and geographical locations. Authors including Woodward (1958), Perrow (1967) and Galbraith (1973) view organizational structure in terms of technology and its impact on performance.

While the above dimensions are undoubtedly structural, they are insufficient for our purpose. For example, Woodward, Perrow and Galbraith have a somewhat micro perspective more suited to 'job design' or 'process engineering'. While Hatch's perspective is broader it excludes the potential impact of environmental and strategic issues on organizational design.

Mullins (1996: 332) introduces a notion of the purpose of structure: 'Structure makes possible the application of the process of management and creates a framework of order and command through which the activities of the organization can be planned, organized, directed and controlled'.

A useful metaphor for organizational structure and design is the performance of a musical composition. The product is a song, which on the one hand may have a simple repetitive structure such as a pop tune. On the other hand, the composition may have a more complex design, as heard in a Mozart symphony for example.

In each case, the configurations of music are different. The pop tune may be performed by only one to four people, whereas the symphony has an infinitely more complex structure with many players divided into different sections (strings and woodwind for example, each of which may be further differentiated into smaller parts). Undoubtedly both compositions need co-ordinating and controlling but the process becomes increasingly difficult with more players and more instruments.

Organizations are no different and for our purpose, structure and design is reflected in the definition favoured by Bartol *et al.* (2001: 267): 'the formal pattern of interactions and co-ordination that managers design to link the tasks of individuals and groups to achieve organizational goals.'

Key point 2.1

Effective organizational design is based on the principle that structure follows strategy. This allows potent co-ordination of activities and optimizes organizational direction.

The remainder of this chapter is divided into two sections. The first looks at strategic structure and design by introducing two models of organizational extremes. Key contingencies are introduced and their potential impacts discussed. The second section focuses on some basic principles of structure and organization of work.

Organizational extremes

Mechanistic organizational structures tend to exist in firms with:

- 'sizeable' and complex operations
- many departments (horizontal differentiation)
- several levels between the highest and lowest positions (vertical differentiation)
- a centralized configuration; in other words, (strategic) decision-making exists only at the highest level with virtually no input from lower-level members
- formalized rules, policies and procedures are also more evident in these organizations.

Mechanistic structures have similar strengths and weaknesses to those of bureaucracies. For example, there may be some difficulty in adjustment to external changes and problems with internal communication. However, co-ordination and control are easier to accomplish compared with organic designs which may be considered as the structural opposite of mechanistic ones.

Organic organizations have:

- fewer levels of authority
- simpler structures
- less formality
- a decentralized configuration
- employees with generalist skills rather than being highly differentiated through work
- employees with more discretion in decision-making and performing their jobs.

Furthermore, lateral communication and co-ordination are emphasized which minimizes centralized management direction. A comparison of mechanistic and organic structures by way of summary is shown below in Table 2.1.

Both of these organizational types are, more or less, a firm's design response to contingencies. For example, mechanistic structures are appropriate in 'placid' conditions where there are only minor and, usually, slow environmental changes. Organic

	Complexity	Formalization	Centralization
Mechanistic	High	High	High
Organic	Low	Low	Low

Source: adapted from Hatch (1997: 170).

Table 2.1 A comparison of mechanistic and organic structures

designs work best where these conditions are dynamic and there is a need for continual flexibility to cope with fluctuating changes.

Robbins (2001) holds a similar view and suggests that organizational structures are best suited to the following strategies:

- organic – innovation: loose structure with low specialization, low formalization, and decentralization
- mechanistic – cost minimization: tight control with extensive work specialization, high formalization and high centralization
- mechanistic and organic – imitation: mix of loose with tight properties including tight control over current activities and looser control for new undertakings.

Another view alerts us to the idea that organizations undergo a natural process of development and increased sophistication by virtue of their own success. Greiner (1972) first conceptualized this organizational 'evolution', and the major phases are summarized as:

- entrepreneurial – leadership which brings the organization through its first crisis and provides goals and direction
- collectivity – autonomy
- delegation – control
- formalization – red tape
- collaboration – renewal which leads to either a new form of organization or into decline (adapted from Hatch, 1997: 174–7).

Implicit in the above is the notion that each stage is dominated by a different focus fraught with crises. Once these crises are addressed, the organization passes into the next developmental stage. However, Greiner's model is introspective and is more concerned with leadership than environmental dynamics. In addition, it does not deal with major contingencies identified by many other theorists. The following subsection introduces some of these contingencies and explains their meaning in a leisure services context.

Contingency factor one – environment

According to Robbins (1998) the environment includes forces outside the organization that potentially affect its performance. This is a fairly obvious assertion but it is worthwhile stating that this typically includes customers, pressure groups, suppliers, competitors, government regulations and so on. All these elements combine and conspire to produce an environment which is unpredictable to a lesser or greater extent. In fact, it is the uncertainty that compromises the effectiveness of organizational structures rather than environmental factors *per se*.

Managers must therefore try to reduce uncertainty through prediction and making subsequent adjustments to organizational structure and design. Popular ways of analysing environments include use of techniques such as:

- strengths, weaknesses, opportunities, threats (SWOT)
- political, economic/environmental, social, technological (PEST)
- mnemonics whereby all appropriate variables are considered.

Gerloff, Muir and Bodensteiner (1991) posit a different typology, which considers environmental uncertainty to be determined by three main dimensions shown in Table 2.2.

Dimension	Characteristics
Capacity	Extent to which growth may be supported; growing environments create excess resources allowing organizations to make mistakes and remain successful. For example, many tourism and hospitality firms were inappropriately structured but thrived in UK resorts prior to 'continental' competition for cheap package holidays until the mid-1960s
Volatility	Extent of environmental instability ranging from extreme dynamism to extremely stable
Complexity	Extent to which there exists heterogeneity and concentration among environmental elements; simple environments are homogeneous and concentrated. For example, newer purpose-built resorts in Australia tend to be owned and operated by only one company; by contrast older resort areas in the UK are a conglomerate of individual owner-operators and others, with organizations emerging and declining continuously

Source: adapted from Robbins (1998: 500–1).

Table 2.2 Environmental classification according to three key dimensions

These authors conclude that environmental uncertainty correlates strongly with organizational design. Accordingly, a scarce, dynamic and complex environment should give rise to organizations with organic-type structures, whereas mechanistic designs are more suited to conditions which are abundant, stable and simple.

Another useful approach is to classify geographical regions as products. Resorts or destinations may be viewed from a marketing perspective as 'products' subject their own life cycle. Butler's (1980) model or 'sequence' attempts to explain identifiable stages in these terms.

Essentially, Butler proposes that tourist destinations experience five distinct growth stages: exploration, involvement, development, consolidation and stagnation. Each stage of the cycle requires a specific managerial approach, and thus organizational structure, to remain effective and efficient.

The basic tenets of the Butler sequence are shown in Figure 2.1. Although this construct has been criticized, it is popular because of its simplicity, intuitive appeal and overall robustness.

Customer demand and expectations also play a fundamental role in the way organizations are structured. In the leisure sector, one only has to consider the impact of 'seasonality' to validate this idea. There can be little doubt that the operating conditions for hospitality, tourism and leisure service organizations are dynamic.

Despite their organization charts giving a mechanistic impression, delivery of the product relies on individuals being cross-functional because provision of service is

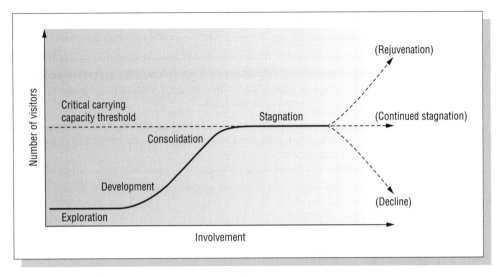

Figure 2.1 Butler's S-shaped resort cycle model
Source: Weaver and Opperman (2000: 371).

more akin to process delivery rather than manufacturing a product. To cope with these pressures, these organizations (especially in resort areas) have adopted an organic structure – the 'flexible' firm, also known as a 'core-ring' or 'shamrock' structure.

Key point 2.2

Organizations have structures which are determined by internal and external factors.

Flexible firm ● ● ●

Interest in labour flexibility dates from the 1980s from which Atkinson's (1985) 'ideal' model of the flexible firm was developed at the Institute of Manpower Studies in the UK. This model classifies workers as either 'core' or 'peripheral' and is linked to Doeringer and Piore's (1971) notion of primary and secondary labour markets.

Core workers are defined as those who conduct key activities of the firm (Atkinson and Meagre, 1986). They require organization-specific skills and are therefore comparatively difficult to recruit from outside. Their jobs are usually well paid, autonomous, carry a degree of responsibility and have identifiable opportunities for career progression.

Peripheral employees, on the other hand, are less likely to have permanent contracts, have fewer career opportunities and their jobs are often unskilled with limited job security and lower pay. They also have skills which are not organization specific or central to the organization's success and are relatively easy to recruit externally (Simms, Hales and Riley, 1988). In effect, they form a buffer, insulating core employees from changes in demand.

Flexibility	Characteristics
Numerical	Employment opportunities vary directly with economic activity; job tenure is usually part-time, temporary/seasonal, casual or some other form of short-term contract
Functional	Employment opportunities not linked directly to economic activity, multiskilled, jobs enriched, similar to more 'traditional' full-time employment

Table 2.3 Flexible categories

Table 2.3 shows how core and peripheral workers allow structural flexibility in leisure service organizations.

In an applied sense, leisure organizations in resort areas typically draw core employees from a professional national or international pool. Conversely, they may recruit locally and provide in-house training. These individuals are normally supervisors or managers and work the whole year round. During the 'off' season their job tasks are likely to change from service delivery to maintenance of the physical property.

This scenario is particularly appropriate in the small to medium-sized unaffiliated sector. Core workers thus become multiskilled in areas other than service delivery and help ensure consistency of product during the busy season.

An organizational structure which delivers consistent product quality from season to season is clearly important because peripheral workers are recruited from a traditionally 'unskilled' national or local labour pool.

In addition, they are offered little training and do not enjoy the employment conditions of their core counterparts. On a cautionary note, the description of peripheral employees and the 'unimportance' of their jobs run counter to their role in the leisure service sector.

These individuals often are employed at the customer interface and these encounters are now regarded as key result areas (Jones and Lockwood, 1989: 110). For example, absence of training provision is an inappropriate strategy for managers particularly in geographical areas where labour is in short supply or there are no reputable agency supplies of skilled banqueting staff. The use of agencies to supply peripheral workers is akin to a strategy of 'distancing'.

This is another example of how the structure of leisure organizations is becoming increasingly flexible. The rationale for adopting this approach ranges from skilled labour shortages to firms deciding to concentrate on their most profitable areas. In the case of hospitality organizations, this would be selling rooms.

Hotels have always applied distancing strategies or had a 'networked' structure in one form or another (although this could hardly be described as a 'virtual' structure in the contemporary 'cyber' sense). Popular strategies include use of:

- engineering and maintenance contractors
- laundry services

- more recently, dividing accommodation from catering with the latter being operated by another company.

Indeed, in the USA, Australia and increasingly in Europe, hospitality, tourism and leisure companies provide a range of separate services at particular locations and destinations. For example, in the USA, supply of roadside accommodation and catering may be divided between Motel 6 and Wendy's or Red Lobster; in Australia, similar accommodation is provided by the independent sector or affiliated accommodation and Red Rooster or Sizzler restaurants.

Furthermore, popular Australian winter tourist destinations such as Thredbo may be serviced by a variety of affiliated and unaffiliated organizations. For example, Novotel, Pender Lea and Valley Lodge supply accommodation and the Thredbo Resort Centre Pty Ltd take care of heritage and village walks, skiing and snow-shoeing. This arrangement is similar to that found in Aviemore (UK) and Chamonix (France). However, these configurations are better described as networks which is not strictly a distancing strategy.

Some advantages of distancing include a focus on core business, appropriate use of expertise and cost savings. Conversely, the company adopting the distancing strategy loses control of activities. This may cause problems particularly if there is a difference in quality standards between the organizations concerned.

Key point 2.3

Environmental conditions for hospitality, tourism and leisure service organizations are often dynamic, therefore structures and designs are based on organic principles. One important organizational form in this sector is the flexible firm.

In addition to the vagaries of the environment, there are other important issues, which influence organizational structure and design; these are technology, size and structure. We will address each in turn beginning with technology.

Contingency factor two – technology

Technology may be viewed as the way in which an organization manufactures its product. Kats and Kahn (1966) mapped these elements and processes abstractly as inputs, transformation process and outputs. Their 'open systems' view considers the manufacture or delivery of a product similar to a process which is shown in Figure 2.2.

At this level, technology or the transformation process is viewed as a 'black box'. In other words, it represents all of the interplay, interaction and complexity between organizational and environmental variables necessary to produce or deliver the final product.

Robbins (2001: 430) summarizes the thrust of numerous related studies and comments: 'The common theme that differentiates technologies [and thus organizational

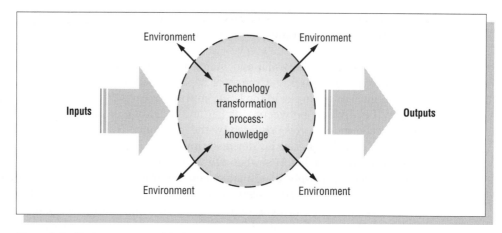

Figure 2.2 Basic systems model of organizational technology

structures] is their degree of routineness.' In other words, the extent to which organizations deliver or produce a customized or automated product has an impact on their technological and structural design.

His comment is rooted in the earlier work of Woodward (1958) who claims that organizational structures tend to vary or can be predicted according to the technology 'types' in most frequent use. In the case of leisure firms, technology may be considered as the processes involved in service delivery, including tangible elements of the product; for example, food and beverage.

Bartol et al. (2001: 314) reproduce Woodward's (1958) original typology which divides and classifies routineness of production as 'unit and small batch' – customized; 'large batch and mass' – large quantities, assembly line; and 'continuous-process'. These categories are shown below with illustrations from the leisure industry:

- unit and small batch – all frontline service exchanges with customers
- large batch and mass – table d'hôte items for catering functions such as weddings, banquets and other special events; fast-food restaurants
- continuous-process – there are no true examples of this type of process although centralized 'factory-type' preparation of cook-chill and cook-freeze items for airlines, hospitals and prisons come close.

In the leisure sector, customized service provision dominates the product and this can be clearly identified in the first category. Indeed, it could be argued that even the production of tangible goods such as menu items only extends to the 'large batch' area of category two. According to Woodward (1965) organizations occupying the first two categories should have relatively simple organizational structures; centralization and formalization should be similarly low. Both of these elements are minimal in autonomous work groups and may, in part, explain a simplification of organizational structures where empowerment has been extended to leisure workers as discussed earlier in this chapter.

However, the suggestion that a 'simple' organization structure parallels a simple service delivery process would be inappropriate. Even Bryant's (1986: v) astute characterization that the UK hospitality sector is 'low tech' gives a false impression. Leisure services are multidimensional, subject to varying perceptions of quality and are a conglomerate of tangibles and intangibles.

Consistent and appropriate service delivery has proved something of a conundrum for leisure organizations because:

- the service is intangible and cannot be seen or experienced beforehand by customers
- quality is a purely subjective concept and differences may exist between individual service providers and individual customers
- identifiable stages of the delivery process must be completed in a particular sequence if the service is to be satisfactory. The number of necessary stages depends on the sophistication of the service, but each has the potential to fail.

A number of authors have taken up the challenge of modelling and explaining the process (see Kandampully, Mok and Sparks, 2001, for a summary of major contributions). While some differences exist between theories, all concur that the service provider becomes an important part of the overall product. Frontline employees often find themselves in complex customer exchange situations and behave accordingly. These exchange encounters are:

- 'key result areas' (Jones and Lockwood, 1989: 110)
- managers need an appropriate method of controlling the process
- thus, decision-making is pushed to 'lower' levels of the organization in order to maximize the chances of success.

Some hotel jobs are easier to differentiate than others, but in certain areas autonomous work groups may be more productive than individuals undertaking highly differentiated tasks. This is a theme which Lashley (1997) extends in his work on fast-food restaurants and argues with the relatively recent research into frontline hospitality tasks such as 'service encounter management' (for example, Sparks and Bradley, 1997).

Plausibly, Kandampully (2002) considers that most hospitality functions may be re-engineered into a seamless service experience. This requires a considerable amount of multiskilling and cross-functional capability to be achieved. In addition, hospitality, tourism and leisure-based research into revenue maximization or 'yield management', for example, stresses the importance of increased autonomy if these systems are to prove effective (see Ingold, McMahon-Beattie and Yeoman, 1999). The underpinning philosophy is that customers require immediate satisfaction for a range of demands, not all of which are strictly the responsibility of one employee.

Effective delivery also relies on (reciprocal) inputs from other areas of the organization. Thompson (1967) classifies this situation as 'reciprocal interdependence' where Katz and Kahn's (1966) notion of outputs from one system become inputs for another and vice versa. For example, the service of a restaurant meal requires reciprocal arrangements between reservations, dining area and kitchen. Bartol *et al.* (2001) illustrate this relationship using the roles of maintenance and flight crew for passenger aircraft.

The concept of autonomous work groups, team and cross-functional working has now been wholeheartedly embraced by a multitude of non-service organizations such as General Electric, DaimlerChrysler, 3M, Federal Express and so on (Robbins, 2001:

257–8). The rationale for this shift is chiefly because of heightened global competition and the need to secure and maintain competitive advantage in an increasingly dynamic marketplace. In simple terms, organizations must satisfy customer expectations or fail.

There is no doubt that the delivery of intricate and multidimensional leisure services is a highly complex affair; it is processual, and for this reason the initial views of both Woodward (1958) and Katz and Kahn (1966) give a more informative picture than that conveyed by an organizational chart. Indeed, it is tempting to suggest that organizational charts (discussed in the final section of this chapter) for hospitality, tourism and leisure firms give a false impression of authority, structure and order. This is despite the seemingly clear-cut departmental and hierarchical form they detail.

Key point 2.4

Organizations which produce on a unit and small-batch basis and have operations characterized by reciprocal interdependence are complex and require horizontal co-ordination. Similarly, non-routine or low-level technologies, which are typical in leisure service provision, rely on specialized knowledge and delegated decision-making authority. These are characteristics of organic organizational structures.

Contingency factor three – size

Evidence suggests that size impacts significantly upon organizational structure and design; for example, in large organizations standardization of formal rules and procedures is a necessary mechanism for co-ordination. Thus, large organizations will tend to have more rules and regulations, departments and vertical levels than will small organizations.

There are a number of negative outcomes associated with large organizational structures, including increased absenteeism and job turnover and decreased job satisfaction (Porter, Lawler and Hackman, 1975). Furthermore, evidence for superior economic performance of firms with complex multi-layered structures is equivocal.

In the hospitality industry, there is strong evidence to suggest that the larger and more complex organizations become, the less that formal rules and procedures are used for communications and operations at unit level (Shamir, 1975).

Currently across all industrial sectors (with some public sector exceptions), large organizations are downsizing. In part this is because of retrenchment, but also there is an acknowledgement that small simple structures resonate more easily with dynamic environments. Furthermore, employees tend to perform more effectively with increased autonomy and fewer vertical levels of authority.

Contingency factor four – strategy

Strategy is no less important than the three contingencies already discussed. Leisure organizations can only truly maximize effectiveness by matching an appropriate structure with their chosen strategy (in that order). There are several ways to categorize organizational strategy but each focuses on innovation, cost-minimization and imitation. Table 2.4 shows each of these strategies with examples of each.

Clearly, some of the examples in Table 2.4 could appear in more than one category; for example, Virgin Blue is currently a new innovation in Australian air travel which at the moment is dominated by the more expensive Qantas service.

Strategy	Example
Innovation – emphasizes introduction of major new products and services	Virgin Blue, Australia; Disney World, Orlando, USA; Formule 1, Europe
Cost-minimization – emphasizes tight cost controls, avoidance of unnecessary innovation or marketing expenses and price cutting	Novotel, UK; Motel 6, USA; Balti Curry Restaurants, Birmingham, UK
Imitation – emphasizes movement into new products or markets only after their viability has already been proven	Alton Towers Theme Park, UK; Warner Brothers Theme Park and Studios, Gold Coast, Australia; Hungry Jack's, Australia; any number of franchises

Table 2.4 Strategies and structures

It is an innovator because of new 'no frills' transport, but the novelty exists chiefly because of cheap fares; this is a feature of cost minimization. Furthermore, Alton Towers would have been considered an innovation in the UK when first introduced. However, it is an imitation of an earlier Disney World, Orlando, USA (which itself is a replica of Disney Land established earlier in California).

Figure 2.3 summarizes the major contingencies impacting upon organizational structure and design.

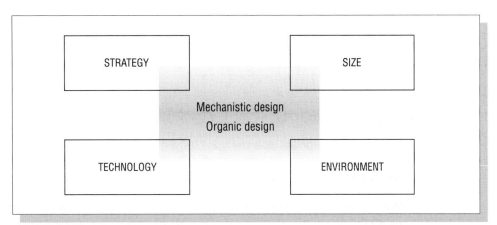

Figure 2.3 Contingencies influencing organizational structure and design

So far, we have discussed some of the key factors which are said to impact on organizational structure and design. These are:

- the nature of the product
- the nature of the labour force
- four major contingencies summarized in Figure 2.3.

Ideally, with the foresight that such knowledge permits, managers should now be in a position to structure their organization appropriately. However, to do this there are a number of crucial design fundamentals that need to be considered.

Reflective practice

1 Evaluate whether both internal and external factors impact equally on organizational design.
2 Using examples, illustrate any two stages of Butler's S-shaped cycle model.
3 Using two leisure services organizations of your choice, estimate the proportions of core and peripheral workers for each.
4 Do you think peripheral workers require similar training to that of their core counterparts?

Case study 2.1

Jayne Booth is the general manager of a large 500-bedroomed chain hotel in a major Australian city. It is the most successful in the company and she has a reputation for running a 'tight ship'. Jayne is therefore understandably unconcerned when she learns of an impending visit by the company's chief executive officer (CEO) to discuss strategic matters including the hotel's structure and design.

Their meeting is now well under way. The conversation turns to the role played by the hotel's structure and design in achieving customer satisfaction and good financial performance. Jayne knew this would be an important part of the meeting. She deals with these questions by first presenting details of the hotel's structure and design using its organizational chart.

Reflective practice

1 Using the scenario in Case study 2.1, how much importance would you place on the organizational chart when attempting to explain profitability and customer satisfaction to the CEO? What other issues does it illustrate?
2 Do you believe it represents the structural reality of the hotel?
3 Would you classify the hotel structure as mechanistic, organic or something else?

Basic principles of structure and design

To obtain an overall 'feel' for how organizations operate, who holds power, makes decisions and so on, it is helpful to think of your own work experiences. Consider the nature of the product, to whom you report and how information is communicated. Also think about just one person as an organization and build from that point, introducing more products, increased demand and more employees.

Imagine a chef who decides to open a small restaurant offering a limited menu. Later, the restaurant becomes popular, creating demand for longer opening hours, more menu items (although not necessarily) and a requirement for more help in the kitchen and more staff to serve the food.

How do these additional demands impact on the structure of this organization? Will the operation need to divide jobs into specific tasks undertaken by more than one person, for example? This is known as division of labour and is adopted to increase effectiveness and efficiency of the production process.

Although this example may appear overly simple, it is in fact an accurate reflection of how many large organizations begin (after all, Lord Forte began operating what was to become arguably the largest hospitality company in the world from one simple 'Milk Bar' in London, UK, just after the Second World War). However, not all entrepreneurs have such lofty ambitions.

It is often said that organizations employing between one and ten staff dominate the secondary and service sectors of most developed nations. This is certainly the case in the UK and Australian leisure industries, particularly in tourism and hospitality where even small to medium-sized firms occupy 97 per cent and 90 per cent of market share respectively (Lee-Ross, 1998). Several explanations are usually offered and most include:

- low barriers to entry
- chance to be your own boss
- status in the local community
- preference for staying small and family-run, and making mediocre but satisfactory profits.

Whatever the reasons for setting up in business, most small organizational structures are simple, with owner-operators undertaking most of the technical work and making all the decisions. There is little or no delegation of authority and power because there are only a few employees (or none at all) and who are often family members prepared to defer to the family head.

Characteristics of this particular design are short lines of communication, flexibility and an absence of formal rules and regulations. Indeed, the organization often becomes a 'personification' of the employer's personal aims and objectives. If they are particularly effective, the organization is likely to prosper but, if the patron is ineffective, the business is likely to fail or enjoy only limited success.

Our organization has now expanded and offers a wider range of leisure services. It is unlikely that a single individual can provide and manage all of these items effectively. Production and service of menu items will need to be divided between several employees. Similarly, accommodation and recreational facilities will need to be managed by specialists. Each of these areas will also require staff with the technical competence to deliver the product.

Furthermore, as the organization grows, individuals will need to manage areas, which facilitate or support the provision of core products. There is now a requirement for expertise in planning and control of marketing, finance, staffing and maintenance. Thus, the organization becomes more complex structurally.

The owner-operator can no longer rely on intuition for marketing plans or informal unwritten policies and procedures for service co-ordination, provision and control. As the organization increases in size, these issues become more elaborate and the design of the organization changes. The theoretical structure of firms is underpinned according to:

- work specialization
- division of work
- chain of command
- span of control.

Work specialization

An archetypal example of work specialization is the 'assembly line' which was largely responsible for the success of Henry Ford's Model T which could be 'any colour so long as it was black'. This production design is rooted in Taylor's (1947) scientific approach which considers that all work processes can be separated and analysed to identify a 'one best way'.

These tasks are then rearranged and combined with only a few performed by each worker to maximize efficiency. Until recently, most manufacturing-type production processes were undertaken in this manner. However, by the 1960s, worker diseconomies such as increased absenteeism, boredom and stress were beginning to emerge. Current thinking has shifted emphasis away from jobs which are highly specialized to ones which encourage group and team participation and increased autonomy.

There is no doubt that in an economic sense, the tenets of the scientific design work well and are present in a number of service organizations. Visit any KFC, Hungry Jack's or McDonald's outlet and you will see that the production process is based on such work specialization (tempered with measures designed to address negative outcomes of the process).

However, it is difficult to imagine many jobs in the leisure sector are appropriate for this kind of treatment except for those that mirror a manufacturing process. Even in many hotel kitchens food production is no longer highly differentiated. Indeed, there has been a move away from specialization even in fine-dining restaurants.

Until recently the service of meals was broken down into its constituents and separate food items. Meats, vegetables and sauces were 'silver served' to the customer; sometimes a waiter or waitress would be responsible for each of these items. With the advent of Nouvelle Cuisine, Cuisine Nouveau and so on, chefs now cook and arrange complete menu items. Thus, they are responsible for presentation and, to some extent, service style. Effectively, the job of chef has been enriched because of the increased responsibility afforded by more contemporary approaches to fine dining.

This is an example of a contingency which has changed the design of these production-type jobs. Moreover, this shift has happened by virtue of fashion and because the job of chef has become deskilled due to the increasing use of convenience products.

> **Key point 2.5**
>
> In most hospitality, tourism and leisure organizations, frontline jobs should be structured so that employees require a minimum of direct input from management. This empowerment allows service to be customized every time it is delivered.

Division of work/departmentalization

At a broad level, work may be divided by product or service whereby specialists have responsibility for each. This configuration is usually found in large organizations that produce several different (or related) products. For example, the Accor group has a range of service products targeted at different market segments including Go Voyages (air travel packages), Formule 1 (budget accommodation) and Sofitel (prestige accommodation). These products may also be structured according to geographical region. Several Accor hotel brands are international; for example, Novotel, Suite and Ibis.

Within organizations work may be divided by a common logical attribute, such as relative importance of a specialization, use of same resources or shared expertise. A common grouping is based on the major purpose or function of the organization; for example, finance, marketing, operations and so on.

Span of control and chain of command

This key feature of structure is basically a classical approach to organizational design. It concerns authority and refers to the number of workers who report directly to a particular manager or supervisor, or the number of employees a manager can direct effectively.

Despite the early effort of Graicunas (1937), who provides a formula for calculating span of control, the number of employees who can be supervised effectively varies according to:

- the nature of the organization
- the nature of the product
- complexity of work
- available time
- personal qualities of management
- training needs.

Span of control also helps determine the number levels, and thus managers, in organizations. Consider two organizations each having around 4100 operative employees. If one organization has a span of four and the other eight, the latter would have only five levels and approximately 600 managers; compared with seven levels and around 1300 managers.

Companies have now moved towards flatter designs (or wide spans of control) in order to get closer to customers and empower employees. However, it must also be said that these structures are more productive because they require fewer middle managers.

Flatter organizational designs work best when employees are trained to cope with the new responsibilities which accompany empowered roles. Thus, co-workers instead of managers may be consulted for advice, and to some extent leadership. In the case of hospitality industry frontline workers, evidence suggests that many prefer working autonomously with a minimum of management intervention. However, this is not always the case. For example, a banqueting service requires more direct co-ordination and control by a supervisor or manager than an informal dinner.

- Most of these basic design principles are communicated in a firm's organization chart which shows its structure at one particular point in time and, although hackneyed, still prevails.
- Usually, details of departmentalization, activity groupings, relationships and authority are all included in organizational charts.
- Information tends to be shown in varying detail depending on the organization's requirements.

Figures 2.4 and 2.5 show two charts: Figure 2.4 (Boulton, 2003, personal communication) is for a large medium-quality hotel and Figure 2.5 (Teplys, 1996, personal communication) is for a large luxury-style resort. Both have a similar design and show division of work by function, a chain of command and a span of control. In addition, the figures also suggest formal relationships between different areas, which Mullins (1996) summarizes as:

- Line – downward vertical flow of authority from directors to managers, supervisors to operational staff; line relationships associated with departmental division of work and control; line managers have authority for all matters within their own section or department.
- Staff (sometimes referred to as functional) – relationship between specialists or advisers and line managers and their operative workers; for example, a personnel manager will offer a common service throughout all organizational departments but has no particular authority over any, although line managers will be expected to take the advice of this specialist.

Essentially, there are few differences between Figures 2.4 and 2.5 except that the former is smaller and understandably has a marginally wider and flatter structure. However, these charts have their limits and fail to show the extent of delegation from managers to operatives (although a simple flat structure may give this impression) and the precise nature of relationships between people.

Organizational charts remain popular because they:

- are relatively easy to understand
- supply a seemingly coherent plan of the organization
- provide a convenient point of reference from which other structures can be explained.

The latter issue is important because, often, actual organization structures bear little resemblance to anything shown in their organization chart, especially in the leisure industry.

The hierarchy, division of labour and authority explicit in these figures are rooted in Weber's (1947) model of bureaucracy. In some respects, this organizational design has been fashionably maligned by many writers for reasons of inflexibility and overreliance on rules and regulations, both of which stifle the

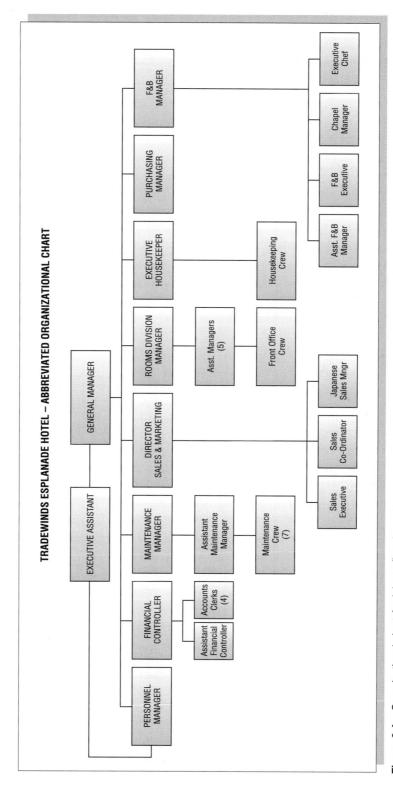

Figure 2.4 Organizational chart for leisure firm 1
Source: Boulton (2003).

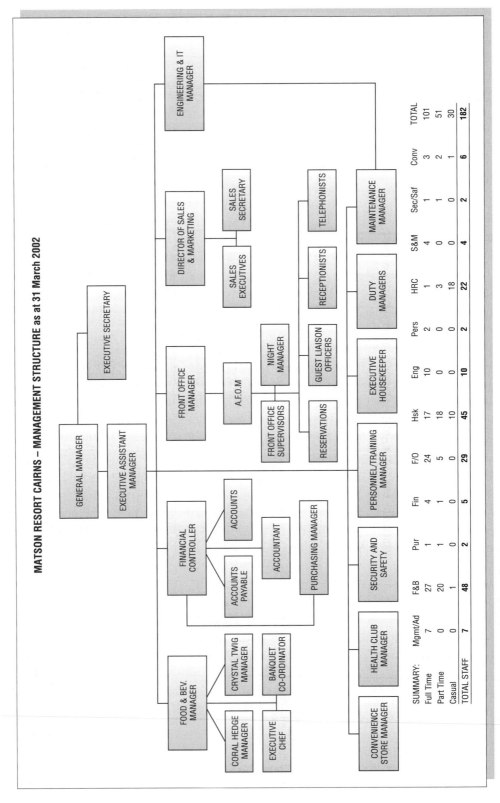

MATSON RESORT CAIRNS – MANAGEMENT STRUCTURE as at 31 March 2002

SUMMARY:	Mgmt/Ad	F&B	Pur	Fin	F/O	Hsk	Eng	Pers	HRC	S&M	Sec/Saf	Conv	TOTAL
Full Time	7	27	1	4	24	17	10	2	1	4	3	3	101
Part Time	0	20	1	1	5	18	0	0	3	0	1	2	51
Casual	0	1	0	0	0	10	0	0	18	0	0	1	30
TOTAL STAFF	7	48	2	5	29	45	10	2	22	4	2	6	182

Figure 2.5 Organizational chart for leisure firm 2
Source: Teplys (1996).

organization's response to environmental stimuli and compromise individual creativity. However, there is no reason why autonomy cannot be afforded to employees within these structures.

Furthermore, there is compelling evidence to suggest that in a contemporary context this occurs in any case, through official policies of employee empowerment. This is similar to Hatch's (1997) notion of de-differentiation where semi-autonomous work groups replace management responsibility and control. Even in an informal sense, this way of working has been identified by hospitality researchers such as Shamir (1975). He notes that despite the bureaucratic and mechanistic appearance of hotel structures, the tasks involved in service provision are based on informal autonomy and communications due to the service element of the product.

Other research identifies worker traits such as entrepreneurialism and non-supportive management styles (Johnson, 1980; Leinster, 1985) as powerful reasons for autonomy in hospitality organizations. The former seems to be a pivotal employee 'orientation to work' whereas the latter is brought about as a coping mechanism because of poor supervisory technique.

Thus, in the leisure services sector, hospitality organizations behave organically rather than mechanistically. Figure 2.6 is a tongue-in-cheek comparison of a formal organizational structure with a more realistic one.

The static organizational structure (shown in the first part of Figure 2.6), conceived by early theorists such as Adam Smith, Frederick Taylor and Max Weber, might now be considered almost illusory. These models were mainly concerned with economic rationalism and adopted a unitarist stance. This traditional perspective paid little heed to diverse work attitudes and motivational requirements. Instead, employees were considered as a collection of individuals pursuing a common economic goal established by management.

Although the second part of Figure 2.6 is an exaggeration it illustrates a serious behavioural construct known as the 'informal organization'. This is where issues of employee communications, group norms and culture determine the smooth running of the firm. When you consider that 'working to rule' is used as a legitimate form of employee protest, the potency of structural informality in the workplace can be appreciated. Despite the early classicists' attempts to rationalize structure and design by economic logic, make no mistake, organizations are social systems where employees establish their own rules and regulations.

The matrix structure ● ● ●

As organizations become larger, progressing from a simple structure to a necessarily more complex and differentiated one, there is potential for inefficiency. Chiefly, communications can become distorted, response rates sluggish and departments too competitive (with each other) thereby creating a situation of 'suboptimization'. This means that departmental or section goals become more important than those of the organization. There are various ways suboptimization can be minimized and we have already mentioned a few techniques and approaches, including autonomous work groups and teams, empowerment and flatter organizational designs.

A more formal organizational design said to mitigate certain organizational inefficiency is know as a matrix structure. This is where a set of divisional horizontal

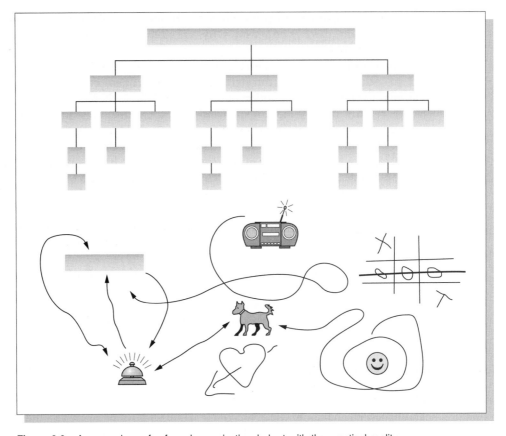

Figure 2.6 A comparison of a formal organizational chart with the practical reality

reporting relationships are superimposed onto a hierarchical functional structure or where functional departments are combined with units that integrate activities of different functional departments on a project or product basis.

There are both vertical and horizontal chains of command. The former flow downwards from functional departments whereas authority and responsibility of the project manager is horizontal across the organizational structure.

Matrix structures are appropriate where there is:

- more than one critical orientation to the operations of the organization
- a requirement for simultaneous processing of vast quantities of information
- a need for sharing resources
- environmental pressure for focus on both functional and divisional dimensions
- unpredictable demand for the product.

While a matrix structure has a number of theoretical strengths, including flexibility and staff development opportunities, several disadvantages have been identified. The ones of major concern are high administrative costs, role ambiguity due to dual reporting and responsibility and overemphasis on group decision-making.

There is also evidence to suggest that, for matrix structures to work, organizational culture must be predisposed to accommodate them. If this is not the case then cultures must be adapted correspondingly. As we will see in Chapter 8, bringing about cultural change in organizations is notoriously difficult to achieve.

Key point 2.6

In many service organizations, the mechanistic, hierarchical structure suggested by organizational charts is an illusion. While many service firms are moving towards flatter structures, employee orientations to work and management styles have already created this design.

Conclusion

There can be no doubting the importance of organizational structure and design. Structure reduces ambiguity and clarifies roles and task expectations. In addition, it affects the attitudes and behaviour of members and the productivity of the organization as a whole.

Organizational structures are many and varied, often with two or more design features incorporated into the same firm (elements of bureaucracy and flexibility, for example). These forms change for a number of key reasons. On the one hand, there is evidence to suggest that organizations experience a natural development with transition between stages punctuated by some sort of internal management 'crisis'. Another perspective holds environmental characteristics responsible for structural change (or adaptation).

The latter view is popular and classifies organizations operating within these dynamics as extremes of either mechanistic or organic structures. The former have formalized rules, specialized procedures and protocol. There is usually an adherence to a visible chain of command with limited delegation of responsibility. This design is best suited to unchanging and predictable operating conditions. Organic structures have the opposite features and succeed in dynamic conditions where adaptation and flexibility are required.

In addition to environment, other contingencies of technology, size and strategy are also held as key determinants of organization types. In the leisure service sector, seasonal demand, nature of the product and integrated processes necessary for service delivery all have a crucial impact on organizational design. For example, firms operating seasonally have a 'flexible' structure whereby extra staff are employed to supplement the existing core worker complement during busy times. However, this flexible model is different to that used in other industries because peripheral workers require training and empowerment if they are to operate effectively at the customer interface. In addition, the service product is intangible and often uses a complex staged delivery process. This requires staff who are multiskilled and able to communicate and operate cross-functionally.

Distancing strategies are also used frequently by leisure service organizations for reasons including, risk minimization, focusing on core and profitable areas and so on.

Of course, this also has the impact of flattening the overarching network of firms or modular organizational structure.

Thus in the leisure services sector, more fluid and flatter organic designs are appropriate. Structures should engender production through autonomous work groups and self-managed teams using common activities to differentiate, rather than functions or departments. Jobs with increased empowerment are more effective than high specialization with each task being completed by one person. These proposals challenge earlier assumptions of basic principles of specialization, division of work and span of control/chain of command indicated in traditional organizational charts.

Furthermore, the attitudes and behaviour of people and groups in organizations are not explained fully by formal structure, nor are they detailed in organizational charts. The manner in which employees interpret jobs, operationalize tasks and work within formal structures becomes the actual organizational design. Despite this, organizational charts still remain popular probably because they are easy to understand and give an idea of a seemingly coherent structure.

Reflective practice

1 Discuss the objectives of organizational structure and design.
2 Identify and explain the major contingencies impacting on the structure of hospitality, leisure and tourism firms.
3 Discuss the essential differences between mechanistic and organic organizational structures.
4 Explain why organic structures are appropriate for hospitality, leisure and tourism organizations.

CHAPTER 3

Organizational politics: legitimacy and opposition

- identify models of political rule in organizations
- discuss ethical issues in organizational behaviour
- describe the collective forms of opposition
- evaluate oppositional behaviour in leisure service organizations.

Most of us have a general interest in politics. It is popularly understood to be about the State and its affairs including societal issues like inflation, unemployment, exchange rates and so on. At both national and international levels, politics creates many heated discussions across a range of issues. For example, you probably have an opinion on who should run your country. Likewise, a friend may have an equal but opposite view. Both perspectives are valid and will have been influenced by your background and upbringing, facts, figures and persuasive argument. This outlook is known colloquially as politics with a capital 'P' and is what most people perceive the term to mean. However, this is only partially correct and other factors need to be identified before politics can be understood fully, especially within organizations.

Morgan's (1986) models of political 'rule' are shown in Figure 3.1 and help us appreciate how organizations try to govern their members. They are by no means mutually exclusive and several are often present simultaneously in the organization.

Autocratic – absolute government where power is held by an individual or small group.

Bureaucratic – ruling by the written word which promotes a logical or rational 'rule of law'.

Codetermination – rule by a combination or joint management of opposing parties for mutual benefit.

Representative democracy – officers elected and mandated to act on behalf of electorate for a certain time period.

Direct democracy – everyone has the right to rule and are involved in all decision making with the principle of self-organization.

Figure 3.1 Models of political rule in organizations
Source: adapted from Morgan (1986: 145).

Although helpful, Morgan's constructs have much in common with capital P politics and do not explain the nuances, power struggles and pursuit of personal objectives by organization members.

- The practical organizational reality is that within each of these apparently 'rational' models, individuals have their own agendas and seek ways to advance their careers, often at the expense of others.
- It is the manner in which members perceive their position in the organization and how they try to achieve personal objectives which is important for our purpose.

This chapter is broadly divided into two sections. The first defines and explains organizational politics. This should allow you to appreciate its nature, prevalence and potency. Moreover, you should also gain an understanding of the political way people behave in order to achieve personal goals. The second section deals with the ways that organization members oppose the current political power regime.

Reflective practice

1 Over the next few days, pay attention to the media and note any major (or minor) political debates and developments. Try to apply these principles to an organization with which you are familiar. Outline your thoughts in small groups or feed your ideas to the class for general discussion.
2 In a capital P sense, who has most power, a nation's treasury or the premier's department/cabinet?
3 Which department has the most power in an organization where you have either worked or are familiar with?

What does 'politics' mean in an organizational context?

The *Collins English Dictionary and Thesaurus* defines politics and politic respectively as 'The art of government' and 'expedient and cunning'. Interestingly, appearance of the word 'art' in the first definition suggests that politics is a subjective process.

Thus, perspectives of what constitutes establishing and maintaining appropriate 'order' is a matter of opinion.

This 'human' explanation of politics is not surprising if you consider even large P politics. None are objectively more appropriate than others. Think of the vast array of political parties in your own country; each argues that they hold the panacea or cure-all for unemployment, low productivity, crime and so on.

As with politics in society, perceptions of what is political and what constitutes a legitimate political issue is a matter of values, attitudes and beliefs. Using categories outline by Fox (1973), people holding different views of organizations will have different expectations and perceptions of legitimate behaviour. Disagreements over the allocation of resources in organizations are a fundamental concern.

Take, for example, disagreements over frontline members' pay:

- A person with a *unitarist* view will argue that organizations in a market economy are run to maximize to social good. Giving too much pay to workers will make the organization too costly and this will either lead to increased prices paid by customers, or to the ultimate closure of the firm and the unemployment of workers. In these circumstances, the organization's managers are making economically rational decisions that benefit society as a whole. Opposition and action to support opposition are irrational and due to a failure to 'understand the realities of business'. Large pay differentials between senior and junior members of the organization are a reflection of their different market positions.
- A *pluralist* might view pay claims as reflecting an interest group's claims on scarce resources. Managers and shareholders, along with customers, all have different interests and these sometimes conflict with each other. It is therefore important for organizations to manage these different demands on scarce resources in a way that ensures even treatment and fair processes. Sometimes compromise results in mutual dissatisfaction, so it is important to have in place procedures that are open and transparent for all to see. It is also important to ensure that differentials in pay between senior managers and junior staff are not too excessive.

- A *radical pluralist* might view pay claims as reflecting the nature of conflict within a capitalist enterprise. The surplus created by workers is taken by shareholders. Claims for a pay increase are the result of the conflicting relationship between owners and workers in an organization. Ultimately, the uneven power relationship of owners/shareholders means that workers are exploited. Differentials in pay rates between senior managers and junior organization members are an indication of the uneven distribution of power. Powerful senior staff work in the interests of themselves and the shareholders, and the only defence for the workforce is collective action or, ultimately, alternative ways of organizing the production of goods and services.

Another definition is helpful because it suggests that politics is about achieving something effectively and efficiently. In addition, 'cunning' is a human trait which once again infers that politics is subjective but may have an additional and negative connotation (depending on who benefits from the act of cunning). Indeed, in a work-a-day sense, individuals frequently talk of organizational politics in this way as a barrier to personal goal achievement, personal development and success.

Having read through the chapters in this book, you will realize that organizations are an extension of the human psyche; that is:

- they are irrational and fraught with contradictions and frailties
- the workplace lives and breathes, contains paradoxes and conflicts because of the individuals who inhabit them
- in a service context this metaphor is particularly appropriate because of the role members play in service delivery (for example, see Chapter 4)
- indeed, many writers consider that organizational politics exists and thrives because of the differences between the goals and aspirations of individual members (in addition to contextual matters).

Thus, by way of summary, both Robbins's (2001) and McShane and Travaglione's (2003) definitions seem wholly appropriate for the purpose of this chapter: 'Activities that are not required as part of an individual's formal role in the organization, but that influence, or attempt to influence, the distribution of advantages and disadvantages within the organization' (Robbins, 2001: 362); 'The attempts to influence others using discretionary behaviours to promote personal objectives' or 'It [organizational politics] is the exercise of power to get one's own way, including acquisition of more power, often at the expense of others' (McShane and Travaglione, 2003: 411).

Key point 3.1

Organizational politics concerns more than simply acknowledging models of political rule; rather, it is about understanding the infinite complexities and interplay between organizational members for their personal gain.

Organizational politics: good or bad?

Whether politics is inherently good or bad for organizations is a difficult question to answer. Indeed, political manoeuvring in one particular establishment may not be regarded as such in another. It simply depends on who is doing the politicking and who are the beneficiaries.

For example, an aggregate of evidence suggests that service organizations are moving away from the old-fashioned autocratic rule of law to a more democratic and open framework. These organizations often advocate empowerment and team working as the enlightened way forward. It is claimed that this promotes harmony and employee wellbeing, and has a positive impact on profitability and productivity (for example, UK-based Harvester and TGI Friday Restaurants; see Lashley, 1997).

However, ultimately these strategies are highly political and Legge (1995) points out that for teamworking, replacing management with a peer (or peers) for the purpose of control is downright unethical. She contends that this type of domination over workers is achieved without them ever realizing what is taking place. Thus, from a management perspective, these political strategies are of benefit to the organization. Conversely, other members might disagree if they discover how they are being manipulated.

Table 3.1 shows how a number of fashionable management initiatives are viewed from two alternative political perspectives.

Table 3.1 presupposes that all managers think alike. In practice, this is not the case nor is it true of other organizational members. Nonetheless, it helps us appreciate

Politics of management	Politics of other members
Customer first	Market forces are sovereign
Total quality management	Trying to achieve more with less
Lean production	'Mean' production
Flexibility	Management does what it wants to
Core and periphery	Reduction of organization's commitments to employees
Devolution/delayering	Reduction of middle managerial level
Downsizing/right-sizing	Redundancy
New working patterns	More part-time jobs at the expense of full-time equivalents
Empowerment	Someone else takes risk and responsibility
Training and development	Manipulation
Employability	No employment security
Recognizing contribution of the individual	Erosion of union power and process of collective bargaining
Team-working	Reducing individual's discretion

Source: adapted from: Sisson (1994: 5).

Table 3.1 Sisson's model of rhetoric and reality

differences of opinion about seemingly 'harmless' management strategies. The saying that beauty is in the eyes of the beholder seems appropriate here.

Reflective practice

1 Using the above technique, explain whether you agree or disagree with the comments of Karen Legge about teamworking and empowerment.

Key point 3.2

Whether political behaviour is good or bad in an organizational context depends on who is doing the politicking and who receives the benefits.

A commonly held view of organizational politics is that it interferes with the work process and as such should be diffused. After reviewing the evidence, McShane and Travaglione (2003) note that political behaviour plays a major role in work stoppages and other delays. They also categorize 'problematic' political behaviours as:

- lack of trust
- reduced willingness to collaborate
- reduced knowledge sharing
- misuse of resources.

Furthermore, they note that employees who experience organizational politics are likely to report higher levels of stress, psychological withdrawal and an increased propensity to quit their jobs.

Robbins (2001) comments on political behaviours but divides them into two groups of legitimate and illegitimate. *Legitimate political behaviour* includes complaints to supervisors, deliberate obstruction of policies and forming coalitions with other interested and powerful members. Members may also network with people external to the organization, bypass the formal chain of command, work to rule or withhold information from decision-makers. *Illegitimate political behaviours* range from industrial sabotage to whistle-blowing or less extreme measures such as violation of the company dress code.

How can a judgement be made whether political activity is acceptable or not? There is a technique available which enables us to assess it according to three moral principles. Of course, the final judgement depends on whether your perspective is that of management or other organizational members:

- Utilitarian rule – does the behaviour provide greatest benefit for most of the people? If not, does it affect the welfare of others negatively?
- Individual rights rule – does the behaviour infringe the legal or moral rights of others?
- Distributive justice rule – is the strategy fair for all or does it benefit someone at the expense of someone else?

What is the root cause of organizational politics?

It is unfortunate that wherever and whenever organizations exist, so too will their politics because of the variety and number of people working in them. There will always be conflict due to inter-member aspirational differences, goals and personality traits. For example, Biberman (1985) considers that individuals such as entrepreneurs display 'strong' traits of locus of control and a need for power. It would therefore seem reasonable to suggest that politics may be commonplace in the hospitality, leisure and tourism organizations for two reasons.

First, the sector is dominated by smaller owner-operated firms run by entrepreneurs. Second, entrepreneurial characteristics have been identified in many frontline workers of large hospitality corporations (see Chapter 4). This may also be the case elsewhere given the move in large organizations to promote and reward intrapreneurism for the purpose of product innovation (see Chapter 9).

Conflict and thus politicking within organizations also develops for a number of other reasons, which may be considered as contextual or cultural. Indeed, some authors believe this to be the major culprit (for example, see Robbins, 2001). It is alleged that individuals differ to a similar extent in all firms, yet some organizations are more political than others. Although there is little evidence to support this assertion, it would seem churlish to dismiss it totally.

Intuitively, employing organizations must have some impact on political behaviours and a few typical examples include:

- unsystematic allocation of finite resources
- unclear budgeting protocols
- inequitable salaries
- ad hoc performance evaluation systems.

Another often cited 'favourite' is lack of knowledge because decision-making in organizations typically takes place in an imperfect environment. In other words, people make choices without having all the necessary information to hand (this is known as 'bounded rationality'). Often, bounded rationality results in poor decisions being made and induces the decision-maker to optimize the 'facts' or withhold information in support of their own interests.

Key point 3.3

The root causes of organizational politics are the personality traits of individuals and the context in which they work.

As future or current organizational members, we would advise all students to recognize the significant of and often negative impact that politics has in the workplace. Ignorance may well be 'bliss' but failing to become politically aware is a serious misjudgement. Figure 3.2 contains a number of points which may help limit some of the negativity of organizational politics (as far as management is concerned).

Make sure there are enough resources but when scarce specify and communicate usage protocol.

Establish clear flows of information so the organization is not dependent on a minority of individuals.

Manage change in a step-wise fashion ensuring everyone knows what, when, where and how.

Restructure organizational and group norms to reject politicking which appears to obstruct achievement of company goals.

Provide opportunities for open dialogue between members and departments regularly.

Have employees monitor workplace and actively discourage colleagues who engage in political behaviour.

Figure 3.2 How to control political behaviour
Source: adapted from McShane and Travaglione (2003: 418).

Realistically, organizational members will always engage in political behaviour despite the best efforts of prevention. Therefore, Figures 3.2 and 3.3 contain hints designed to improve the political shrewdness of individuals. Some of the information overlaps but the message is clear: if you are not politically astute, you will be unable to either protect yourself from organizational mischief or use the skills for personal benefit.

Frame arguments in terms of organizational goals.

Develop the 'right' image – also known as impression management which is the process used by people when attempting to control the impression others have of them; for example, agreeing with someone else's opinion or doing them favours to gain approval, offering explanations which downplay your mistakes, flattery and so on.

Gain control of organizational resources including information and access of others to that information.

Be visible, make yourself appear indispensable and create obligation.

Develop powerful allies, coalitions and networks to achieve objectives which would be impossible as an individual.

Support your boss

Figure 3.3 How to improve your political effectiveness
Source: adapted from Robbins and Hunsaker (1996).

Avoiding action:

- Overconform by strict adherence to rules
- 'Pass the buck' by transferring responsibility for tasks to someone else
- 'Play stupid' by pleading ignorance or inability
- Depersonalize people by treating them as numbers or objects; this allows you to distance yourself from situations
- Make the job fit the time frame by prolonging it for as long as possible
- 'Stall' by appearing supportive in public but doing little about the matter or situation privately

Avoiding blame:

- Document your activities rigorously to give the impression of competence and thoroughness
- Evade situations which may reflect unfavourably on you; for example, only undertake projects that have a high probability of success
- Develop explanations that minimize your responsibility for a negative outcome
- Place the blame for a negative outcome on someone or something else (computer malfunctions are a particular favourite)
- Manipulate information by distortion, embellishment, deception, selective presentation and so on

Figure 3.4 Defensive strategies
Source: adapted from Robbins (2001: 371–2).

Another form of defensive political behaviour is to do nothing at all or at least try to avoid taking action. Figure 3.4 summarizes several techniques which individuals may use in this respect.

On a more cautionary note, viewing organizations exclusively from a political perspective and adopting the behaviours shown in Figures 3.3 and 3.4 may lead to negative consequences for the individual concerned. On the one hand, if they are used in the long term, individuals will probably experience feelings of isolation and self-estrangement. Moreover, they may lose a degree of respect and trust from their colleagues. In addition, both Morgan (1986) and Bolman and Deal (1997), whose texts adopt several metaphorical views of organizations, warn against holding such a narrow view. They consider that individuals may become obsessed with the perspective and interpret 'innocent' organizational processes with unwarranted suspicion. Ultimately, if members become too politically motivated, jobs become disrupted and less important than their own self-interest.

Key point 3.4

It is extremely unwise to ignore organizational politics, but avoid using this perspective exclusively when analysing the hospitality, leisure and tourism sector.

Opposition within organizations

The preceding section highlights some of the suggestions that have been made to improve personal effectiveness within the political organization. Junior members of the organization are in a position where power and authority are vested in senior members. Individually they have little personal influence, and little personal power to either change things they dislike, or influence decisions towards policies they support.

Ultimately, politics in organizations rest on the distribution of power within the organization. Typically, the organization's owners influence the power distribution within the organization. The owners have ultimate power to appoint people to senior positions, and they in turn appoint others to positions within the organization and decide policies and priorities. As Chapter 7 shows, senior managers have a number of sources of power with which to influence the organization (Ellis and Dick, 2000):

- The role they occupy is by definition a role *legitimized* by the formal structure and, ultimately, they have the agreed authority to make decisions and instruct subordinates. Junior members agree to do what they are told because they support the legitimate right of senior members to instruct them and make decisions.
- They also have, through their control over resources and budgets, an ability to exercise *rewards* in a way that encourages desired behaviour and actions by subordinates. Juniors do what seniors desire because they will gain some rewards now or in the future.
- In addition, they have authority to *coerce* subordinates through threat of discipline or dismissal from the organization or through just bullying as discussed in Chapter 6. Juniors obey instructions because they fear the consequences of not obeying.

The approaches discussed in Figure 3.1 provide insights into the broad strategies that organization managers adopt to exercise these different sources of power:

- Autocratic organizations are chiefly relying on coercive power though there is some element of legitimate power.
- Bureaucratic organizations are largely relying on legitimate power though have both rewards and coercive aspects to the way rules and procedures are managed.

Faced with the power of senior members to both define the organization's priorities and enforce their perceptions on the organization, how do junior members of the organization react to something with which they disagree? There are two potential strategies. The first involves collective opposition by taking action with other organization members. The second strategy takes a non-collective form.

Research by Lashley, Thomas and Rowson (2002) provides some insights into the experiences of employment in some leisure service organizations. Interviews with recruitment agencies revealed some interesting insights on the issues that can cause conflicts between organizations and new recruits. The following summed up many of the points from their interviews:

> Yes we get feedback from employees placed with clients. Moans about pay and conditions are the most common complaints. On the pay it's not always the level that's the problem, it's that the people are being asked to do extra

hours but for the same weekly pay. Poor working conditions is another that crops up on a regular basis, and 'being thrown in the deep end' not shown what to do properly and what's expected of them. Many of the kitchen staff often complain of verbal abuse from the chefs and such. In fact I've had a couple of people we have sent for posts as kitchen assistants ring up after a few days and say I've finished there; I wasn't going to put up with that 'crap' for that pay. I've had people complain that they went for the interview, were asked to start the next day, were not shown what to do properly and then had the chef ranting and raving at them for not doing the job properly. (Ibid.: 12)

Collective opposition within the organization

Collective action with other organization members relies for its effectiveness on the power of the groups to have a greater influence than individuals. Typically collective opposition requires organization of the individuals round a set of agreed actions and objectives. Organized collective action is usually co-ordinated through the activities of a trade union.

A *trade union* is a formal organization created to represent the interests of the employees of work organizations with government, employer organizations and employing organizations in collective bargaining.

Patterns of industrial relations and collective bargaining vary in different countries. In the UK, for example, collective bargaining has evolved over a long period and tends to be based on bargaining within each organization. In Germany collective bargaining was reorganized post-1945 and involves formal procedures at industry level.

Collective bargaining involves representatives of a group of employees negotiating with representatives of their employers. Within an organization collective bargaining can take place over a range of issues and involve different groups of workers. Typically, and at its simplest, a leisure service organization will negotiate with one trade union on matters covering such issues as:

- pay and bonus schemes
- hours of work
- employment
- contracts of employment
- interpretation of national agreements
- consultation and participation in organizational decisions.

In addition, the trade union will typically represent individual and collective organization members in disputes with the organization's management or part of the organization's consultative processes. Here the trade union might be involved in representing the individual in the following issues (Maghurn, 1984).

Individually:

- disciplinary hearings with management
- grievance procedures with individual managers

- discrimination disputes
- over redundancy and dismissal
- at industrial tribunals (where appropriate).

Collectively:

- on health and safety committees
- on consultation committees
- on quality circles
- on works councils.

Membership of the trade union in most leisure service organizations is *voluntary*. In the UK the 'closed shop' used to compel new recruits to the organization to join the relevant trade union. Nowadays most organizations working with trade unions would expect the union to represent and bargain on behalf of an identified group, if not for the workforce as a whole, and new recruits would be advised to select that trade union if they wish to take up union membership.

Collective pressure is the key bargaining strength of the trade unions. The direct or indirect power of the collective actions of its members is what provides the trade union with its power in negotiations with senior organization members.

Individuals join trade unions because they feel trade union members:

- provide insurance against unfair treatment
- help to gain better terms and conditions than they could achieve individually
- provide expertise over employment and negotiation matters
- provide a collective voice representing the workforce
- act as a counterbalancing force against management.

Solidarity and collective action are of key significance for the trade union and its members. Where membership is voluntary there is a concern to ensure that most organization members are members. Clearly, the trade union is able to claim greater authority when it can be seen to be speaking for the majority of an organization's frontline employees (Mars and Mitchell, 1976).

When a dispute occurs and the trade union members take some kind of collective action, their efforts are more effective if they all act in common and other organization members are not working normally.

Collective action taken by the workforce has both a *demonstration effect* and an *economic effect*. The demonstration effect shows the employer organization the strength of feeling and support for the position being advocated. The economic effect aims to increase costs, reduce revenue or generally cause disruption to the normal workings of the organization.

Forms of collective action

The approaches taken by employees in dispute with leisure retail organizations include forms that might be found in many other organizations but also include some that reflect the service context. Here are some examples.

Withdrawal of labour or *strike*. Here the organization members in dispute stop working and attempt to put economic pressure on the organization. The quicker the economic pressure takes effect the more quickly the organization will come under pressure to negotiate a settlement with their striking members. Strikers are not paid when they withdraw their labour and the strikers, too, are under pressure to reach a quick settlement.

Strikes are potentially effective in leisure service organizations because the nature of services prevent easy replacement of lost production. Unlike manufacturing where lost output can be replaced later or from another source, services are time specific (perishable) so, once lost, cannot be replaced.

Strikes are less effective when striking organization members are easily replaced by other staff, or where there are ideological differences between striking and non-striking organization members. Mars and Nicod (1984) report on a culture of 'individualism' among waiters in London hotels and restaurants, and this has proved to be a barrier to trade union recruitment and collective action.

Go slow or working to rule involves employees working at a deliberately slow pace or following every organization procedure to the letter, which has the effect of slowing work rates. From the members' point of view, the go slow has the benefit of causing economic pressure on the organization by reducing sales while they continue to be paid. The build-up of effect is slower than with the strike.

Smile strikes involve frontline staff deliberately giving a glum appearance to customers. It is the opposite of the 'have a nice day' approach required by most leisure service providers. The aim is to create customer dissatisfaction thereby having an economic impact, though it also has an important demonstration effect. Members in dispute with the organization continue to be paid.

An overtime ban, whereby members refuse to work overtime, can result in lost output and greater inflexibility to meet fluctuations in demand. Lost revenue or added costs can lead to economic pressure on the firm, thereby adding pressure to negotiate

Key point 3.5

Disagreements about management decisions and policies are likely to occur in most organizations. Junior member opposition to organization policy can be registered in collective forms.

Barriers to collective organization in leisure services

As we have seen, leisure service organizations are vulnerable to collective organization by junior members because of the 'perishable' aspect of leisure services. That said, there is not a strong record of strikes and collective action in the sector internationally. The picture does vary somewhat between countries (Windmuller, 1987), but the sector does not have a record of high trade union membership and collective action. The factors listed below are some examples of influence on these patterns of trade union membership and collective action. However, it is important to remember the national setting and legislation in different countries is influential in explaining variation.

1 *Small numbers employed on any one site.* The numbers of people employed does have an influence on patterns of union membership and thereby the degree of collective opposition that can be brought to bear on the organization's management. Many leisure service organizations employee thousands of employees but on many sites. This presents a logistical problem for a trade union organization attempting to recruit members and for organizing collective action across many units (hotels, restaurants, shops and so on).
2 *Numerical flexibility* as a result of fluctuations and uneven demand for labour mean that many organizations employ part-time, seasonal or casual staff, and this creates barriers to encouraging collective consciousness among individuals who are rarely on duty at the same time. In some cases, these jobs are being undertaken for short-term motives and staff have less commitment to the long-term improvement of conditions.
3 *Small firms* tend to dominate the provision of leisure services and may represent paternalist tradition relationships within the organization. Being part of the 'family' may have an effect on establishing a less oppositional perspective among employees.
4 *Tips and other non-wage benefits* can form a significant element of the total reward package in some sections of leisure services. Wages are nominally low, but other benefits such as tips or service charge payments add to 'take home pay'. Accommodation and free meals are also a 'perk' for some leisure sector employees and these add to the total benefits package that might stifle dissatisfaction and opposition. In the case of accommodation, the potential loss of job and home as the result of a dispute might also reduce the willingness to take collective action.

For these and other reasons organizational members who are unhappy with policies and other aspects of their relationship with the organization are less likely to belong to a trade union and become involved in collective action. More frequently their action takes individual forms.

Case study 3.1

Staff working in the Berwick Hotel had been unhappy for some time. They had seen wage levels cut by the management. Full-time staff were being asked to work more hours than they were paid and part-time staff frequently had their hours cut at short notice. Whenever they tried to complain, the managers said they were under pressure from head office to increase profitability.

Over recent months a trade union had been recruiting staff and now all kitchen staff, housekeeping, restaurant and bar staff below the level of supervisor were members of the union. One day Alice who worked in the kitchen told her mates, 'I've had my hours cut again. The boss said he would not pay me for the same number of hours in future. I need the money from this job, our Don is unemployed and we can't manage without it'. Several other people from other departments said they had been told the same thing. Alice said, 'This is a job for the union, let's get 'em in'.

Reflective practice

1 What actions would you advise the employees in Case study 3.1 to take if you were the trade union official brought in to advise these union members?
2 If you were the hotel manager how would you respond to a meeting with the trade union official?
3 Discuss the strengths and weaknesses of taking strike action as a way of putting pressure on the hotel management.
4 Which of the two parties – management or union members – are in the strongest position and why?

Individualized forms of opposition

Junior members of leisure service organizations are often in a position where they are unhappy with pay and conditions and other employment practices in their organizations but have limited power to change things. They are typically employed in 'routine unskilled jobs' where few skills are required and they can be easily replaced by the organization. In these cases opposition takes an individual form because:

- managers, who could do something to resolve their problem, are the cause of it
- there is no trade union in their organization and no way of getting support to resolve the difficulty
- there is no independent process whereby they can air grievances in a non-threatening environment.

Here are some ways that individuals register their opposition on an individual basis:

1 *Staff leave the organization.* Staff turnover is a major problem for some leisure service organizations. Lashley and Rowson (2000) report that this can average 300 per cent in some firms. Withdrawal is a natural response to unpleasant situations. Organization members simply register their opposition to the organization by removing themselves from it.
2 *Staff absence* from the organization in an unplanned manner causes disruption, reduces moral among other staff and can cause extra costs when agency staff are brought in. As with staff turnover, this is psychological removal from an unpleasant situation.
3 *Poor quality working* or working without enthusiasm has an impact on service quality. Customers wait longer for the service and they are treated in a way that is unpleasant. In effect the person withdraws emotional labour and this impacts on customer satisfaction, or increases cost through increased wastage.
4 *Sabotage* of the organization's products or services involves deliberately causing damage and results in customer dissatisfaction and added costs. Here the behaviour is quite deliberate. Sometimes groups of service employees sabotage products together, or develop a sabotage culture. The employee perceives themselves as 'getting their own back' for the way they are being treated by the organization.
5 *Fawning and sucking up,* although not directly oppositional to organization managers and senior members, individuals play a 'political' game by attempting to win

favour with the boss. Ultimately, they are trying to resolve personal dissatisfaction through individual actions rather than collective ones.

Individualized forms of opposition, unlike collective forms, are not aimed at resolving the problem or producing a desired outcome. They are emotional expressions of opposition. They either remove the individual from the organization or make them feel better through the sense of redressing the feeling of injustice that they perceive. The emotions of unjust treatment in organizations are discussed further in Chapter 6.

Key point 3.6

For a number of reasons individuals in leisure service organizations register their opposition to organizational practices through individual actions.

Conclusion

Politics is commonly thought to concern the State and government. While this is true, it has many other nuances and dimensions, all of which may be considered organizational politics. This is the way people vie for power and position to satisfy personal objectives. It involves consideration of how power is distributed and in whose interests it is exercised. Organizations, like societies, are often in a situation where there are scarce resources, or at least insufficient resources to satisfy all the demands upon them. Organization politics is fundamentally concerned with how these resources are allocated, with whom and in whose interests?

Political behaviour within organizations is entirely subjective and commonly regarded as destructive. However, a benchmark against which these activities can be deemed ethical is available and uses three criteria of utility, individual rights and distributive justice.

On a personal level, political behaviour takes a number of forms including impression management, networking, blaming others and avoiding doing anything at all. These responses are provoked due to the personality traits of individuals and the context in which they work. For example, some people have a need for power and see no reason why this should not be achieved using political manoeuvres. Alternatively, a sense of inequity may permeate the organization for reasons of ad hoc performance appraisals, unclear budgeting protocols, unsystematic allocation of resources and so on.

Organization politics is also concerned with opposition to the formal power, reward and decision-making structures in organizations. In a situation where organizational members may well disagree with the way resources are allocated and how decisions are made, organizational politics is concerned with organization and management of opposition. As we have seen, some people are able to play the political game but others, particularly employees in the most junior positions, have limited opportunities and employ either collective or individual behaviours that register their opposition.

Ultimately, all organizations are political and related behaviours are difficult to diffuse. Individuals can either make a decision to try to ameliorate political phenomena or take steps to advance their own careers by engaging in such behaviours. If they choose the latter, it is unwise to do so in the long term because of the negative responses that overtly political individuals induce among their peers.

Reflective practice

1 What is the relationship between power and politics?
2 What causes political activity in organizations?
3 Why does political behaviour appear to be the norm in organizations?
4 You are the manager of a small national chain of medium-sized and middle quality hotels which has recently seen a decline in sales. Discuss four defensive behaviours which you could use to limit the negative personal consequences of this development.
5 Organizational politics must be avoided because it has the potential to increase employee stress levels and labour turnover. Moreover, if employees engaging in organizational politics are rewarded, their job tasks will not become a priority. In groups of three, discuss this statement using personal or hospitality, leisure and tourism examples.
6 Table 3.2 comprises an exercise is designed to assess the extent to which you view your work environment in political terms. The exercise includes statements which may (or may not) describe an organization with which you are familiar. If you are having difficulty, relate this activity to your college or university.

Scoring key ● ● ●

Assign the appropriate number to each question as shown in Table 3.3 and then add the numbers together. Individuals who score seven or above on the 'general political behaviour' dimension believe that their chosen organization has a politicized structure. People scoring 25 or higher on the 'go along to get ahead' dimension consider that employees get ahead by avoiding disagreements with the organization's administrators or managers.

Write your scores for each item on the appropriate line below (statement numbers appear in brackets) and add each scale.

General political behaviour ———— + ———— = ————
                                      (1)   (5)   Subtotal A

Go along to get ahead ——— + ——— + ——— + ——— + ——— + ——— +
                            (2)   (3)   (4)   (6)   (7)   (8)

——— = ———
(9)   Subtotal B

Total score ————————————— + ————————————— =
                (Subtotal A)   (Subtotal B)

—————————
    Total

Indicate the extent to which you either agree or disagree with the following statements about the administration of your chosen organization	Strongly agree	Agree	Neutral	Disagree	Strongly disagree
1 Administrators/managers in this organization tend to build themselves up while tearing others down	5	4	3	2	1
2 Employees in the organization are encouraged to speak out even when they are critical of well-established ideas	5	4	3	2	1
3 There is no place for 'yes' people here; good ideas are encouraged even if it means disagreeing with superiors	5	4	3	2	1
4 Agreeing with powerful administrators/ managers is the best course of action in this organization	5	4	3	2	1
5 There have always been a few powerful administrators or managers here that no one ever crosses	5	4	3	2	1
6 Sometimes it's easier to say nothing than fight the system in this organization	5	4	3	2	1
7 It's best not to rock the boat in this organization	5	4	3	2	1
8 Telling others what they want to hear is better than the truth in this organization	5	4	3	2	1
9 Employees must follow orders rather than making up their own minds in this organization	5	4	3	2	1

Source: adapted from Kacmar (1997).

Table 3.2

For statement items 1, 4, 5, 6, 7, 8 and 9	For statement items 2 and 3
Strongly agree = 5 Agree = 4 Neutral = 3 Disagree = 2 Strongly disagree = 1	Strongly agree = 5 Agree = 4 Neutral = 3 Disagree = 2 Strongly disagree = 1

Table 3.3

CHAPTER 4

Individuals in organizations: personality, perceptions and learning

- define personality and perception and explain their impact upon behaviour
- explain the 'big five' dimensions of personality
- identify and explain the key elements which shape perception
- define learning and explain the essential differences between cognitive and behavioural theories of learning.

A major conundrum in hospitality, leisure and tourism organizations is recognizing and rewarding individuals who exhibit novelty, creativity and flair. For example, on the one hand, frontline employees are encouraged to be original and creative when dealing with customers. On the other hand, organizational members must also be able to get along with others and behave according to rules and regulations. These staff may base their responses on a formal 'script' but will need to remain individually dynamic when dealing with customers.

The aim of management is to encourage individualism tempered with appropriate deference and a willingness to get along with others. In order to achieve this we need to understand some of the major influences on individual behaviour. In an OB context, understanding individuals is essentially an attempt to predict their behaviour accurately in the workplace. This area is complex, demanding and often contradictory.

Consider for a moment how you behave in certain situations. Do you always react in the same way to given stimuli? The answer could be 'Sometimes yes and sometimes no' depending on the circumstances. Contexts can vary widely depending on situational specifics. You too will have changed through learning and the influence of experience since you were last in a similar position. Other features also affect your behaviour, including personality, perceptions, values, beliefs and so on.

Case studies 4.1 and 4.2 are based on interviews with managers/owners of two independent seasonal medium-sized hotels in the UK. Both suggest that (situational or) 'external' and 'internal' issues have a bearing on behaviour. In each case, the manager has made assumptions and errors of judgement in dealing with people, resulting in minor 'organizational disasters'.

Case study 4.1

Interviewer. I understand that many hospitality organizations experience problems of high labour turnover. How have you found the situation?

Manager. Yes the staff come and go regularly.

Interviewer. What do you think the main issues are?

Manager. Well, they just don't want to do a hard day's work.

Interviewer. What do you mean?

Manager. You'd think they'd be grateful for a job but seem happier to scrounge off welfare or the 'dole'. They're all bone idle. In the slack times I have a hard job to meet their wage costs and then when the pressure's really on, they quit, turn up when they want to or call in sick. I don't consider that fair at all.

Interviewer. How do you select your staff?

Manager. Sometimes I don't have the time to interview – I'm a very busy man you know – and accept what the Job Centre sends me, after all that's what they're there for isn't it?

Interviewer. Do you have any motivational programmes or incentive schemes for your staff?

Manager. No, they get well paid and have the chance of picking up extra in 'tips'.

Interviewer. Do you mind if I ask their rate of pay?

Manager. The basic minimum set for this industry.

Interviewer. What type of jobs do you offer these individuals?

Manager. Well we run seasonally so I suppose most of the jobs are part-time, split-shift, temporary.

Interviewer. So you make them redundant at the end of the busy season?

Manager. Yes.

Interviewer. Are you able to offer your staff a continuous position with some sort of career path?

Manager. No, but the good ones are always welcome to return the following year to pick up their old job. You know, I've busted a gut to get where I am today. How do they expect to get anywhere without putting in some effort. I did it, why can't they. The trouble with youngsters these days is that they don't want the work. It was different in my day.

The following statements and comments have been extracted from this situation to illustrate key behavioural issues; some of which appear later in this chapter:

- 'You know, I've busted a gut to get where I am today' (locus of control)
- no career structure, only basic minimum wage and no incentive scheme, abdication of responsibility for proving 'liveable' wage in favour of tipping (motivation)
- 'youngsters these days' (stereotyping and attitudinal differences based on generation)
- 'you'd think they'd be grateful for a job' (failure to recognize individual perceptions)
- manager socialized to believe that any job, however poor the working conditions, is better than receiving welfare payment (generational differences)
- 'Sometimes I don't have the time to interview' (job fit).

Case study 4.2

A manager explained that he was becoming rather angry with a particular chef. Every night after dinner service had finished he would leave kitchen equipment turned on including cookers and fluorescent lighting, extractor fans and so on. In desperation, the manager left the chef written instructions: 'Before you leave this kitchen at night please make sure everything is turned OFF'

The following morning, much to the dismay of the manager, the chef had done so but had also disconnected all refrigerators and freezers.

Although the above situation is unusual and somewhat humorous, it allows us to identify issues in addition to those shown in Case study 4.1, including:

- poor means of, and ambiguous, communication
- erroneous presumption on the part of the manager
- individual rebellion shown through abdication of responsibility for 'obvious' outcome of disconnecting power in the kitchen.

Case study 4.2 also illustrates the idea of role perception, which may be explained as an individual's view of how they are supposed to act in a given situation (including job tasks). Clearly, the chef's idea of his duties and tasks were different to that of the manager. This drove the manager to write instructions and communicate (poorly) with the individual. The unfortunate notice written by the manager reveals a failure to understand the chef's perception of his role.

Reflective practice

1 Think of a typical work situation in which you have found yourself on more than one occasion.
2 How have you behaved in response to stimuli present?
3 Were there any differences from time to time?
4 If 'yes' explain your behaviours.
5 If 'no' identify why your behaviour did not change.

What is individual behaviour?

As shown in both case studies, individual behaviour is essentially an outcome of a number of stimuli. These can be external or internal to the employee. Moreover, behaviour can be dynamic or relatively stable depending on the experience and learning which has taken place between one episode and the next. Simply, the behaviour of individuals is influenced by a multitude of variables. Both stimuli and responses have a propensity to change to a lesser or greater degree depending on context and a person's 'internal state'.

While classifying these variables as external and internal is useful, it does not really add much to our understanding of behaviour; it only helps us begin a mapping process. Similarly, the definition of behaviour provided by the *Collins English Dictionary and Thesaurus* – 'Act or function in a particular way' – gives no clue of the complexity and major influences affecting individual behaviour.

McShane and Travaglione (2003) suggest a 'MARS' mnemonic which provides clues about key behavioural 'triggers':

- M – motivation
- A – ability
- R – role perceptions
- S – situation.

However, their model appears to omit the dimensions of personality and perception. This is surprising because perception underpins all behaviours in the workplace. In an attempt to partially explain the actions of individuals, this chapter continues by discussing four important components or triggers of behaviour (shown in Figure 4.1) beginning with personality. Other factors affecting behaviour are discussed in Chapter 5.

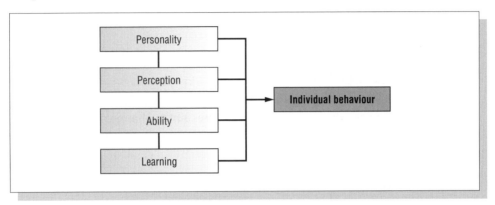

Figure 4.1 Individual behaviour: key influential factors

Personality

How often have you glanced through the jobs section in newspapers or other media and noticed employers asking for people who are 'energetic', 'outgoing', 'friendly' or have some other such personality trait? Frequently, frontline jobs in the leisure services sector are advertised using these descriptors. Do you have classmates or work colleagues who may be described in this manner? There will definitely be some you might consider as 'timid', 'loud', 'enthusiastic' and so on.

Furthermore, you probably know someone who has an uncanny knack of getting along with people or, despite adverse situations, always appears to manage it to their advantage. Why is it that some people seem to be innately 'good at selling', 'shy and retiring' or 'eager to please'? Whether your impressions of these people are entirely accurate is not important. The main issue here is that these examples focus on an individual's personality.

In general, personality studies can be divided into those which collect data about:

- specific personality traits and then attempt to measure them. This approach is known as the 'nomothetic' perspective and presumes that personality traits are constant over time and are resistant to change
- the other or 'idiographic' perspective, which considers personality holistically and suggests that it is dynamic and influenced by a number of environmental and social stimuli. It is also something which is continually developing. This approach also considers the measurement of traits inappropriate and limited in the way it presents potentially rich data in a shallow manner.

The authors believe that both perspectives are valid and should be considered as complementary rather than exclusive. The nomothetic view has intuitive appeal and tends to be more popular with managers. This is because traits or types become measurable and appear to have predictive value, so appropriate matches can be made between people and jobs.

The *Collins English Dictionary and Thesaurus* define personality as: 'Distinctive character'. While this does little to help break the concept into understandable component parts, many researchers believe it is best described in this way. For example, Robbins (2001: 92) opts for a holistic perspective when he explains personality as '[the] Sum of the ways in which an individual reacts and interacts with others'.

Key point 4.1

Approaches to the study of personality are either nomothetic or idiographic. The former considers personality to be resistant to change and measurable; the latter believes it to be dynamic and susceptible to change through environmental and social stimuli.

Personality formation is a complex and dynamic affair. Writers agree there is no single source of influential variables; rather, there are many and they are rooted in three generic areas which are summarized in Figure 4.2.

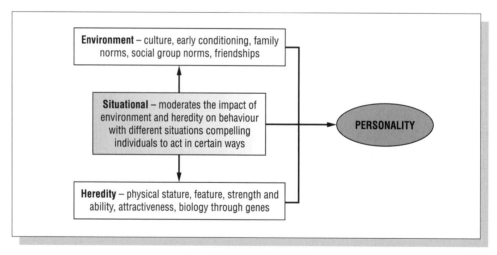

Figure 4.2 Determinants of personality

There are literally hundreds of variables which manifest themselves in an almost equal number of 'personality traits'. Their sheer volume has forced researchers to reduce them to a lesser number which does not lose the essence of individual traits. For example, Cattel (1973) tries to explain personality by using sixteen 'source traits' said to determine behaviour in particular circumstances and they appear in Table 4.1.

Eysenck (1960) sought to explain and measure personality by applying the four classical 'humours' (melancholic, sanguine, phlegmatic and choleric). He proposed

Reserved	versus	Outgoing
Less intelligent (logical)	versus	More intelligent (abstract)
Affected by feelings	versus	Emotionally stable
Submissive	versus	Dominant
Serious	versus	Happy-go-lucky
Expedient	versus	Conscientious
Timid	versus	Adventurous
Tough-minded	versus	Sensitive
Trusting	versus	Suspicious
Practical	versus	Creative
Forthright	versus	Shrewd
Self-assured	versus	Apprehensive
Conservative	versus	Radical
Group dependent	versus	Self-sufficient
Uncontrolled	versus	Controlled
Relaxed	versus	Tense

Source: adapted from Mullins (1996: 107).

Table 4.1 Cattel's source traits

that a person's personality could be understood according to four major 'types' composed of traits expected to affect behaviour:

- extroversion
- introversion
- neuroticism
- stability

His typology has an intuitive feel and forms the basis of many subsequent instruments designed to identify and measure personality. The popular Myers–Briggs Type Indicator (MBTI) has some consistency with Eysenck's earlier construct.

The MBTI is essentially a personality test used as a means of identifying links between personality type, occupation and management style. This helps individual better to understand:

- the way they make decisions
- how they communicate and relate to each other
- their learning styles
- the jobs for which they are suited.

Individuals who complete the MBTI 100-question test obtain results which are then expressed according to sixteen personality types. For example, someone could be classified as any of the following:

- practical, analytical, realistic and decisive
- having a drive to realize their own original ideas

- sceptical, independent, critical and stubborn
- good at conceptualizing, innovative and attracted to entrepreneurial ideas.

Key point 4.2

The MBTI is used to identify personality along four dimensions of extrovert–introvert, sensing–intuition, thinking–feeling and judgement–perception.

There are a number of anomalies in predicting behaviour based on personality assessment. For example, typically you would expect frontline workers in the leisure services sector to be extrovert because they have to interact directly with customers. However, not all individuals in this situation do so naturally. Paradoxically, some employees and many actors (and lecturers, for that matter) are introverted innately but manage to effect a persona in public. The following situation is based on an interview with a hotel manger and illustrates this point.

Case study 4.3

A few years ago, we used to have a resident entertainer who had this terrible stammer. It took him an enormous amount of concentration and energy even to ask for a cup of coffee. But as soon as he stepped up to the microphone to begin his 'patter' he was like a different person. He never faltered or tripped over his words at any time. It was absolutely amazing to watch him.

While this example is not strictly about a hotel worker, many frontline employees consider themselves as performers, likening their work to that of the theatre, so the story is more appropriate than you would at first think. Jung (1968) explains this phenomenon by invoking four overarching aspects of personality:

- a darker self
- a self-actualizing self
- masculinity and femininity
- a persona or role we can play.

Reflective practice

1 In certain situations (work or social) do you effect a behaviour that is different to how you normally act?
2 If 'yes', explain why you do so and how you feel about behaving this way.

Despite the apparent vagaries of predicting behaviour from personality traits or types, Robbins (2001) concludes that the 'big five' model underpins all other personality dimensions and is reasonably successful in predicting behaviour:

- extraversion – someone who is assertive, gregarious and sociable
- agreeableness – someone who is co-operative, trusting and of a 'good' nature
- conscientiousness – someone who is dependable and responsible
- emotional stability – someone who is self-confident, calm, positive and secure
- openness to experience – someone who is imaginative, artistic, sensitive and intellectual.

Other personality attributes found to explain workplace behaviour are shown in Figure 4.3.

Internals, externals and locus of control – people who believe that they either control what happens to them or do not; degree to which people believe this to be true

Machiavellianism – degree to which people are pragmatic, maintain 'distance' and that ends justify means summarized by the adage, 'You cannot make an omelette without breaking a few eggs.'

Self-esteem – a person's propensity for self-liking

Self-monitoring – a person's ability to adjust their behaviour in response to external situational factors

Type A or B personality – type A struggles relentlessly to achieve at all costs, highly competitive; type B is the equal opposite

Figure 4.3   Key personality predictors of behaviour patterns in organizations
Source: adapted from Robbins (2001: 96–9).

Nowhere is an understanding of personality theory more important than in service industries. Workers are required to interact with customers and, during this time, become a key part of the product. The service encounter is the point at which management effectively loses 'control' of the process. Instead, it has to rely on employees to manage the encounter and take responsibility for ensuring delivery of a quality product.

Despite the many indirect techniques available for managing service encounters ('scripting' and selection procedures, for example), personality plays a crucial role in ensuring that customers are satisfied. Services are notoriously difficult to provide and each has the potential to differ because of individual customer demands.

In addition, the inherent complexity and integrated nature of some highly customized services makes 'failure' all too common. Therefore, frontline employees must have the capacity to recover the service (as well as those actionable behind the scenes). Clearly, someone who is predisposed to do this by virtue of his or her personality is a valuable asset to the organization.

Indeed, if you consider the key element of service industries as product delivery, then employees' personality becomes at least as important as their objective physical capabilities. It is therefore not surprising that 'personality inventories' are becoming increasingly popular in the hospitality, leisure and tourism sector for staff selection purposes. In Australia, it is now common practice for leading national hotel companies to use a variety of such instruments before choosing their employees.

Matching people with jobs is known as 'job fit' or, more recently, 'organization fit' to account for increasing dynamics and extra pressure exerted on employees to be functionally flexible; that is, to undertake a number of jobs competently. Holland (1985) suggests that personality type and occupations have an ideal match and his typology is presented in Table 4.2.

Type	Personality characteristics	Congruent occupation
Realistic – prefers physical activities requiring skill, strength and co-ordination	Shy, genuine, persistent, stable, conforming, practical	Mechanic, drill press operator, assembly-line worker, farmer
Investigative – prefers activities that involve thinking, organizing and understanding	Analytical, original, curious, independent	Biologist, economist, mathematician, news reporter
Social – prefers activities that involve helping and developing others	Sociable, friendly, co-operative, understanding	Social worker, teacher, counsellor, clinical psychologist
Conventional – prefers regulated, ordered and unambiguous activities	Conforming, efficient, practical, unimaginative, inflexible	Accountant, corporate manager, bank teller, file clerk
Enterprising – prefers verbal activities in which there are opportunities to influence others and attain power	Self-confident, ambitious, energetic, domineering	Lawyer, real estate agent, public relations officer, small business manager
Artistic – prefers ambiguous activities that allow creative expression	Imaginative, disorderly, idealistic, emotional, impractical	Painter, musician, writer

Source: Robbins (2001: 102).

Table 4.2 Personality and congruent occupations

Reflective practice

1 Based on Holland's typology, suggest appropriate personality types for jobs of local government tourism officer, hotel manager, food and beverage attendant, and adventure tourism guide.
2 Do you believe that matching personality with occupation is important or worthwhile?

In sum:

- Personality is a complex amalgam of traits which can be grouped into specific types.
- This grouping helps managers to predict employee behaviour in the workplace.
- Underpinning each personality type are variables rooted in broad categories of heredity, situation and environment.

The latter affects personality formation because it exposes the individual to a variety of influences including those of culture, family and society.

Predicting individual behaviour exclusively from personality is unreliable because of the factors that moderate the relationship. Arguably, the most important of these factors is the process of perception. The association between personality and perception is dynamic, with some people arguing that the former influences the latter and vice versa. Identifying exact causality is not helpful but there can be little doubt that perception plays a key role in the way people organize and interpret their surroundings in order to make sense of things.

The following section considers personality in more detail.

Key point 4.3

The relationship between personality and behaviour is unclear because it is moderated by other variables.

What is perception?

The *Collins English Dictionary and Thesaurus* defines the word 'perceive' as, 'To obtain knowledge of, through senses'. This definition is limited because it alludes only to physical senses. Perception undoubtedly begins in this way but the process is complex and includes selective attention and internal prioritization and interpretation of stimuli. These processes then affect values, beliefs, attitudes and behaviour (see Chapter 5).

Acknowledging that objects and situations may be perceived in a number of ways is to suggest that:

- 'objectivity' does not exist. Instead 'reality' is experienced according to how we make sense of it which, in turn, is influenced by learning, culture, upbringing and so on
- human beings continually strive to make sense of a chaotic world of information.

Accordingly, our perceptions help to confer order, to prioritize and to 'clarify' what is communicated to us through our physical senses.

Thus, what we are actually doing is trying to understand and predict people's behaviour based on what their perceptions of reality are. Unfortunately for managers, there are few constants in organizations. In other words, we can rely on organizational members to perceive many work-related issues differently from each other.

Everyone has a unique picture of 'reality' because individuals are not passive but, instead, receive information, analyse it and then make judgements. For example, managers attempting to improve profitability would no doubt perceive the industry's appropriate trade union with suspicion or outright hostility.

On the other hand, employees would be positively disposed to such representation. Similarly, there were extreme and opposing perceptions of the benefits of 'scientific management' techniques when Frederick Taylor first introduced them to the manu-facturing process to standardize and improve productivity. Guess which group perceived the new principles positively?

Key point 4.4

An individual's behaviour is based on his or her own perceptions of the world, that is, their reality.

What affects perception?

It is curious, but true, that individuals can see the same object, situation or target and perceive it in any number of ways. This may be explained by considering three important elements, which appear in Figure 4.4.

When perceiving a target we notice its characteristics, so any extremes of motion, sound, size and so on will affect our impressions of it. In your class, attractive individuals will be more noticeable in a group than others. It is similar for loud people (in the nicest possible way!) over shy and retiring types.

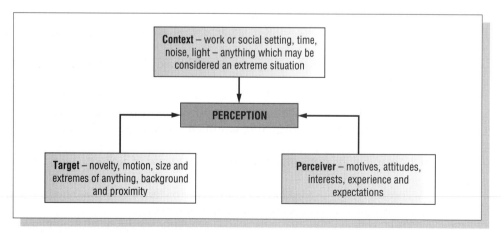

Figure 4.4 Elements shaping perception
Source: adapted from Robbins (2001: 124).

Additionally, targets are perceived holistically or in relation to each other. This is sometimes known as a Gestalt view of the world, whereby things are viewed as composites or partial composites grouping items together if they are visually close to each other.

Also, we identify targets according to the relationship they have with their background. This causes a separation resulting in a particular visual perception of the object. Figure 4.5 shows some examples.

Figure 4.5 Targets: figure and ground and grouping

There are no correct answers to the following questions.

- How many of you first see a young woman before an old one in the top left-hand illustration in Figure 4.5?
- How about the top right-hand drawing; do you see the rat or the bespectacled gentleman first?
- Which becomes immediately apparent in the picture appearing at the bottom left-hand corner of Figure 4.5; two side-profile faces or a candlestick?
- 'The cat' is an interesting one and illustrates grouping and, to some extent, 'closure'.

No doubt there was little difficulty in reading the words 'the cat', but look again; you will notice that the second letter of each word is exactly the same, yet you perceived the first as an 'H' and the second as an 'A'. This is because you grouped the letters in association with each other (you also closed the second letter of the second word to form an 'A' rather than letting it remain as an 'H'). If you return once again to the words, try to force yourself to place an 'A' where the 'H' is and vice versa. You will find this terribly difficult to do without effort.

There are a number of 'internal' factors including personality, motivation and experience which affect an individual's perceptual set. These condition a person to interpret external stimuli in a number of ways with a predictable response behaviour (personality types are discussed earlier in this chapter). For example, the attitudes towards an object or situation will impact on whether something is perceived positively or negatively.

Thus in principle, do individuals react positively towards working part time or full time? This depends on a number of other issues. If working part time is convenient with your other commitments then you would be less likely to have a negative attitude towards organizations offering jobs of this nature. Alternatively, to a younger person who is keen to establish a career in the leisure sector, part-time working may be perceived negatively.

Individuals' needs also play an important role in affecting perceptions. For example, if you are under pressure to complete a piece of written work and are focused on doing so, extraneous noises will probably not distract you. Your most urgent needs therefore affect perception.

In addition, a stimulus, whether an activity or event which is ever constant or has been tried a number of times, will impact on your perception because of the learning experience afforded by its earlier occurrence.

In an organizational sense, members will often reject ideas for a new way of working, product or process because similar has been tried unsuccessfully beforehand; perceptions of a new idea has been affected by previous experience.

Unfamiliar events will also be more noticeable than those which are ever present. This perceptual process is known as 'habituation'. How often have you 'noticed' a sound only after it has stopped (refrigerators, air conditioning and so on)?

Interestingly, insightful use of habituation has been made for the purpose of perceived noise reduction. A company manufactures contraptions which when switched on produce 'white noise' (the nondescript hissing sound which can sometimes be heard on televisions when broadcasting has stopped). The hissing sound covers other more extreme sounds produced by cars, people, heavy machinery and so on. Soon after the unit produces white noise, listeners cease to hear it and the other distractions.

Expectations and motives also have a powerful impact on perception. If a person expects individuals from overseas or ethnic groups to behave in a particular way, they will appear to do so regardless of their actions.

In Case study 4.1, the manager was motivated to see all his seasonal workers as workshy and ungrateful. The reality is that these workers were probably no less lazy or inefficient than the manager. However, a combination of his past experiences caused a fusion effect of habituation and stereotyping.

Essentially stereotyping is when someone is judged according to the perceived characteristics of a group to which they are deemed to belong. In an organization behaviour context, stereotyping is something everyone indulges in because it simplifies complexity.

For example, a manager may consider a certain ethnic group or sexual orientation to be a key predictor of certain types of behaviour and hold that, 'gay employees are ideal for entertaining customers', 'older workers are more reliable than younger workers', 'all chefs are drunkards', 'Italians make great ice cream' and other such nonsense.

The difficulty with stereotyping is that people who make these assertions fail to recognize characteristics they would not associate with them. The scenario therefore becomes self-perpetuating with the person doing the stereotyping having his or her perceptions reinforced rather than exposed as inaccurate.

As you will appreciate, the processes involved in shaping perceptions are complex and, in some cases, unexpected. For example, an individual may have held a strong perception about another person for some considerable time only to change it significantly after experiencing some critical incident or other. This happens frequently because people like to make sense of apparently unconnected issues or complexity. For example, some atheists become religious in conditions of extreme adversity such as warfare or at loss of a loved one.

Key point 4.5

Perception is a 'sense-making' activity whereby individuals are stimulated via the five senses. Stimuli are then processed selectively and organized in order of importance. The individual then behaves in a manner consistent with this process.

This internal sense-making (or reduction of 'dissonance') is constant and in some circumstances helps us to hang on to our own mental 'wellbeing'. Similarly, we also like to understand the behaviour of others. According to Heider (1958) and Kelley (1973) we do this by attributing meaning to another's behaviour by considering whether their actions are a result of perceived internal (ability, skill, effort invested, fatigue and so on) and external forces (rules, policies, behaviour of managers, climate and so on).

Judging whether a person's behaviour is attributable to forces outside their control (external) or not (internal) is known as 'attribution theory' and comprises three major dimensions:

1 Distinctiveness – how different was a behaviour in these circumstances compared with that shown for other situations?
2 Consensus – is the behaviour different or similar to that of others in the same situation?
3 Consistency – is the behaviour the same over time or rather one which is caused by unusual external circumstances?

Table 4.3 shows a hypothetical situation where a hotel manager has failed to meet a particular performance target. In row 1 we have made an internal attribution (poor performance is manager's fault); in row 2 we have made an external attribution (poor performance is not manager's fault).

Another issue in the evaluation of performance is whether behaviour has resulted from ability or ease of satisfying a performance goal (stable factors) and exertion of effort, or luck (unstable factors). Based on the work of Bartunek (1981), Mullins (1996) combines these factors with internal and external attributions to give another perspective on the interpretation of behaviour (Table 4.4).

Despite the seductive qualities of attribution theory it is by no means flawless. For example, there is overwhelming evidence suggesting that people overestimate the influence of internal or personal factors, of themselves or others.

	Distinctiveness	Consensus	Consistency
Internal attribution	Manager fails to meet all performance targets	This manager is the only one not to meet this target	Manager also fails to meet a renegotiated target
External attribution	Manager satisfies other performance targets	All managers perform poorly for this performance target	Manager satisfies renegotiated target

Table 4.3 Attributions for hotel performance

	Internal attribution	External attribution
Stable factors	Ability	Task difficulty
Unstable factors	Effort	Luck

Source: Mullins (1996: 156).

Table 4.4 Attributions and 'stability'

A leisure centre manager may therefore wrongly attribute the failure of a promotion campaign to marketing and public relations ineptness rather than a superior product offered by a close competitor.

Similarly, from the turn of the twentieth century (until the 1980s), UK coastal resort towns produced many successful hospitality, leisure and tourism entrepreneurs operating thriving small businesses. The success derived from satisfying the demands of mass tourism had little to do with strategic business acumen. Rather, good fortune and being in the right place at the right time explained this entrepreneurial success. During this period, demand consistently exceeded supply. However, it is doubtful whether these entrepreneurs would recognize their good fortune because evidence suggests they have a strong locus of control which gives rise to a 'self-serving bias'; that is, they regard success as solely due to their own efforts.

There are a number of other biases which come into play when we judge the behaviour of others. Robbins (2001: 126) calls them 'shortcuts' and they may be summarized as:

- selective perception – we interpret stimuli on the basis of our background, attitude, experience and interests
- halo effect – we draw an overall impression of someone based on a single characteristic (appearance, enthusiasm, sociability and so on)

- contrast effects – judgement of characteristics by comparing with recent others ranking differently for same characteristic
- projection – of one's own characteristics onto others.

Reflective practice

1 Can you think of any leisure service sector examples of where these short cuts are made?
2 As a guide, you might like to consider areas of employment interviewing, performance expectations, self-fulfilling prophecy, performance evaluation, employee effort and loyalty.

Perception is a highly subjective internal process where stimuli are received, selected and prioritized in order for individuals to make sense of their environment including the behaviour of others. These interpretations are unique because of objective sensory limits, motivations, experiences and the individual's need to reduce dissonance.

People often use short cuts in their sense-making; some of which are learned and some are innate. The latter views may be rooted in culture, upbringing, poor education and so on – racial, ethnic and gender stereotyping are typical perspectives in this respect. Some perceptions are more difficult to change than others but, ultimately, they and associated attitudes may be changed by learning and methods of 'modification'. The following section introduces and discusses these issues.

Learning

The *Collins English Dictionary and Thesaurus* defines learning as to 'Gain knowledge of or acquire skill in something by study or practice'.

We cannot actually observe learning but it is reasonable to assert that it has taken place if someone's behaviour has changed permanently. In some cases it would appear that, despite the best efforts of managers, some employees have difficulty in changing or modifying their behaviour. Why is this so? There are usually several reasons including, perhaps, a person's negative attitude towards a behaviour or because the new behaviour may violate norms of the work group to which they belong (see Chapter 7). However for the purpose of this chapter, there are chiefly two reasons why behaviour remains unchanged: the appropriateness of the learning or training programme and the individual's ability.

There are two broad theories of learning. The first is behavioural and the other cognitive. Behavioural theories may be divided into three areas:

1 Classical conditioning (reflexive; from within) – individual responds to a stimulus which is not intuitively linked to response type (Pavlov, 1927).
2 Operant conditioning (learned; from without) – desired voluntary behaviour is rewarded and reinforced, undesired voluntary behaviour is punished (Skinner, 1953). Examples include certain behaviours at customer interface to obtain reward in the form of tipping.
3 Social learning (extension of operant conditioning) – through observation of others and from own experiences. Examples include the 'buddy system' so

that behaviour patterns may be incorporated into new employee's role (Miller and Dollard, 1955).

The behaviourists played a significant early role in the understanding of learning processes and their constructs still form the basis of many learning and training programmes. For example, in the leisure sector reinforcement is an important way of changing the way people act in the workplace. Robbins (2001: 43) refers to this as 'shaping behaviour' and considers the following to be suitable techniques:

- positive reinforcement (promotion for good performance)
- negative reinforcement (by looking physically busy at work an individual may not be asked by management to perform extra duties)
- punishment (dismissal for repeated incompetence)
- extinction (gradual removal of reinforcement which sustains a behaviour).

Reinforcement may be further divided into two overall categories: continuous and intermittent. These may be varied to maximize the reinforcing effect and can be either ratio (how many responses or certain types of behaviour an employee engages in) or interval (appropriate behaviour shown by employee after a specified time period has elapsed). Furthermore, reinforcement may be either fixed or variable.

However:

- continuous reinforcement soon becomes accepted as the norm and its affect on behaviour modification becomes weakened
- intermittent reinforcement does not have this limitation because it is inconsistent in terms of regularity.

Overall, intermittent reinforcement tends to be more effective because it is perceived to be linked directly with reward for effort.

Reinforcement, whether continuous or intermittent, is only effective if the associated reward is something the employee considers worthwhile. So, in addition to what the organization can physically and practically offer, managers must understand the attitudes of their workers to ensure the reward is appropriate.

Notwithstanding this, learning is only effective if managers have a clear picture of their employee's potential or ability. Behavioural approaches have been criticized for their limitations in this respect. For example, they do not provide an adequate explanation for the 'internal' choices or preferences of employees.

The behaviourally based social learning approach is unable to reason why some new workers choose not to incorporate all behaviours demonstrated using a buddy system for example. There are a variety of reasons for this behaviour being rooted in personality, perceptions, motivations and past positive or negative experiences. Cognitive learning theories account for these variables and thus allow a more robust explanation of the learning process.

The cognitive perspective recognizes that people have different learning styles and hold learning as a three-staged information processing procedure:

- active perception – full attention to environmental stimuli
- mentally active – making sense of information
- restructuring and storage.

The learning approach on which this book is based is essentially cognitive and the tenets of the model used (Kolbs', 1985, learning cycle) are explained fully in the Introduction. His construct considers that effective learning results from the synthesis between behaviour and evaluation of experiences. Reflection and subsequent experimentation in new situations is vital and allows the learner to become aware of new possibilities.

Participants play an active role in the learning process by interacting and relating to their world. Learning ability becomes a composite of innate ability and social experiences. Importantly, motivation to learn and attitudes held towards learning have a significant effect on the outcome. Although these factors may not be immediately apparent or observable, managers need to be aware of them before they can facilitate effective learning and affect behaviour modification in the workplace.

Consider the range of subjects you study at the moment. Now think of a favourite and whether you are a high achiever in this area. The answer will almost certainly be that you consistently 'score' better in this subject than in those on which you are not so keen because it motivates you above all others.

Indeed, attitudes to learning are shaped by a wide range of influences including, culture, gender, rewards, formal education system and so on.

Key point 4.6

Individuals learn effectively by interacting and relating to their world. A person's ability to learn is a fusion of innate capability and social experiences including the attitudes they hold towards the process.

In an organizational behaviour context, managers need to be aware of the current ability and skill levels of existing and new employees before effective learning can take place. A person's ability may be explained as their innate or learned capacity to perform job tasks or, put more simply, what someone can do.

Abilities are broadly divided into categories of intellectual and physical, and several instruments are available to assess each category. The specific purpose of testing will vary but normally they are useful for:

- training employees to achieve required competencies to modify their behaviour
- job redesign so employees are only given tasks within their capabilities
- achieving 'job fit' for new employees.

Of course before any testing takes place, managers must ensure the subsequent measurement is valid. For example, do tests which chiefly target numerical ability have value for the job of, say, leisure centre manager? The answer is, of course, 'possibly', but there are other abilities which require assessment.

There are other important issues to consider when using standard instruments including:

- Do they discriminate unfairly against anyone?
- Are the skills and abilities targeted by the tests strictly necessary?
- Do they correlate positively with job performance? For example, the ability to speak fluent Japanese would impact on the performance of a hotel manager in Brisbane, Australia. However, this would not be so for a similar role in a northern UK town.

According to McShane and Travaglione (2003), the whole issue of testing for job-specific abilities may be changing, especially in the Pacific Rim region. This is because firms are beginning to recognize the dynamic nature of their external trading environment. Increasingly, generic or generalizable competencies are now considered important because they provide a 'measure' of an individual's overall capability. Competencies are broad ranging and include ability, personality and other characteristics. The practical value of using competencies is that they are expressed as job-related behaviours.

To recap, managers must be aware of the current ability and skill levels of their employees before establishing and implementing consistent training procedures based on appropriate learning strategies. However in some seasonal and unaffiliated small to medium-sized hospitality organizations, the following characteristics conspire against such activities:

- a 'hands-on' management style in response to demand and nature of service product
- semi-skilled jobs
- an over-reliance on 'peripheral' workers to cope with fluctuating demand patterns.

Managers often find themselves undertaking a number of 'hands-on' roles, rather than operating strategically, due to the nature of the product and demand pattern. It has been argued that this effectively prohibits managers from other important duties such as staff training and development. The reason for this style is partly rooted in the pattern of organizational ownership, but also in the skills possessed by contemporary managers.

In short, there are effectively no barriers to owning and running a hospitality organization; anyone can do it. In many cases owner/managers are former hospitality workers who only possess operational skills. These are then internalized by managers and become 'common sense' (see Chapter 8) with a presumption that employees share this knowledge.

Unfortunately, this element of managers' backgrounds perpetuates bad practice. At best there may be some training provision for inexperienced employees working alongside an existing colleague. The aim is to learn chiefly by observing how objective and tacit tasks and duties are performed.

In some organizations there is a perception that certain operational jobs are semi-skilled. In one sense this is true and there has been a definite managerial cost-cutting policy of deskilling because it immediately increases the size of the labour market. This helps prevent labour shortages and ensures lower labour costs.

In addition, semi-skilled jobs help perpetuate the above common-sense myth and 'justify' either little or no training provision. Furthermore, operational skills are also deemed 'transferable' which means jobs are similar across a variety of organizations. While this may be the case, unfortunately it is often used to justify inadequate training provision. High levels of labour turnover are also sometimes linked with and used to explain an absence of training in transferable skills.

Finally, many hospitality organizations have a 'flexible' structure which means they employ a small number of core or permanent workers and a larger body of peripheral and relatively poorly waged staff (see Chapter 1).

Organizations respond to increases in demand by relying substantially on peripherals from the secondary labour market; once demand falls they are made redundant. Peripheral employees are often supplied by specialist agencies to undertake semi-skilled jobs perceived to need minimal training. Furthermore, the skills are deemed transferable and managers would normally expect these workers to be trained externally (by the agency). In these cases, hospitality managers have effectively abdicated responsibility for training provision.

In short, a situation exists in a few organizations whereby the learning preferences and abilities of employees are not fully understood because of these characteristics. Moreover, they way in which they are linked provides managers with a self-perpetuating cycle of logic. This situation is unlikely to improve unless these issues are addressed.

Conclusion

In order to reward individual effort while ensuring employees work together harmoniously, we need to understand something of their individual behaviour. The way individuals act in the workplace is a symptom of a complicated configuration of variables. Personality plays a key role in shaping behaviour and a number of attempts to map its components have been made. Some writers believe personality is too complex to be measured and is continually changing (idiographic), while others consider it to be stable over time and 'testable' (nomothetic).

The latter perspective holds that particular identifiable traits and types help explain personality and thus behaviour. Eysenck's model of introversion–extroversion, stability–neuroticism is arguably the most reliable of these models, with many subsequent instruments being based on its tenets.

However, the relationship between personality and behaviour remains unclear; this is explained in part, by the role of perception. Perception is a function of a target, context and the individual concerned. It is the way in which people make sense of their world using the five senses and through an internal process of filtering and interpreting. We also like to interpret the behaviour of others by attributing it to one cause or another, broadly into internal and external.

Unfortunately, perception is susceptible to bias whereby individuals make erroneous attributions or 'short-cut' a longer process when interpreting information. Typically, these short cuts include selective perception, the halo effect, stereotyping and so on. If decisions are made on the basis of a skewed perception, serious consequences may result.

The concept of learning has an important role to play in attempting to understand and explain behaviour because much of how individuals act in the workplace is learned. Clearly if managers need employees to behave in a certain manner, they have to provide effective training. The best training procedures must be based on a sound understanding of learning theory. In short, two generic approaches exist: one is behavioural and the other is cognitive. Much workplace behaviour can be learned or modified using the former but it does not account for the employee's ongoing cognitive processes. For example, the behavioural approach does not explain the notion of selectivity, motivation and/or attitudes sufficiently well.

Cognitive theories alert us to these individual differences and also encourage an action-learning approach with reflection and application of knowledge to new situations. The effectiveness of behavioural or cognitive modification techniques depends on the job or situation and also on obtaining an accurate assessment of employee skills and abilities. Once a current inventory is established, appropriate training programmes can be devised.

Reflective practice

1 Define personality and perception.
2 List the key determinants of personality.
3 Which view of personality do you prefer and why.
4 Explain the process of perception.
5 Discuss the relationship between personality, perception and behaviour.
6 Explain the common short cuts in which people engage during the process of perception and give examples of when you did similar.
7 Discuss why an understanding of learning theory is important for hospitality, leisure and tourism industry managers.
8 Suggest some key abilities required by: hotel managers, food servers and tourist guides. Are there some common ones?

CHAPTER 5

Individuals in organizations: attitudes, behaviour and motivation

- define values, beliefs, attitudes, behaviour and motivation
- explain the 'theory of reasoned action'
- identify and describe key motivational theories
- explain why behaviour is (usually) the ultimate outcome of the interaction of values, beliefs, attitudes and motivation.

Consider for a moment the plight of Sherlock Holmes engaged in bringing to justice the perpetrator of some dastardly deed. To solve this mystery, the detective required key pieces of information about context, motives and other circumstances. Service managers are no different in their quest to understand their workers. Necessary organizational variables need to be analysed and arranged in a particular order to help managers make sense of them. Only then can informed and effective decisions be made in an organizational behaviour context.

In Chapter 4 we discovered that personality, perceptions and ability have a powerful impact upon individuals and how they act in the workplace. In addition, the process of behaviour modification or learning and its impact on training were also explained. However, there remain other crucial pieces of this complex puzzle which must be positioned before service managers can hope to understand their employees and predict their behaviour. In other words, so far we have only discussed those issues that suggest individuals might hold particular values, beliefs, attitudes and motivations. We have yet to learn about the chronology and true meaning of these elements.

Values, beliefs, attitudes and behaviour

Values

What exactly is the benefit of understanding values in the workplace; why not just look at behaviour? The answer to this question is:

- first, that values are antecedents of (come before) organizational behaviour so managers need to understand them before they can hope to explain how individuals behave
- second, a comprehension of values allows managers to use this knowledge as an alternative strategy to formal command and control protocols. Theoretically, at least, this permits a fostering of commonality among members to help ensure movement in one direction (pursuit of organizational aims and objectives).

The *Collins English Dictionary and Thesaurus* defines values as 'principles or standards' but a more substantial 'feel' for what we mean by values, is provided by Robbins (2001: 62): 'Basic convictions that a specific mode of conduct or end-state of existence is personally or socially preferable to an opposite or converse mode of conduct or end-state of existence'. However, we need to be clear about specifics because Robbins alludes to more than one type of value. Current research concludes that they may be divided into several categories:

- personal – brought into organization, formed from experience and interactions
- cultural – influences personal values with dominant societal beliefs
- organizational – pattern of shared assumptions, values and beliefs
- professional – those held by a particular occupational group
- terminal – desired states of existence (for example, equality and quality of work life)
- instrumental – desired ways of effecting terminal values (politeness, logic, ambition and so on).

Hospitality, Leisure & Tourism Series

Problematically, values, much like all antecedents of behaviour, cannot be seen or easily explained by people who have them. There is no doubt that they are strongly experienced, depending on the situation, but often they either defy or invoke circular logic. For example, an individual may have little idea why they feel the way they do about a situation, person or object. Indeed, they might explain these values by stating something like, 'it's obvious isn't it'; well actually, no, it is not.

Reflective practice

Consider something about which you have conclusive feelings. Is there anything happening nationally or globally about which you have definite views? We guarantee that the following questions will generate strong internal feelings and opinions:

1 What is your opinion of terrorist groups; are they callous murderers or disempowered freedom fighters?
2 Do you believe that national governments have a societal responsibility for ensuring full employment?
3 Is positive discrimination in favour of minority groups in the workplace a reasonable way to redress inequity?

Personal feelings evoked by particular situations are explained by an individual's upbringing, experience and societal influences. These values are often (but not always) stable over time and prioritized into a 'value system' depending on how strongly individuals feel about each one. In the workplace, employees may think nothing of arriving late or leaving early but may not be prepared to steal cash amounts from their employer. Arguably, both of these activities are tantamount to stealing; the former is just an indirect way of doing so (and also a matter of personal ethics).

In this example, these values have been prioritized into a system. The authors are not suggesting that all service employees engage in these activities; we are simply illustrating the point. Having said that, Mars and Nicod (1984) consider this sort of value system and behaviour to be commonplace in the hotel industry.

Mars and Nicod argue that the reward system for employees is effectively divided into official payments of salaries and wages (and tips) and unofficial benefits in the form of stolen merchandise and hotel stock. They name this the 'total reward system'. Presuming that there is some truth in their assertion, a value system emerges. For example, an employee may think nothing of stealing condiments from their employer but would not consider breaking into the hotel safe to steal money or other valuables.

The above example also illustrates that value systems are often shared by specific groups. In this case, Robbins's (2001) categories of occupational and professional values can clearly be identified among hospitality workers. Moreover, the fact that group values are common enables managers to influence organizational members efficiently and effectively in the workplace (provided unofficial values do not become established first).

Another way to illustrate shared values is by using a 'generational' approach applied to working populations. Table 5.1 provides a summary of dominant work values by generation.

The values in Table 5.1 may not apply internationally because it is an aggregate of Western values addressed predominantly by North American studies. We only have to consider Hofstede's (1980) view of cultural values, discussed in Chapter 8, to realize its limitations.

Stage	Year born	Entered workforce	Current age	Dominant work values
Protestant work ethic	1925–45	Early 1940s to early 1960s	55–75	Hard work, conservative, loyal to organization
Existential	1945–55	1960s to mid-1970s	45–55	Quality of life, nonconformist, seeks autonomy, loyal to self
Pragmatic	1955–65	Mid-1970s to late 1980s	35–45	Success, achievement, ambition, hard work, loyal to career
Generation X	1965–81	Late 1980s to present	Under 35	Flexibility, job satisfaction, balanced lifestyle, loyalty to relationships

Source: Robbins (2001: 64).

Table 5.1 Work values by generation

In sum, the values of individuals originate from a variety of sources and are often experienced strongly by the holders. The term 'conviction' sometimes used in common parlance is, in fact, another way of expressing a value or value system. Most people understand the 'power' conveyed by this word; as such it is a useful way of remembering the meaning of values.

So, how are values different from beliefs and attitudes; are they just different words used to say the same thing? The answer to this question is that the first two terms are similar and together help form an individual's attitude to objects, people and situations. These issues are explained in the next section.

Key point 5.1

Values are antecedents of attitudes established and influenced by a number of factors; once held they are prioritized into a value system which is difficult to change.

Beliefs and attitudes

Mullins (1996) differentiates values from beliefs and attitudes in the following way:

- values – what 'should' be and what is desirable
- beliefs – what is known about the world, centring on 'what is', or reality as is understood
- attitudes – a state of 'readiness' or tendency to act in a particular way.

Beliefs are transformed into attitudes once an idea of what is desirable, good and worthwhile is added (values). Rosenberg and Hovland (1960) agree, contending that attitudes are a function of beliefs and values or evaluative statements towards objects people or events. You might find that separating these variables for the first time is tricky because they cannot be seen, neither are they objective. Indeed, we all hold attitudes about a variety of matters but the components and formation of them is a wholly intangible and subjective process.

There are almost no limits to the number and types of attitudes held by individuals in the workplace. Holland (1966) conceptualizes these as 'personality types', and considers that collective attitudes produce specific predispositions to work. He notes: 'The members of a vocation have similar personalities and similar histories of personal development ... it follows that each vocation attracts and retains people with similar personalities [and attitudes]' (ibid.: 5).

Members will bring their own learned, acquired and embodied attitudes to the organization in addition to those that they form as a result of being in the workplace. The former attitudes were first conceptualized by Ginzberg *et al.* (1951), and were confirmed by Goldthorpe *et al.* (1968) in their study of UK automotive workers; these attitudes are described as 'orientations to work':

- instrumental orientation (seeing work as a means to an end, for example salary with which to support a family, leisure time and so on)
- expressive orientation (seeing work as an end in itself, regarding work as a means of self-expression, a source of intrinsic satisfaction)
- social orientation (seeing work as a social activity, as a source of social relationships)
- promotion orientation (seeing work as a ladder, a source of advancement and status).

Both Shamir (1975) and Lee-Ross (1996) have since found similar attitudes present among employees in British hotels.

Attitudes to work may be broadly classified as either core or peripheral irrespective of where they originate (work, culture, upbringing and so on). Typically, the former are more difficult to change than peripherals. This is important to know because managers often have to effect change in the attitudes of their workers for a number of reasons. For example, a decision may have been taken to introduce teamworking into the organization where formerly work was carried out on an individual basis. Similarly, if organizations are moving towards empowering their workers, new attitudes will need to be developed to take advantage of these opportunities. Furthermore, in a macro sense, prevailing environmental conditions are changing significantly and organizations have responded.

Currently, there appears to be a plethora of new developments which have cultural implications (see Chapter 8). Some of these developments are shown below:

- direct foreign investment – Singaporean investment in Brisbane Marriott Hotel, and Tiawanese investment in Sofitel Imperial Hotel in Mauritius
- management contracts – Marriott International, Hilton International, Hyatt International, Accor and Holiday Inn
- joint ventures – Accor with China, Korea, Vietnam, Malaysia and Thailand
- franchising – KFC and McDonald's
- strategic alliances – Telstra with Hilton International, Marriott and Hilton with Pizza Hut, Visa with Marriott, American Express with Accor, Sheraton and Hilton, Holiday Inn with Thrifty Car Rental and Westin with Japanese Airlines (adapted from Kandampully, 2002: 296–300).

These shifts impact on firms and employees in a variety of ways, and former work attitudes may need changing to ensure success in new and increasingly competitive and international environments. In a practical sense, managers are faced with the decision either to effect an attitude change in their employees or not. If attitudes are deemed core, it may be more cost-effective not to make the attempt.

This is often why companies offer individuals redundancy or early retirement packages rather than introducing costly (and ineffective) attitude-change programmes. On the other hand if managers have opted to change workers' attitudes, they must understand:

- their composition
- how to audit or diagnose them
- the relationship between attitudes and behaviour.

Rosenberg and Hovland (1960) explain that attitudes comprise three elements, which appear in Table 5.2.

While the ability to implement organizational change programmes in response to macro environmental shifts is important, managers also need to understand employees' attitudes in order to gauge employee wellbeing or 'mental health'.

Worker attitudes commonly are obtained using questionnaires. These forms can be custom made by managers but there are also several standard instruments available for this purpose. For example, Hackman and Olham's (1974; 1980) Job Diagnostic Survey (JDS) has proved popular and targets job tasks, linking them with the outcome attitude of job satisfaction.

Question statements they use are based on the above three-component view of attitudes and require respondents to indicate their opinions using a Likert-type scale (scale of 1 to 7 with 1 being 'low' or 'poor' and 7 being the opposite). Average employee scores are then calculated to give a summary diagnosis for all elements of work, including job satisfaction.

In addition to job satisfaction, alternative collective terms are also used by other instruments including:

- 'job involvement'
- 'organizational commitment'.

Element	Description	Example
Cognitive	Perceptual responses and verbal statements of belief and opinion	You may believe that split-shift and short-term working in the leisure services sector causes workers to quit their jobs; as such it is bad practice
Affective	Sympathetic nervous responses and statements of feelings or emotions	This is your acceptance or rejection (you either like or do not like) of split-shift and short-term working arrangements
Conative	Overt actions and statements concerning behaviour	This is your statement of intent not to apply for work in organizations which only offer jobs based on the above tenure

Table 5.2 The composition of attitudes

The former represents the degree to which a person identifies with their job, participates willingly in it and considers performance crucial to self-worth. The latter is the degree to which a person identifies with an organization and wishes to remain with that organization.

However, with the gradual but definite erosion of 'jobs for life', the continued use of organizational commitment as a valid outcome attitude is questionable. This is particularly relevant for the services sector because employment patterns have always been 'non-traditional' or part-time, split-shift and temporary. Perhaps job involvement is more important in this sense because jobs are not organization specific. Evidence suggests this to be the case among hospitality workers where occupational communities are rife (see Chapter 8 and Lee-Ross, 1996).

Notwithstanding the collectives of involvement and commitment, job satisfaction remains a popular 'catch-all' and in many respects is a composite attitude. Most people have an intuitive understanding of job satisfaction and the behavioural outcomes ascribed to it. Simply, someone who has a high level of job satisfaction 'usually' has positive attitudes toward their job.

We frequently are led to believe that if employees are satisfied with their jobs behavioural outcomes should include low levels of labour turnover, punctuality and increased productivity. However, someone with low job satisfaction or who is 'alienated' from their work may behave quite differently. Based on Marx, Blauner (1964) explains the concept of alienation as:

- powerlessness – denotes worker's lack of control over management policy, work process and employment conditions
- meaninglessness – due to standardization and division of labour
- isolation – not belonging to an integrated work group or having no group norms
- self-estrangement – work is simply a means to a end.

Behaviour driven by alienation might include quitting, 'loafing', aggression and so on. In one extreme case of alienation, a manager reported to the present authors that a former disgruntled worker returned to his hotel to commit petty acts of vandalism. This resulted in significant and costly structural damage to the building. The individual was charged subsequently with burglary and causing criminal damage.

Key point 5.2

Attitudes are comprised of cognitive, affective and conative elements.

Reflective practice

1 Pick a service-related issue about which you have strong attitudes.
2 Now identify each attitude and express the cognitive, affective and conative elements of each one.

Case study 5.1

Judy Gladwell manages a winter resort complex in New South Wales, Australia. The resort comprises several retail sports outlets, two restaurants, five hotels and a number of self-catering chalets. The business is mainly seasonal with the busy period falling between April and September. Understandably, a majority of the labour force is seasonal, with most workers moving elsewhere during the quieter summer months.

A perennial problem for Judy is the high level of labour turnover, worker alienation and the negative impacts these have on service quality and the 'bottom line'. She brings in Tony Yeoman, an OB consultant, to help resolve the problem.

After diagnosis, Tony confidently announces his recommendations. First, Judy must realize that money is not a motivator and she should focus on her workers' higher order needs including their self-esteem and self-actualization. It may also be beneficial for Judy to have an 'open door' policy whereby workers can meet with her and discuss any problems they have.

After deliberation, Judy agrees and acts on Tony's advice. Some time later, she assesses the impact of these changes on her employees. Much to her dismay, the situation has not changed much. If anything, labour turnover and job dissatisfaction have become worse.

Reflective practice

1 Why do you think the consultant's recommendations failed to reduce labour turnover and worker alienation?
2 What action would you take to resolve these problems in the above scenario?

Attitudes and employee selection

The process of diagnosing worker attitudes and job satisfaction is not exclusive to existing workers; it also applies when selecting new organizational members. This approach acknowledges that orientations to work are an important attitudinal conglomerate present in individuals, however, the focus this time is on service predisposition.

Using a similar diagnostic approach as other techniques, the service predisposition instrument (SPI) (Lee-Ross, 2000) identifies whether frontline job candidates are predisposed to working effectively with customers. Simple summary calculations are used to build and compare an applicant's profile (based on their scoring of crucial service attitudes) with previously established job norms for the industry.

The SPI is specifically designed for hotel, leisure and tourism organizations, and provides crucial information about whether potential workers hold appropriate attitudes. This and other attitudinal-based diagnostic instruments have an important role to play in staff selection and assessing other employee attitudes in the leisure service sector. These questionnaires are popular and becoming increasingly available on line. A selection may be found on the Australian-based 'Testgrid' website at http://www.testgrid.com/; http://www.mindtools.com/index.html; http://tara.unl.ac.uk/~hydzmartinw/tests.htm; http://www.psychometrics.co.uk/; and http://www.homeworking.com/library/psychom.htm

Behaviour

Notwithstanding the popularity of the above instruments, there is some doubt that behavioural outcomes are consistently predictable from attitudes. As intuitively sound as the relationship appears, it is (unfortunately for managers) not simple and other factors must also be considered. For example, workers in Lee-Ross's (1996) study of British seaside hotels indicated high levels of job satisfaction, yet levels of labour turnover were high. This behaviour seems inconsistent with a positive work-related attitude. These apparent anomalies were pointed out earlier by writers such as Sherif (1936) and Jones and Gerrard (1967). In response, Ajzen and Fishbein (1980) modelled the attitude/behaviour relationships in their theory of 'reasoned action' and these are shown in Figure 5.1.

This theory is based on the idea that people consider the implications of what they do before they decide to behave in a particular way. The individual's intention to perform (or not) a behaviour is the immediate determinant of the action. A person's behaviour depends on two determinants, one is personal and the other reflects social influence.

The former is the person's positive or negative evaluation of performing the behaviour (attitude toward the behaviour – in favour or against performing the behaviour). The latter is the perception of social pressures to perform or not perform the behaviour and is termed the 'subjective norm'. Thus individuals will perform a behaviour when they evaluate it positively and when they believe important others approve (co-workers for example).

The relative weighting of each will impact on behaviour. In other words, a person who believes performing a given behaviour will lead to positive benefits will hold a favourable attitude toward performing that behaviour. A person who believes the

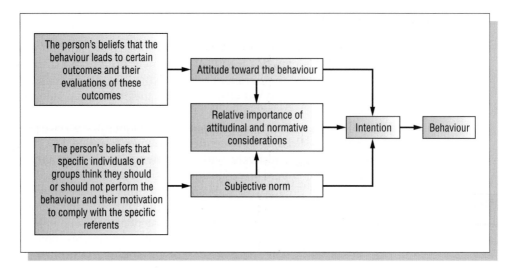

Figure 5.1 Factors determining a person's behaviour
Source: Ajzen and Fishbein (1980: 8).

opposite will hold a different attitude. The beliefs that underlie a person's attitude toward the behaviour are termed 'behavioural beliefs'.

The key part of Ajzen and Fishbein's theory is that individuals always 'reason' before they act. This is most probably true in a majority of behavioural episodes. However, where situations are unexpected, unusual or novel, behaviour often becomes 'non-thinking'.

Robbins (2001) reminds us that in these situations (especially important for new employees) individuals act first and then justify behaviour retrospectively. This phenomenon is known as 'self-perception' and is used to make sense out of a particular behaviour. Managers need to be aware of this because it helps us understand how attitudes are formed in these situations.

Similar to self-perception theory, another phenomenon also applies to individual behaviour. How often have you changed what you say (attitude) in order to justify what you do (behaviour) and noticed others doing similar? For example, as a food service worker, you may believe that the prevailing management style in your organization is overly 'autocratic' (dictatorial and non-supportive).

Now assume you have been promoted to restaurant manager and find yourself using the same approach. It is likely that you will justify the practice by changing your former attitude into one which is consistent with the autocratic management style. Where once you considered it necessary to offer workers constructive support and autonomy, you now believe that tight management control of job tasks is more appropriate (probably defending your new attitude using time and cost constraints).

According to Festinger (1957) this is known as 'cognitive dissonance' and is said to exist when differences exist between two or more attitudes or behaviour and attitudes. Individuals feel 'uncomfortable' internally with these incompatibilities and tend to re-establish balance to reduce or eliminate dissonance.

Key point 5.3

The theory of reasoned action suggests that our behaviour is influenced by the relative importance of subjective norms and the opinions of significant others (referents).

Reflective practice

1 In small groups, identify and explain individually an occasion where you experienced either cognitive dissonance or an episode of self-perception.
2 Do you still behave in this manner?
3 If yes, explain why.
4 If no, why have you changed your behaviour?

In sum:

- attitudes are a multidimensional collection of values and beliefs which, in their turn, are influenced by upbringing, culture, experiences, learning, personality and perceptions
- attitudes may be divided into categories of core and peripheral with the former being difficult to change.

It is commonly thought that attitudes predispose people to behave in a particular way. However, this is not always the case because behaviour is a function of intention to act. This, for our purposes may be expressed as an individual's motivation to behave. Motivation at work has been a popular subject for enquiry over the most recent seventy years or so, with a number of constructs emerging. The following section introduces and discusses some of the major contributions to the area.

What is motivation?

Robbins *et al.*'s (2000: 549) definition of motivation includes key factors about which there is a general consensus: '[A] willingness to exert high levels of effort to reach organizational goals, conditioned by the effort's ability to satisfy some individual need'.

It is also important to note that workers possess a variety of needs, in varying proportions, which change depending on the situation. Thus, if an individual's requirement for something is urgent or overwhelming, they will be highly motivated to direct their behaviour to satisfy the need. Managers must therefore be able to align an individual's needs with the objectives of the organization for the benefit of both employer and employee.

In an attempt to understand and predict organizationally based attitudes and behaviour, motivation has commanded substantial attention and a number of ideas have emerged. Overall, theories can be separated into two groups depending on

Hospitality, Leisure & Tourism Series

whether they focus on the content of an individual's needs or the cognitive processes involved when individuals prioritize their motivational needs.

The former type or 'content' theories seek to explain motivation by considering an individual's requirements and what must be present in the workplace in order to satisfy them. The other perspective contends that it is essential to understand the process of motivation in addition to knowing why people have different (content) needs at different times. The following subsection reviews a number of popular content and process theories of motivation.

Content

Maslow's (1954) 'pyramid' is one such content theory and it holds that individuals prioritize needs according to a distinct 'internal' hierarchy. According to Maslow, the above needs range from the 'lower order' basic physiological needs (food, drink, shelter and sexual needs) to more esoteric self-actualization needs (the drive to realize one's full potential). As each level of need is satisfied in individuals, so their requirements change and the next level becomes important, and so on.

It is interesting to note that, despite the intuitive logic of Maslow's theory, empirical testing was limited and more recent studies show that its predictive power is equivocal. However, it remains arguably the most famous of all motivational theories because of its 'common-sense' approach and ease of application. Table 5.3 illustrates the theory with an organizational application.

Some time after the initial development of the needs hierarchy model, Aldefer (1972) suggested that all five levels were unnecessary and could be represented more concisely as 'ERG':

Needs	Attributes	Organizational attributes
Physiological	Food, water, sex, sleep	Pay, good basic working conditions
Safety	Safety, security, stability, protection	Safe working conditions, company benefits, job security
Social	Love, affection, belonging	Cohesive work group, friendly supervisors, professional associations
Esteem	Self-respect, self-esteem, prestige, status	Social recognition, high-status job, job feedback
Self-actualization	Growth, advancement, creativity	Challenging job, opportunities for creativity and originality, work achievements and advancement

Table 5.3 An application of Maslow's hierarchy

- existence – human existence, survival, physiological, safety and material
- relatedness – relationships, love, belonging, affiliation and interpersonal relationships concerning safety or esteem
- growth – development of potential, self esteem and self-actualization.

Furthermore, although individuals are alleged to progress from lower to higher order needs, these requirements may also be inverted. In other words, higher order needs may become more important than lower ones, especially if the latter have little chance of being satisfied.

Alternatively, if higher order needs become frustrated, then individuals may seek satisfaction of those lower on the scale. Similar to Maslow's (1954) hierarchy, the 'ERG' theory has not been validated successfully.

Hertzberg, Mausner and Snyderman's (1959) 'two-factor' or 'motivation – hygiene' theory (often known as simply Hertzberg's theory) is another important contribution to the content approach in understanding workplace motivation. This construct proposes that the primary determinants of employee satisfaction are factors intrinsic to the work undertaken:

- achievement
- responsibility
- advancement
- recognition
- personal growth in competence.

These factors are called motivators, because employees are motivated to obtain more of them through good performance. The theory also reasons that another category of variables exist, known as 'hygienes'. They are said to be extrinsic to the actual work undertaken and, as such, their presence does not cause job satisfaction but, rather, prevents the onset of dissatisfaction.

Typically these hygienes include supervision, company policy, salary, working conditions and relationship with supervisors. The theory specifies that work will enhance motivation only if motivators are designed into it. Changes to work which only deal with hygiene factors will bring no motivational gains.

Amusingly, in Fred Hertzberg's video, *Jumping for the Jellybeans*, he comments that many have misunderstood the importance of hygiene factors. He quips 'they say get Fred in to present his theory or do some consultancy or something, 'cos he works for nothing. So, I just had to raise my consultancy fees to prove how important hygienes really are; I love hygienes'.

Robbins (2001) includes levels of pay as a key motivating factor under the above circumstances. Weaver's (1988) study of the motivating power of pay levels in the hospitality industry concludes that managers must not underestimate the potential of wages and salaries. Indeed, the oft-quoted notion that pay is not a key motivator is utter nonsense. Its power depends on context and whether workers earn enough to cover their basic needs. One only has to consider Maslow's hierarchy of needs to appreciate how important remuneration is in these circumstances.

However, McShane and Travaglione (2003) warn that financial rewards are 'quick fixes'. This reward type detracts workers from the intrinsic value of the job and their position within the organization. There is some doubt that financial rewards alone are effective motivators. To have any chance of significance and longevity, financial rewards must be integrated into a comprehensive and robust motivational strategy.

Despite its merits, problems have been identified with the Hertzberg's construct because of the methodology used to elicit its major tenets. For example, the theory on interviews where respondents were asked to describe occasions in which they felt particularly 'good' or 'bad' about their jobs is known as a 'critical incident' approach and has a number of inherent weaknesses.

Nevertheless, the body of evidence refuting the validity of Herzberg's theory is counterbalanced by that which supports it. Moreover, for our purposes this theory is important because it is one of the first accounting for work-related factors rather than only physical and social contexts.

Many of you with work experience will know that the leisure services sector is almost characterized by jobs which could be described as 'physical' or 'hands on'. Thus, managers need to be aware of the motivating potential of necessary and inherent service-based job tasks.

Case study 5.2

David Bolan is the president of a regional tourist association comprised of tour operators, hoteliers, attractions managers and other local traders. Around twelve months ago, at their annual general meeting, David had much to say about the motivating potential of money. In particular, he was keen for all to realize the beneficial impacts that performance-related pay has on worker motivation and profitability. He based his opinion on recent supporting evidence from the USA and UK manufacturing sector. Furthermore, he saw no reason why similar tactics should not prove successful in hospitality, leisure and tourism organizations.

Reflective practice

1 Why do you think that companies are using performance-related pay (PRP) to motivate their workers?
2 Do you think that PRP is an appropriate approach in the hospitality, leisure and tourism sector?

Another contribution to the content view of motivation is often ascribed to McClelland (1961) who, instead of looking at primary needs, considers those which are secondary or learned. He concludes there are three key sources of motivation for individuals:

- learned need for achievement (nAch) – accomplishment of reasonably challenging goals through individual effort under competitive circumstances and like to know exactly how they are performing, not motivated by money, for example, entrepreneurs

- learned need for affiliation (nAff) – seek others' approval, conformist avoiding conflict, good at mediating and supporting others, sales and striking long-term relationships with customers, less effective at decision-making which may generate conflict such as resource allocation
- learned need for power (nPow) – seek to control own environment, including people and other resources, for own benefit or that of others, need to acquire and maintain power, for example, corporate and political leaders.

Reflective practice

1 Consider three leisure service sector roles and, using McClelland's typology, recommend the most appropriate category for each job.
2 In the form of a diagram, show the relationship between Maslow's, Aldefer's, Herzberg's and McClelland's models of motivation.

In sum, the above content theories focus on *what* motivates individuals. If managers can identify the needs of workers, they will be in a strong position to affect policies and procedures to satisfy these needs. To be effective this presupposes managers understand:

- that needs are dynamic and will vary between individuals
- know how to effect work environments appropriate to individuals and the organization
- what it is possible to offer employees to satisfy their needs.

However, to obtain a robust and reliable view of worker motivation, managers must appreciate the reason why individuals react and behave in a certain manner. In other words, it is essential to understand (the process of) motivation in addition to knowing why people have different (content) needs at different times. Process theories attempt to do this by focusing on needs deficiency and resulting behaviour. There are several extant process theories of motivation which are reviewed in the following section.

Key point 5.4

Content theories seek to explain motivation by considering an individual's requirements and what needs to be present in the workplace in order to satisfy them.

Process

Probably the best known process theory of all is that of Victor Vroom (1964) and, later, Porter and Lawler (1968). Basically, Vroom's original 'expectancy theory' concentrates upon the worker's perceived relationship between effort, reward and performance, and the effect of this relationship upon motivation. In theory, high motivation is achieved if a worker perceives that effort and consequent performance produce adequate rewards.

Reviewers of Vroom's model raise objections to its underlying assumptions. For example, writers question whether behaviour changes can always be predicted from expectations and anticipated evaluations. However, after reviewing the evidence, Mullins (1996) concludes that the expectancy model appears as valid as other constructs and appears in Figure 5.2.

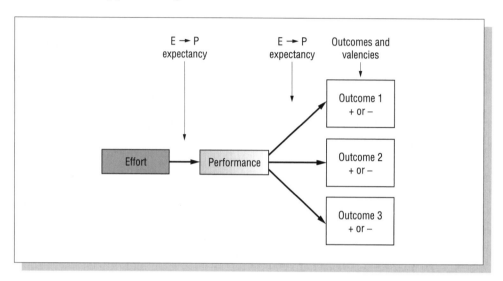

Figure 5.2   Expectancy theory of motivation
Source: McShane and Travagllione (2003: 157).

In brief, effort to performance expectancies concern self-esteem and previous experience in similar situations. Thus, individuals should be trained to achieve appropriate competencies, have unambiguous role perceptions and working conditions so they can perform according to their expectations. Performance to outcome expectancies concern having a clear understanding of job requirements and how they are linked to rewards. Valencies are about ascribing appropriate reward types for each employee. Try answering the following questions, they should help clarify your expectancy perspective of motivation:

● How hard must I work to perform at a certain level and can I do it?
● What do I get for performing at this level?
● Is the reward attractive and does it help me achieve anything?

On a cautionary note, it is important to remember that individuals do not have the capacity to evaluate every possible outcome. So, while an individual's behaviour may appear inconsistent, this may not actually be the case because they will probably have evaluated different outcomes resulting in dissimilar behaviours.

For example, you may be motivated to negotiate travel arrangements successfully with a client because of the commission you will ultimately receive. However, you may already have received a quota of commission payments from your employer and instead be keen to complete the deal quickly because of another pressing engagement.

Reflective practice

1 Using examples from the hospitality, leisure and tourism industry, outline how you would increase an employee's 'beliefs' for each stage of the expectancy theory of motivation?

Equity theory

How often do you make comparisons between yourself and others? Probably more than you might at first imagine because it is something individuals engage in naturally. Comparison is the way we make sense of much that is seen and experienced.

How do you feel if you compare favourably with a peer or competitor over some issue? The chances are you will be happy with the result. However, you may not be quite so delighted if the judgement criteria are flawed or if you believe the result is undeserved (in the case of someone else making the decision; a manager for example). Alternatively, if the situation is reversed and you think management have been unfair in their appraisal of your worth or efforts you will experience a similar but probably more intense sense of injustice.

The basis on which Adams's (1965) 'equity theory' rests suggests that workers make comparisons between job inputs and outcomes, and then consider this ratio with that of peers or 'referents'. In other words, as a receptionist you might consider the benefits derived (could be salary, promotion and so on) in relation to the effort you have invested in the job.

You will then compare your situation or ratio with that of others engaged in similar work. If these comparisons are deemed fair by the individual, then a sense of justice will exist. However, if evaluations are perceived as unfair (negatively or positively), a feeling of inequity prevails and the employee will attempt to reduce this in a number of ways:

- induce others to make changes to inputs or outputs
- change own inputs and outputs
- choose a different referent
- quit their job.

Operatives usually make comparisons within the workplace or company; managers and executives tend to compare externally because they have fewer or no peers. Referents also include the official organizational pay policies and procedures, one's own past experiences and the influence of friends, contacts and family.

This is an example of another theory of motivation which is partially validated but makes intuitive sense; we have all experienced feelings of inequity at some time or other. However, in a sense there is a highly subjective element to this construct which can be traced to the inherent frailties and weaknesses of the human psyche.

It is always difficult for managers to establish and sustain equity in organizations because people's perceptions and expectations are subjective and dynamic. Managers often only become aware of these perspectives when inequity is experienced and communicated. These dynamics are exacerbated in hospitality and tourism organizations because of inherent organizational structures and the corresponding nature of the workforce. For example, employees are either core or peripheral, and both have different rates of pay and working conditions.

Under normal circumstances, members from one or other of these categories would not be used by individuals; that is, core workers would compare their input–output ratio within the same group. However, the nature of the product demands that both groups are involved in key service delivery areas and often undertake similar roles. Therefore, inter-group comparisons are made, resulting in feelings of inequity because core employees are rewarded more handsomely that peripheral workers for what is effectively perceived as the same job.

Some managers have attempted to reduce inequity by striking 'individual contracts' (a reward system which is an alternative and more favourable than the 'officially' sanctioned one and also includes 'unofficial' remuneration) with workers. However, if peers discover that customized working conditions and rewards are more favourable than their own, inequity develops. Furthermore, employment in the leisure services sector is low paid by most national and international standards, therefore 'absolute' inequity is a very real consequence. Some argue that this is why high levels of labour turnover exist in hospitality, tourism and leisure organizations. Whether this is only partially true does not divert us from the proposition that feelings of relative and absolute inequity are common in this sector.

Goal-setting

Goal theory is chiefly attributed to Locke (1968) who posits that an individual's intentions (goals) play a key role in determining their behaviour. The construct acknowledges expectancy theory's perceived value but adds that goals create emotions and desires. The employee will seek to achieve goals so that emotions and desires can be satisfied. In turn, these goals will drive work-based responses and behaviours. An individual's effort is moderated by how difficult the actual goal is and how dedicated the incumbent is to achieve it.

People tend to perform more effectively if goals are moderately difficult to achieve, are clearly defined behaviourally, include completion deadlines and a timely feedback mechanism (which can be used to redefine some goals if necessary). Goal-setting forms the basis of a system of management known as 'management by objectives', although the latter was devised before the theoretical development of goal-setting. Goal theory is shown in Figure 5.3.

After reviewing the evidence, Mullins (1996) concludes that Locke's (1968) construct, much like all theories of motivation, finds partial empirical support. However, once again this theory is intuitive and reasonably simple to apply in the workplace. In addition, it is probably judicious to view goal-setting as a motivational technique rather than a theory. Much the same may be levelled at other approaches including Hackman and Oldham's (1974; 1980) 'job characteristics model' (JCM).

Job characteristics theory

Turner and Lawrence (1965) and Hackman and Lawler (1971) first introduced the idea of building into jobs attributes alleged to create conditions for high work motivation, satisfaction and performance. Hackman and Oldham (1974) developed this idea into

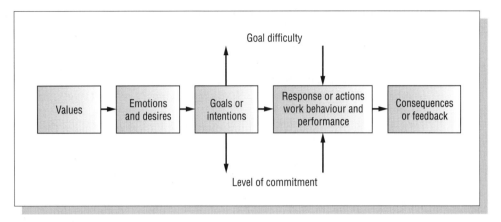

Figure 5.3 Goal theory
Source: Mullins (1996: 511).

'job characteristics theory' (JCT) upon which their JCM is based. Their construct deals with internal work motivation, whereby the presence of certain job attributes motivates workers. It postulates that the more effort expended by workers on their jobs, the more motivated they become, creating a self-perpetuating cycle of motivation. It also accounts for individual differences conceptualizing them as someone's desire to 'achieve and grow'. Hackman and Oldham refer to this as a worker's 'growth need strength' which moderates the relationship of model specified variables.

The JCM focuses upon the interactions between three classes of variables:

- psychological states of employees that must exist for internally motivated work behaviour to develop ('critical psychological states')
- characteristics of jobs that can create these psychological states ('core job dimensions'), that is, skill variety, task identity, task significance, autonomy, job feedback, agent feedback and dealing with others
- attributes of individuals that determine how positively a person will respond to a complex and challenging job irrespective of their psychological state (employee growth need strength).

An advantage of Hackman and Oldham's JCM is that it can be modified to include new variables which are deemed important in specific study areas, thus improving its accuracy. Therefore, as well as accounting for the motivating impact of work factors and individual worker differences, the JCM may also be modified to consider the motivating effect of work groups.

This is particularly important for the leisure services sector because teamworking and the formation of informal groups are common particularly in hospitality organizations (for example, see Chivers, 1971; Lee-Ross, 1996; Shamir, 1975; Wood, 1992).

In addition to grouping the above models of motivation into categories of content and process, they may also be classified as 'distal and proximal'. Proximal and distal allude to how near models of motivation are conceptually to 'action'. The former tend to consider an individual's goals first rather than the factors which may have formed them.

These theories focus on the processes and variables that affect the goal behaviour/performance relation. They are termed proximal because their immediate outcome typically exerts a direct influence on behaviour.

Proximal models of motivation attempt to address how cognitive representations of outcomes gain salience and control over behaviour and how choices are translated into action. The dominant research model has been Locke's (1968) goal-setting framework discussed earlier.

Distal constructs, such as achievement motivation emphasize the impact of non-cognitive individual differences upon attitudes. These are considered distal because their impact on behaviour and performance is often indirect. These processes determine an individual's intentions rather than behaviour and performance.

Key point 5.5

Process theories contend that it is essential to understand the cognitive impact of motivation in addition to knowing why people have different (content) needs at different times.

Reflective practice

1 Which theories of motivation discussed in this chapter would you categorize as proximal or distal respectively?

So how do these theories actually work in practice and which are the most reliable and popular? There are no simple answers to these questions because what works for some may not be effective for others. Furthermore, in leisure service organizations work in progress, working conditions and the perishability of the product may prohibit the effective use of certain techniques and applications. For example, managers may want to begin proceedings by trying to engender a sense of collectivity, openness and honesty among workers.

Theoretically, techniques such as 'open door' policies, debriefings and after-work activities may be effective. However, shift-working, territorialism and the formation of groups and informal hierarchies (Chivers, 1971) within leisure sector organizations are practicalities which may prevent such policies from being effective.

Reflective practice

1 How would you motivate the following categories of employee:
   (a) contingent or temporary
   (b) diverse including women, singles, international, disabled, senior citizens and others low skilled
   (c) those involved in repetitive tasks
   (d) professional.

There is no magic formula when it comes to motivating workers. The key to success lies with managers having a comprehensive knowledge of theoretical constructs, an ability to customize them in accordance with the different and dynamic needs of workers, and an understanding of how practical constraints will impact on good intentions.

Conclusion

In order to understand the way people behave in the workplace there are several fundamentals which managers need to consider. These variables may be arranged chronologically so the outcome of one is explained by its antecedent (that which comes before). Grasping this concept is important because it prevents managers making rash and ill-informed decisions based on symptoms rather than real causes.

People tend to hold a variety of attitudes across a wide range of issues and are classified as types, for example, instrumental, terminal, personal and so on. Employees bring strong personal attitudes to their workplace, formed from a number of influences including experience, learning and upbringing. These attitudes are difficult to change and together are known as orientations to work of which four types are said to exist.

Grouping attitudes in this way is useful but it is vital that service managers also understand how they are formed and whether they can be changed. Evidence suggests that attitudes are formed by the combined effect of values (what is desirable) and beliefs (reality as it is understood). This knowledge is vital, especially in the prevailing context because of increasing global dynamics, competition and resultant structural changes to organizations. In the event of organizational change, managers must be able to impose these programmes effectively; often this requires an attitudinal change on the part of employees.

A useful way to begin any change programme is first to obtain an idea of common and currently held worker attitudes. A popular approach is through distribution of questionnaires such as the service predisposition instrument, job diagnostic survey and others. These instruments are designed to collect data about key job aspects and usually include questions about overall employee satisfaction, commitment and involvement. The design of these instruments is often based on a three-component view whereby the cognitive, conative and affective components of each work-based attitude are targeted.

The link between work attitudes and behaviour is complex and, sometimes, people reflect upon and use behaviour to justify an attitude (cognitive dissonance and self-perception). However, employees usually reason before they decide to engage in a particular act. This process is conceptualized as the theory of reasoned actions and posits that we undertake behaviour types due to the interaction of two key phenomena. These are whether individuals are in favour of behaving in a certain way and whether the individual believes 'important others' would approve of the behaviour. This theory has major implications and alerts managers to the key influence work-based groups can have upon the behaviour of individuals.

There are a number of motivational theories and each has something valuable to offer. Some theories seek to explain motivation by identifying what should be present in the workplace to satisfy the needs of individuals. The other but equally important perspective draws attention to the cognitive processes employees engage in before being 'moved' to act or behave in a certain way.

The former constructs are known as content theories and the others as process. Another useful way of conceptualizing theories of motivations is to view them as being either proximal or distal, which essentially refers to them being conceptually near (or not) to 'action'. Whether one uses theoretical labels for these theories is relatively unimportant. The main issue is to understand what each construct says and then apply the tenets appropriately into a work situation.

Individuals in organizations have the potential to hold unique values, beliefs, attitudes and behaviours. They are likely, therefore, to be motivated by different things. The hospitality, leisure and tourism industry relies on the efforts of a disparate workforce. Thus, a clear understanding of the attitudes, behaviour and motivation of employees is key if service managers want to engender strategies for increased collective employee wellbeing, productivity and organizational success.

Reflective practice

1 Define values, beliefs and attitudes.
2 List the three elements of which attitudes are combined.
3 Discuss the relationship between attitudes and behaviour.
4 Define the terms 'distal and 'proximal' and then discuss the appropriateness of each approach to the leisure services sector.
5 List and explain four ways of motivating employees in the leisure services sector and identify the major theory(ies) underpinning each application.

Emotions in leisure service organizations

After working through this
chapter you should be able to:

- understand the emotional organization
- define emotional labour in leisure service organizations
- identify steps needed for managing emotional labour
- critically discuss the attempts to value the emotional climate.

The emotional dynamics of organizational life emerged as a subdiscipline in the study of organizations and work over the last couple of decades of the twentieth century (Fineman, 2000a). So, any study of organizational behaviour needs to consider the emotional aspects of the behaviour of organization members, but the centrality of frontline staff performance to customer satisfaction makes this crucial for the study of leisure service organization.

The provision of 'emotional labour' to meet customer needs to feel welcome and positive about the service encounter requires employees to display emotions defined by the organization. Hochshild's (1983) seminal text recognized the impact of having to provide emotional labour among flight attendants, and other studies have subsequently explored many aspects of working life in leisure service organizations (Anderson, Povis, and Chappel, 2002; Ashforth and Tomiuk, 2000; Leidner, 1993). In addition to the emotional displays of service workers, leisure service organizations use emotional stimuli in their offer to customers, through branding and the use of physical building design features.

Reflective practice

1 In an organization of which you are a member, identify your feelings about membership.
2 What were your feelings when you first joined your course, or employer?
3 What are your feelings about studying this topic?
4 Are you able to identify why you feel this way? Explain your answer.

The emotional organization

Traditional organization theory has regarded emotions as deviant (Fineman, 1993), because rationality was assumed to be dominant and the rules of organization structure and work design were not subject to emotional considerations. Work organizations had no place for emotions.

Classical management theorists such as Weber (1984) and Taylor (1947), introduced in Chapter 2, stress that organizations are rational goal-seeking bodies, efficient and rational; and the careful use of organizational resources is required of all organization members.

Bureaucracies, hierarchy, experts and 'scientific management' are rational and, by implication, managerialism is opposed to the 'logic of sentiment' (Karmel, 1980).

It is interesting how so many commentators use the language of science and rationality when discussing organizational structures, work design and work behaviour, and dismiss emotional displays as inappropriate. 'Emotion had no place in work. Be emotional at home, on the bus, whatever. But in my office, I expect cool unemotional workers' (Mann, 1999: 1).

Putnam and Munby (1993: 36) sum up a common view among practitioners and many organization theorists alike, 'Emotional reactions at work are often seen as disruptive, illogical, biased and weak'.

Sandelands and Boudens (2000) state that many of these assumptions about the rational organization have their origins in the history of Western thought as far back as Aristotle and Plato. In more recent times the theory of organizations has been justified by these notions of rational thought to the point that they assumed a scientific, and thereby unchallengeable, status. As a consequence, organization problems such as low morale, conflict, poor motivation and ineffective communication were assumed to be the result of some ailment, to be cured through the application of science and rationality. Rarely were emotions and emotional causes sought for these problems.

Understanding organizations as emotional arenas

More recently there has been a recognition that organizations represent an 'emotional arena' (Fineman, 1993). These emotional arenas provide organization members with both emotional support and challenge. 'Workaday frustrations and passions – boredom, envy, fear, love, anger, guilt, infatuation, embarrassment, nostalgia, anxiety – are deeply woven into the way roles are enacted and learned, power is exercised, trust is held, commitment formed and decisions made' (Fineman, 2000a:1).

Key point 6.1

Emotions are not a deviant and unacceptable aspect of organizational life; they are present in all aspects of the interactions that characterize an organization.

The interplay of personal emotions and the emotional displays required of people in different roles – serving customers, managing others, acting as security guard – often produce emotional conflicts that can result in frustration at work. The way these demands are made on the emotions that employees 'should' display and how these impact on the feelings of employees is a major consideration for understanding emotions in organizations. This will be discussed more fully later in the chapter because many leisure service organizations aim to create 'positive' emotional responses in customers through the emotional displays of employees.

Apart from these obvious displays required of service workers, organizations also create cultures that may impose emotional displays that are seen as appropriate or not appropriate in everyday working relationships. The relationships between colleagues, the use of the right kind of professional conduct have emotional elements. Ball and Johnson (2000: 205) refer to research where, 'Only 1 per cent of 200 executives questioned believed that quips are appropriate in internal office meetings, while 39 per cent consider them inappropriate even in informal conversations with colleagues'. They also quote the reaction of one senior director of a FTSE-100 company to their research into the use of humour in hospitality organizations. The executive was shocked at the suggestion that humour had any place in the serious world of business. He even questioned the funding of their research as 'yet another waste of public funds by out of touch academics'.

The emotional impact of organizational control is also an issue that can be revealing. The very act of managing others may well be founded on emotional needs for status and power over others. Similarly, the emotions of those who are managed also are reflected in emotions of fear or anger or admiration. The more extreme forms of autocratic leadership styles do instil a sense of fear and domination over other organization members. In other cases, charismatic leadership styles aim to produce feelings of love and admiration, while democratic approaches aim to produce feelings of pride and self-worth in those who are led. In extreme forms managers can descend into bullying and domination that produce reactions in employees that can be destructive and damaging. These will also be discussed in more depth later because some of the labour retention problems experienced by many leisure service organizations can be better understood by reflecting on the emotions involved.

The supposed rational decision-making that is typical of the idealized picture of the organizations and their managers can also be better understood with reference to the emotional dimensions within which they are associated. Fineman (2000a) identifies three sets of views on the relationship between rational thought and emotions:

- The *first* takes the traditional perspective that emotions interfere with rational thought. From this perspective emotion prevents rational decision-making. Fear, jealousy and greed, for example, prevent managers from making the most rational decisions, and the key to successful decision-making is to remove or control emotions.
- The *second* view states that emotions serve rationality. Emotions make rational thought possible because they provide intuitive support that decides priorities and aid in the decision-making process. Decisions, once made, feel right. 'What is important, worth thinking about, is cued by feelings – including the gut' (Fineman, 2000a: 11).
- The *third* view is that emotions are entwined with rationality. Neither rationality nor emotions drive decision-making. Rational thought cannot take place without some emotional input. The processes involved in thinking, planning and prioritizing involve these thinking/feeling elements.

The act of learning, both for individuals and as organizations, has an emotional dimension. Givens (2002) identified that the emotional learning system is one of five learning systems that support learning. The emotional learning system in particular 'sets the stage' for how individuals act with others, and how they learn and reflect on experiences. Negative emotions interfere with learning while positive emotions can boost knowledge and skill acquisition. Givens goes on to state that the emotional learning system has to be in balance with the other learning systems – social, cognitive, physical and reflective. People who rely exclusively on emotional learning system are 'self absorbed, egocentric and fail to see the other person's point of view' (ibid.: 130). People who do not engage their emotional learning system lack passion and motivation to learn or work.

These same concepts can be said to be at work in leisure service organizations, because organizations operating in dynamic and fast-moving markets need to learn from the experiences and knowledge of frontline staff. Positive feelings of pride and personal worth will assist in that learning process; negative feelings of anger and fear will inhibit that learning.

Key point 6.2

Organizations are an emotional arena and the study of leisure service organization needs to consider the nature of emotions in every aspect of organizational life.

Emotional intelligence

Emotions increasingly have been seen to play an important part in organizational life with an economic value. Indeed, future work organizations are predicted to account for their emotional capital in the same way they currently account for their physical assets (Thomson, 1998). Emotional capital is defined as having two core elements:

- *External emotional capital* describes the way that important external stakeholders such as customers, suppliers, communities and investors feel about an organization. This traditionally has been accounted for as being 'brand value' and goodwill. The value of brands is seen as important because they result in customer loyalty, and recommendations and referrals to potential customers.
- *Internal emotional capital*, according to Thomson (ibid.), is held by 'internal customers' and relates to the way people operate within the organization – 'the feelings, beliefs and values held by everyone in the business. It results in behaviours that result in actions which generate products and services'.

Service quality and enthusiasm to delight the customer, employee commitment and empowerment are central issues when considering the emotional capital within service organizations. For Thomson, emotional capital provides the 'heart' that is the essential working of the 'mind' that creates the intellectual capital now becoming recognized as an accountable asset of the organization.

Many organizations in the financial services and management consultancy arena already recognize that their assets are primarily knowledge assets, or that competitive advantage is gained by having access to, and managing, knowledge. In this sense some organizations describe themselves as a 'giant brain', but 'giant brain will only function if it is driven by a giant heart' (Thomson, 1998: 12). The broad thrust of Thomson's approach builds on the general view of organizations that recognize that people are the 'key asset' because they are aiming to build competitive advantage though quality, or uniqueness (Johnston, 1989), or that are working towards being a 'learning organization' (Senge, 1990).

Emotional intelligence has been described as key to organizational success, with particular relevance in organizations like leisure service, where employee (internal customer) relations impact so directly on external customer experiences. Goleman (1998: 13) puts emotional intelligence at the leading edge of business success: 'The business case is compelling: companies that leverage this advantage [emotional intelligence] add measurably to their bottom line.'

The notion of an 'emotional intelligence quotient' is being widely promoted by many consultants and is said to underpin the most effective business performance and successful lives (Cooper and Sawaf, 1997). Those who are emotionally intelligent are said to have abilities in five domains. They:

- know their own emotions
- manage their emotions
- motivate themselves
- recognize emotions in others
- handle relationships.

Fineman (2000b) criticizes many of these claims for being oversimplistic, feeding a managerial desire for quick business fixes. The same desires are witnessed in other initiatives such as empowerment (Lashley, 2001). This current interest in emotional intelligence could be described as another 'flash in the panaceas' (Lashley, 2001: 258) whereby managers, investors, consultants and business academics are looking for the latest quick fix to solve long-term and complex problems.

Reflective practice

1 Critically discuss the importance of understanding organizations as emotional arenas.
2 Critically discuss the suggestion that there is no place for emotion in rational decision-making.
3 Describe emotional intelligence.
4 Explain the meaning of the term 'a flash in the panaceas' when used to describe management fads and fashions.
5 Analyse Case study 6.1 from an emotional perspective.

Case study 6.1

In January 2002, the *Caterer and Hotelkeeper* reported on customer perceptions of service quality in London hotels. In most cases they reported that in the last quarter of 2001 customers reported that service quality had dropped. The same report also claimed that employee satisfaction scores had also dropped during the same period. With few exceptions most hotels in the survey reported that they had made redundancies after events in New York on 11 September 2001.

Emotion and customers

Emotional dimensions inform customer relations in leisure service organizations. Successful service encounters are said to involve the creation of positive customer responses. In many cases service organizations now link the emotional wellbeing of 'internal customers' with those of external customers:

- Ball and Johnson's (2000) work exploring the use of humour in hospitality retailing organizations reveals much about the use of 'fun' as a specific offer to external customers and as a way of coping with stress among employees. It's a Scream, a Bass brand, deliberately uses humour because it sees its target market as 'students and like-minded people seeking fun'.

- Similarly, TGI Fridays is an organization that sells a party atmosphere in which fun and party celebration are important ingredients in the offer to customers (Lashley, 2000a).
- The F. W. Marriott oft-quoted phrase 'linking happy customers to happy workers' is another example of attempts to link the emotions of internal and external customers. External customers are encouraged to feel welcome and cared for by the happy workers who are pleased to serve them.
- Ball and Johnson quote several examples from other companies where the emotion of fun is being used as a device for influencing employee behaviour. The HR Director of Radisson SAS told the authors: 'Where managers and employees enjoy a working atmosphere of serious FUN, stress levels are decreased as well as employee turnover. Employees enjoy less formal relationships with guests which leads to the personal touch being emphasized and encourages empowered attitudes when dealing with difficult situations' (Ball and Johnson, 2000: 210).
- A senior executive at Gardner Merchants also felt that humour is important as a stress release, as a way of build a team spirit and as away of building a shared vision of service standards.
- Emotion at work involves consideration of the impact of group membership on individuals. Working life typically involves individuals in a number of formal groups, as a consequence of the organization of jobs, and informal groups that arise out of the social dynamic, perhaps bringing people together from several different formal groups.
- In addition, people at work belong to groups whereby they have a face-to-face relationship with all the members. They are also members of secondary groups that are larger, like the organization itself, and one individual is unlikely to know all the other members personally. Organizations try to tap emotional responses through both types of group. They understand that group membership helps to shape individual behaviour. One of the consequences of working in teams is that group membership helps to influence individual behaviour as individuals tend to conform to group norms. The Harvester Restaurants model used autonomous work groups and teamworking to create an emotionally supportive environment in their restaurants.
- Leisure service organizations are increasingly using design to create emotional responses in customers. The work of Wasserman, Rafaeli and Kluger (2000) suggests that the design of restaurants and bars have different emotional responses on customers. Furthermore, they suggest that design and its impact on employees and customers is increasingly seen as a subject of research. Their findings suggest that customers do respond differently according to the design features of restaurants and bars. Lovell (2001) suggested that hotel entrances generate emotional responses and these can be both positive and negative.

Key point 6.3

Leisure service organizations apply a number of different approaches to develop positive emotions and feelings about the organization with both internal and external customers.

Emotional labour

Branded leisure service organizations are selling some form of standardized service to their customers. They all rely on the emotional displays of frontline employees to match the expectations of their customers. Many of them require what Mann (1999: 20) describes as the 'Have a Nice Day culture'.

Although some see this approach to service interactions sweeping the world through the McDonaldization of society (Ritzer, 1993), different occupations require different emotional displays – doctors, accountants and solicitors need emotional displays that are seen as serious minded though caring. In other cases, workers have to deliver 'Have a Rotten Day' emotions. Hochschild's (1983) seminal work provided case studies using debt collectors. Mann also suggests that police are another example. We could also include security guards and 'bouncers' outside pubs and clubs as requiring emotional displays that are different, though nonetheless important, aspects of their labour.

- The 'have a nice day' approach is one shared by large numbers of people working in leisure services. In some cases, these are scripted and the employee is required to run through a pre-written dialogue to ensure that the message given to customers is consistent and that individual performance conforms to an agreed standard.
- In many service establishments, those answering the telephone will use a set-piece dialogue. In some cases, it is printed on a notice by the telephone. In other cases, the scripted is learnt off by heart and then used during the service of each customer to ensure that the appropriate level of welcome or 'upselling' is taking place.
- In other cases, such as TGI Fridays, the emotional display has to be fun and party-like, but it cannot be scripted in the same way. Similarly, the emotional display at Harvester Restaurants or in Marriott Hotels require emotional displays that do not lend themselves so readily to scripting but still do require emotional displays that engage customers, making them feel wanted and welcome.

Many service organizations suggest a strong service culture in which staff performance is seen as a key feature of the offer to customers: 'A strong service culture means that staff are happy and pleased to help, enjoy their work, like the company and will always deal pleasantly with customers' (Mann, 1999: 22). Conversely, organizations are unlikely to be tolerant of displays of the wrong emotions. Displays of temper or aggression, frustration and anger, or whatever else is deemed to be inappropriate, are not tolerated.

Key point 6.4

Employees are frequently in a position of having to display one set of emotions when they actually feel some other emotion, say when dealing with an unreasonable customer.

The rules of the display may vary between organizations depending on how the expectations of managers and customers define the appropriate behaviour for that service occupation. In most cases, smiling is an important aspect of the 'have a nice day' performance. Certainly in most UK and US organizations the smile is a key element of the 'HAND' culture, as Mann calls it.

While the service organizations are pushing frontline employees to be friendly and smile, there is potentially a difficulty both for the service deliverer and the customer. Does the stewardess really like me, or is it that she is very good at the display of appearing to like me? Do we resent the false friendliness of many of these service interactions?

That said, Mann (1999: 28) quotes research in which 84 per cent of UK customers wanted 'Have a Nice Day-ness', even when this was acknowledged to be false. 'A substantial number of people . . . want the forced *bonhomie*, the fake smiles, the phoney grins that typify the HAND culture' (ibid.: 29). Of the people surveyed in the UK, Mann reports 57 per cent, 'reported being happy if the smiles and warmth from service personnel are faked' (ibid.). One interviewee summed up this customer perspective: 'I'd rather have someone say "Have a Nice Day", and not mean it, than someone say "Fuck off" and mean it.'

Employees have to exercise 'emotional management' in their interactions with customers, managers and other staff. Service employees particularly, are required to display emotions that are appropriate to the job – in the HAND culture, smiling and patience with customers even when they are unpleasant and insulting.

In varying ways we use lips and eyes, body language, facial expressions and tone of voice to create the display we want or think is right for the situation. In service work, staff are often trained to deal with conflict by 'neutralizing' the strong emotions of others.

When dealing with angry and aggressive people the natural response is to become angry oneself, but neutralizing involves adopting a quiet and calm manner. In other cases, emotions are expressed and released 'back of house' where these displays would not be allowed 'front of house'. Many leisure service organization employees will display the 'right emotions' in front of the customer but then release their anger in the kitchen or non-public areas.

At heart emotion management requires acting. Service workers have certain roles to act and even within these jobs there are variations.

The way that each organization defines service and the appropriate service performance alters the details of the 'act', but many ways require the same techniques so as to '*hide what they feel and fake what they don't*' (Mann, 1999).

Even people who are naturally cheerful will have times when they do not feel cheerful, welcoming, hospitable, pleasant or friendly, but they will be expected to manage the emotional performance required by their employer.

Looking to the techniques used by professional actors shows that there are two main approaches. The first, the technical school, involves the actor adjusting his or her physical appearance to display the emotion(s) required. So this *surface approach* to displaying the emotions does not need the service worker to actually feel the emotion, they just create the impression they do. While this is less demanding of the individual, it is difficult continuously to display these appearances over a prolonged period or when the person is tired or when the person's feelings actually felt are opposite to the ones intended.

The second approach requires the actor to produce the feeling required by calling on a past experience or imaging how it would feel to have these experiences. Service workers often use this *deep approach* when dealing with a client. They imagine how it would feel if they were in the customer's place. So there is an attempt to get the service worker to empathize with the customer. 'Treating the customer as a guest in your own home' is an example of this technique being encouraged.

The more professional leisure service organizations adopt recruitment practices that involve appointing the 'right sort of person', and in some cases can involve role-plays and psychometric tests as a way of evaluating the individual's 'service predisposition' (Lee-Ross, 2001). Most organizations in the HAND culture have training programmes that include customer care programmes which focus on the behaviours that the organization wishes to promote in frontline staff.

Though this may vary in detail a substantial element of the content, whether expressed or not, is about managing the emotional display defined by the brand. This is further managed by the organization through staff appraisal, further training and development, and reward systems that reinforce the performance required. Employees are further encouraged by being able to select their shifts and areas of the restaurant in which they work.

The problem that most employees face is that emotional management requires emotional labour as each person works on making the appropriate emotional display required in their work. Mann (1999: 69) reminds us that emotional labour has three components: 'It involves the faking of emotion that is not felt, and/or hiding of emotions that is felt. This emotion management is performed in order to meet social expectations – usually as part of the job role.'

Emotional labour, therefore, requires the faking of emotions or the hiding of emotions felt typically in work situations. Mann (1999) defines three potential situations regarding the match between emotions felt and emotional display, particularly in work roles:

- *Emotional harmony* is said to exist in situations where the individual actually feels the emotion required of the display rules and social expectations. In this case, no emotional labour is taking place because the individual is not having to hide or fake emotions.
- *Emotional dissonance* takes place when the emotions displayed for the purposes of the job role are not the emotions felt.
- *Emotional deviance* occurs when the person displays the emotions felt, but these are not ones that are expected to be displayed.

Again this does not require emotional labour because individuals are not having to display emotions that they do not feel, though they may find that they are in a disciplinary dispute with the employer because they are displaying the wrong emotions. Table 6.1 provides a simple overview of these three different situations at work.

Emotional harmony involves the least stress because the emotions felt match those displayed and these are consistent with the displays required in the role. In the HAND culture of many retail organizations, the service worker who feels happy and helpful, and displays these emotions, is not providing emotional labour because they are not having to display emotions they do not feel.

Similarly, the individual who displays emotions that they feel but which are inconsistent with displays required of the role are not providing emotional labour because they are displaying what they feel, even though this is in conflict with the expectations of the role. The emotional display does not cause stress, though there may be some problems created through the performance being at odds with the display rules.

	Emotional harmony	Emotional dissonance	Emotional deviance
	Displayed emotion is the same as felt emotion and expected emotion	Displayed emotion is the same as the expected emotion but different from the felt emotion	Displayed emotion is the same as felt emotion but different from expected emotion
Emotion actually displayed	Happy	Happy	Unhappy
Emotion really felt	Happy	Unhappy	Unhappy
Emotion expected by company or society (display rule)	Happy	Happy	Happy

Source: Mann (1999).

Table 6.1 Emotional harmony, dissonance and deviance at work

Emotional labour is supplied, as we have seen, when emotional dissonance occurs; that is, a person acting within the confines of the expected displayed emotions provides a display of emotions that are not felt. Here, stress stemming from this emotional dissonance can lead to 'Have a Nice Day Syndrome' (Mann, 1999: 84); that is, the psychological effects of providing emotional labour. Mann suggests that the effects of working in a situation where emotional dissonance is an almost permanent feature of the work experience are likely to produce stress-related behaviour.

Emotional labourers are likely to be less satisfied with their jobs, more likely to leave or be absent from work, suffer minor illnesses, complain of being 'burnt-out', and 'have an increased susceptibility to serious conditions like coronary heart disease'(Mann, 1999: 85). At root, dissonance causes mental strain that cannot easily be reduced. Though, it is hoped that changing the way people are managed might result in reduced dissonance. In other words, happy employees are happy to make happy customers in the Marriott mode.

Coping with the stress of emotional labour is a skill that varies between individuals, though some approaches can be developed and managers can be trained to assist employees cope better. Anderson, Povis and Chappel (2002) suggest that the employee's ability to cope with the stress of emotional dissonance and resist the effects of burnout will be a by-product of *coping strategies* and/or *coping resources*. Figure 6.1 provides a view of how the manager might influence individual employees' ability to cope with emotional labour and the emotional stress it can cause.

- *Coping strategies* relate to the way the individual processes the experience. These can be *emotion focused* that involve avoidance, minimization of distancing and creating positive value out of a negative experience. Taking your mind off the problem,

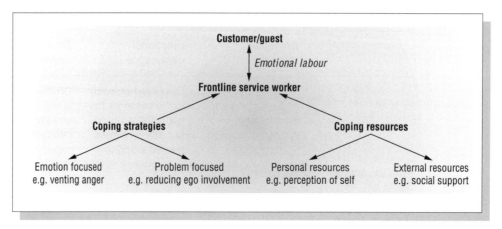

Figure 6.1 Conceptual framework for understanding emotional labour coping strategies
Source: Anderson, Povis and Chappel (2002).

venting anger elsewhere, having a drink to relax, and seeking emotional support from others are examples of coping strategies. Coping strategies may also be problem focused through reducing their own emotional involvement or learning new skills or procedures.

• *Coping resources* refers to the resources on which an individual can draw so as to cope with the emotional stress caused by emotional dissonance. *Personal resources* provide individuals with varying abilities to cope with emotional stress. Education and training, emotional stability, and social skills are likely to impact on the personal resources that an individual has at her/his disposal. In additional *external coping resources* may help the individual cope. Social support through colleagues, or management, are important resources in work contexts. Teamworking can be particularly helpful in providing social support to cope with emotional stress. Management trained to understand emotional labour and the problems faced by employees can be another resource that helps employees to cope.

Reflective practice

1 Read the statements from leisure service workers provided in Case study 6.2 and identify the coping strategies being used in each case.
2 Think of a situation where you have had to cope with emotional stress at work or school or in the family, and describe how you coped. Which strategy do you use?

Case study 6.2

Case 1

'At the end of the day, I'm wrung out, I don't want to see anybody because you've been really nice, it isn't out of character for me to be nice, so I'm not playing a role.

You're thinking about them all the time, you're concentrating on the road, because you don't want to have an accident, and you're trying to point out points of interest to them and chatting with them and making them comfortable . . . till at the end of the day, conversation drops, tiredness kicks in and at the end of the day . . . I don't want to see anybody . . . [at the] end of the day's work, I can't go straight home, I can't go straight home and then the wife says 'OK look, Ben needs new shoes, Ben needs new socks', Uhhhh!, see me later, I mean, because I've spent all day being nice, catering to other people to what they wish, and it's just you know, I've got to switch off, back to normal.' (Ron, limousine driver)

Case 2

'Sometimes, I'll have the worst day at work, but I, I hold it all in, and I'll get home and I'll take it out on my partner . . . Why did I do that? I'm like why, why? Maybe I should have just sat somewhere for ten minutes in the car before I got home and just sort of relaxed, just you know, not talked to anyone, just sat there quietly and sort of let it all just go.' (Rosie, bus tour company)

Case 3

'If I get a bit stressed, I, I don't know what I do, I guess, I just step back and I just go out, I will make myself a cup of coffee or something and then that's you know, a two-minute break or whatever, and then, you know, the stress will be over.' (Beth, bus tour company)

Case 4

'Sometimes some of them [finish at 10 p.m.] . . . then they go off for a couple of hours and come back . . . but they might come back at 11.30 or 12 and if we're here having a drink, they might stop and have a drink . . . It's very good, I think its very good stress management to do it, because it gives those . . . that have had a problem, a chance to tell you. [It] also gives the staff who've had a really good night a chance to tell you how good things went and why they think they went well.' (John, restaurant manager)

Case 5

'If someone comes in and they're particularly difficult, I think just going back to the other staff and we sort of talk about it . . . and just like having that sort of interaction with the other staff, you think, "oh, yea, I might try that way next time".' (Ailsa, tourist information)

Case 6

'I start from the position, in my head, they're not angry with you, 'cause they don't know you . . . I'm just there, I'm just available . . . I also have a really clear plan of action, I'm not really foul-mouthed, but once I've dealt with it, I'd go out the back and when there's no one around I say something absolutely putrid, to help . . . I've got no way of knowing how they've got to this point on that day, so, but, the least likely thing is that I've caused it, and the least likely, the least important person in their life is me, so, you know, let's not over-rate my role in this . . . it's really, really easy to put yourself at the centre of things, but in reality, you know, if they weren't born to you and they're not married to you, you're not really all that important to them, are you?' (Sheena, tourist information)

Source: Anderson, Povis and Chappel (2002).

Where employees feel emotional stress caused by having to provide emotional labour, illness can arise, as suggested by Mann above. However, in other instances it can lead to organizational conflict or separation. Many leisure service organizations experience high levels of staff turnover. Emotional labour can be a cause of people leaving because people withdraw from difficult and stressful situations.

Where conflict arises, employees in leisure service organizations may resort to collective action through a trade union to resolve their problems – strikes, go slows and other actions can be seen as a consequence of emotional labour. New York hotel workers have organized 'smile strikes' whereby employees refuse to supply the emotional labour required.

However, employees in leisure service organizations frequently, are not organized collectively by a trade union, and in these circumstance conflicts are resolved on an individual basis. Individuals just leave, or they commit acts of deliberate sabotage.

Key point 6.5

Emotional labour results from emotional dissonance and can cause stress and conflict if not understood and supported by appropriate management actions.

Reflective practice

1 Identify the most likely causes of emotional labour and stress in leisure service organizations.
2 Critically discuss the steps that can be taken by organizations to overcome emotional stress caused by emotional labour.
3 Critically discuss the responses of employees to situations where they experience emotional stress.

Emotions and employment practice

Emotions and injustice at work

Harlos and Pinder (2000) identify a number of emotional responses that arise from feelings of injustice in work organizations. Emotions can cause or result from perceived injustice in the workplace. The traditional conflict between kitchen and restaurant can be the result of a sense of injustice and can cause a sense of injustice. The head chef's outburst to a member of the restaurant workforce may therefore reflect a sense of injustice when the restaurant worker is reporting a customer complaint, and then might also cause a sense of injustice in the other person. In turn, this might lead to feelings of anger or fear on behalf of the restaurant worker.

In other cases injustice might be felt when individuals are not given the credit they feel they deserve, or do not achieve the promotion they think they deserve. Alternatively, praise or being selected to be 'employee of the month' can result in feelings of joy in the recipient, but feelings of anger and injustice in others.

Case study 6.3

TGI Fridays, the restaurant and bar chain, employs about forty people in each unit. They use an incentive programme that rewards the ten top-performing restaurant staff by allowing them to have first choice of table stations and shifts worked.

The selection process is based on sales generated and is made by managers every three months. The top ten choose to work the busiest shifts and select the table stations that are the most popular. This enables them to maximize their income from the commission-based reward packages. Many of the top ten earn more than double the average wage for restaurant workers. Needless to say, interviews (Lashley, 2000a) with the top ten reflect emotion of pride and satisfaction with this arrangement. There is a high level of staff retention among this group. Interviews with other employees who are not members of the top ten reveal frustration and anger, based on a widely held sense of injustice. They often report difficulty in breaking into the top ten group. There is a high level of staff turnover among this group.

Harlos and Pinder (2000) give four patterns of injustice experienced by organization members:

- *Interactive injustice* occurs as a result of workplace relationships between employees and authority figures in the organization.
- *Systemic injustice* is linked to perceptions of injustice that involve the larger organization and stems from a perception of widespread mistreatment by authority figures throughout the organization.
- *Distributive injustice* stems from a perception that organizational rewards and benefits are distributed unfairly, say in the handling of pay and other cash rewards.
- *Procedural injustice* express concerns that the manner in which decisions are made is unfair and create a sense of injustice.

Harlos and Pinder's interviews with individuals in a wide range of work contexts suggest that the most significant experiences of injustice occur as a consequence of interactions or of the systemic relationships.

Interactive injustice involves relationships between organizational members who are in uneven power relationships; for example, the use of the power of a supervisor or manager to bully and browbeat subordinates. It can take a number of forms – shouting, slapping a person's buttocks, telephoning at unreasonable times of night, continually criticizing and rarely praising employees. Harlos and Pinder (2000: 258) state that interviewees reported, 'These events often occurred over several months and were reported by participants as significant sources of fear, depression and stress.'

Table 6.2 reproduces the dimensions of interactional injustice as identified by Harlos and Pinder. The eight dimensions relate to the relationship between subordinates and their boss. They include intimidation, abandonment, inconsistency, degradation, criticism, inaccessibility, surveillance and manipulation. The study found that intimidation and degradation were the most frequently reported source of injustice.

Definition	Perceived interpersonal mistreatment by a hierarchical superior or authority figure
Intimidation	Use of physical, verbal and/or emotional means to instil fear and induce control in employees *Key acts*: threatens (directly or indirectly) employees with dismissal, or discipline and/or violence, yells at staff, throws property
Degradation	Communicating (directly or indirectly) in disrespectful and hurtful manner. *Key acts*: publicly shames or humiliates employees; displays impatience and/or judgement about enquiries; personally and professionally attacks employees; gossips about or disparages other employees.
Other dimensions	
Criticism	Frequently finding fault with employees' performance, ideas and personal qualities, and neglecting positive performance
Abandonment	Neither enquiring about nor responding to employees' physical, social or emotional work needs
Inconsistency	Arbitrarily changing direction, focus or standards for individual performance, poorly communicating changes to employees
Inaccessibility	Restricting physical and/or emotional availability, discouraging contact with employees
Surveillance	Close monitoring and directing employees, providing them with minimal autonomy and authority
Manipulation	Managing employees' skills, values, hopes and emotions for personal and work-related outcomes

Source: Harlos and Pinder (2000: 259).

Table 6.2   Dimensions of interactional injustice

Harlos and Pinder's findings demonstrate that employees' perceptions of injustice are a result of manager/supervisors' displays of anger and a widespread lack of emotion through the organization. Employees felt emotions were a reflection of these perceptions of injustice. The long-term experiences of injustice can be both displayed or felt and not displayed. In some cases, the lack of displayed emotions in the workplace resulted in personal problems and domestic relationship difficulties.

Overall the two most dominant emotions resulting from perceptions of injustice were anger and fear. Bosses' behaviour both displayed anger and caused anger in employees who considered their treatment to be unfair. The study also suggested that both male and female bosses were equally capable of causing these perceptions of injustice, though males were more likely to use *intimidation*, while females used *manipulation*, *criticism* or *abandonment*.

Fear was also a major emotional response to feelings of injustice. This, in turn, could lead to emotional stress and 'burnout'. While the perception of injustice can lead to high levels of staff turnover as people engage in 'flight' from difficult situations, surprising numbers seemed to stay and put up with their ill treatment. Harlos and Pinder suggest that traumatic bonding might take place: 'Traumatic bonding is a social psychological explanation for the paradoxical dynamics in abusive relationships when women and children not only stay, risking further abuse, but strong bonds between abuser and victim, similar to between captor and hostage' (ibid.: 273)

Key point 6.6

Employee perceptions of injustice can add considerably to negative emotions felt by employees. In turn, these impact on service worker performance and workforce stability.

Empowerment and emotions

Service organizations increasingly require frontline service personnel to manage their emotions so as to be appropriate to the given situation and to be consistent with the offer being made to be customers (Leidner, 1993). 'Through recruitment, selection, socialization and performance evaluation, organizations develop a social reality in which feelings become a commodity for achieving instrumental goals' (Putnam and Munby, 1993: 37).

The use of employee empowerment might also be added to this list. Empowerment takes a variety of forms. It is hoped that initiatives which involve employees, enabling them to participate in decisions and generate high levels of commitment, will result in an increased sense of ownership of the service encounter and generate the expected emotional display more easily. Through empowerment, employees are expected to be able to genuinely feel the warmth to customers required by the organization. Empowerment is discussed more fully in Chapter 9, but employment practice that uses empowerment could have an impact on emotional labour:

- Emotional labour can be stressful and produce negative behaviour in employees. However, by definition, emotional labour exists in an environment of emotional dissonance; that is, having to display one set of emotions while feeling something else.
- If an employee experiences emotional harmony, he or she will feel and display the emotions expected by the company and social definitions of their role. It is here that empowerment has the potential to 'square the circle'.

- By managing people in a way that develops their sense of self-efficacy, convinces them that their tasks are meaningful and that they are able to effect outcomes through the exercise of choice, employees are more likely to feel the emotions that have to be displayed. Hence, emotional labour is no longer needed because the service worker is in emotional harmony.
- Case study evidence suggest that empowerment is easy to discuss and hard to achieve. Being emotionally engaged in an empowered way requires careful and sympathetic planning by management. It is unlikely to come from a few superficial name changes that are driven by the need for a quick fix.

Key point 6.7

Some employment practices, such as the empowerment of organization members, can create positive emotions that may reduce emotional dissonance, but only if they are introduced in a planned and consistent manner.

Reflective practice

1 Apart from the emotional impacts of organizational life and emotional labour, employment practices within leisure service organizations can have both positive and negative effects. Highlight some of the employment practices that are likely to have positive and negative emotional effects on organization members.
2 Many leisure service organizations have problems retaining employees. Suggest some causes of staff turnover from an 'emotional' perspective. Highlight the actions that might lead to higher levels of staff retention.

Conclusion

This chapter has provided a brief introduction to some of the issues relevant to the analysis of organizations from an emotional perspective. We have argued that far from being a deviant and illegitimate aspect of life in leisure service organizations, emotions form a permanent feature of everyday human interactions. Organizations are, therefore, emotional arenas and need to be perceived as such. The nature of work organizations is such that work cultures will impose standards and expectations of appropriate emotional displays. These are further compounded in many leisure service organizations where employees are supposed to provide emotional displays that will encourage positive emotional responses in customers. In addition, the emotional underpinning of both managers and the managed need to be understood, as a way of explaining organization behaviour and the supposed rationality of organizational decision-making.

Leisure service organizations increasingly are attempting to create positive responses in customers, because customers who feel welcome and wanted on a personal level are likely to return to the organization and become loyal customers. Employee performance assists indirectly in creating these positive emotional responses in customers and they are being regarded as 'internal customers'. In other cases, the specific offer to customers adopts a 'fun' or 'party' atmosphere through the general image created and the building design features. In addition, there has been a growth of interest in the 'emotional intelligence' and cultures as well as employment approaches that foster 'emotional capital'.

Work life in many leisure service organizations involves 'emotional labour' arising from the prescriptive nature of the emotional displays deemed appropriate. The 'have a nice day' culture can produce emotional dissonance where the employee is required to display one emotion while feeling another. Where emotional dissonance does occur, employees are likely to suffer emotional stress and 'burnout' unless this is understood and managed.

Finally, we featured some employee emotional responses that arise from general management practice. Perceptions of injustice lead to negative feelings. In particular, interactional feelings of injustice arise from the way managers and supervisors interact with subordinates. The anger and fear that can result from these perceptions of injustice can have an impact on employee performance and staff retention. However, employment practice that reflects employee worth and value is likely to lead to positive emotions.

Reflective practice

1 Describe emotional organization and those features that help understand organization behaviour through the study of emotions.
2 Define emotional labour in leisure service organizations.
3 Identify steps needed for managing emotional labour.
4 Critically discuss the attempts to value the emotional climate.

CHAPTER 7

Groups, leadership and power

- understand the fundamentals of group formation and function in organizations

- evaluate teamworking in organizations

- critically discuss leadership through behavioural theories

- appreciate leadership power bases.

Work in leisure organizations involves people working with other people. The service of food and drink, travel and recreational services almost always involves some work with others or is based on a team effort. It is important, therefore, that those wishing to understand the behaviour of people in leisure service organizations understand the influence that group membership has on the way people behave. In fact, organizations, (for example, individual units, hotels, theatres and sports team grounds), departments, work sections and, even, shift groups are all forms of groups that can both influence individual behaviour and individuals who make up the group.

Reflective practice

1 Make a list of words that you might use to describe yourself to a stranger.
2 Would you describe yourself as a student, lecturer, manager or worker?
3 Think about one of the opposite group on the list and describe them in terms of their typical approach to work, values and attitudes, personality, characteristics and so on.
4 Describe the group to which you belong in similar terms.
5 Are there differences and similarities between the two lists? Why?
6 In both cases, are all members the same?

Groups in organizations

People define themselves, in part, through the groups to which they belong. Group membership is in fact a defining feature of society, so we all belong to groups in one way or another – nation, religion or none, gender, ethnicity, region or town of origin, sport team supporter. Group membership provides individuals with a sense of who they are.

Actually we belong to two types of groups. *Secondary groups* are groups like those mentioned above. We belong to them, they give individuals a sense of who they are, and just as importantly, whom they are not. These groups are a reference point that help individuals define themselves and other around them. Not all secondary group members are known to one another. However, they do influence individuals in how they act and what they consider to be right or wrong. In other words, a person may declare that they belong to a national group, say the English, without knowing all other people who make up the nation – the English. Yet membership of this group can result in all sorts of positive and negative behaviour – supporting the football team and being in conflict with supporters of other teams, saluting the flag and fighting others who salute other flags.

Human conflict often can be explained in terms of inter-group relations – war between nations, racism, ageism and sexism, for example, all involve individuals who belong to one specific group holding stereotyped views about members of other groups. Social psychologists talk about 'in-group' (groups to which individuals belong) and 'out-group' (groups to which individuals do not belong) relationships. People typically have positive perception of the group(s) to which they belong and more negative perceptions of groups to which they do not belong.

Reflective practice

1 Think about some of the secondary group types we have mentioned and consider your perceptions of people from others – gender, ethnic backgrounds, nations, sports teams.
2 How do you arrive at these perceptions?
3 Consider a recent event in the news that involves people acting in an aggressive way towards people who are not known to each other individually, but who merely belong to another group.

Key point 7.1

People refer to secondary groups to which they belong for a sense of personal identity. These groups shape self-perceptions and the perceptions of other individuals who belong to other groups.

These secondary groups are important because they aid understanding of individual behaviour, and large leisure service organizations are secondary groups. Not all employees are known to one another in a firm like McDonald's, but that does not prevent individuals feeling pride in, or loathing for, the organization. That said, the study of groups within organizations is chiefly concerned with the second type of groups.

Primary groups are groups where members have face-to-face relationships. All group members are known to one another and have these face-to-face relationships (Mullins, 2002). They typically are unlikely to exceed twelve members in total. Beyond this they cannot maintain group identity and they fragment into two groups. These are sometimes called *psychological groups* (Huczynski and Buchanan, 2001) because they exist not only in interactions between members, but also through the members' perceptions of themselves and other group members and members of other groups. Huczynski and Buchanan (2001: 277) describe psychological groups as: 'people who consider themselves to be part of an identifiable unit, who relate to each other in meaningful fashion who share dispositions through their shared sense of collective identity'.

Thompson and McHugh (1995: 268) define groups as; 'A collection or coalition of people who interact meaningfully in the pursuit of common goals or objectives, and who have a tacit sense of agreed standards, values and common identity'. They form the building blocks of work organizations. Even the smallest employing organization involves some aspect of group dynamics. Larger leisure organizations comprise sections, departments, units, regions, divisions and brands.

Group membership influences individual behaviour in a number of ways:

- *It provides a sense of identity* – individuals define themselves partly by their group affiliations (membership).
- *It develops a structure including roles such as leader* – roles vary but each plays a part in helping the group to maintain unity.

- *It establishes norms and expectations about how members behave* – norms include values, attitudes, beliefs and behaviours.
- *Individuals are pressured to conform to the norms* – group members use a range of techniques from humour, to intimidation, to the threat of expulsion to make individuals conform. This is particularly strong when the group perceives itself to be under threat.
- *It provides individuals with a sense of security* – membership helps individuals when dealing with out-group members.
- *It will defend individuals from threats outside the group* – the sense of security is well placed because groups protect 'their own'.
- *It can improve collective output through mutual support*: individuals support each other to achieve collective goals and to achieve more than the individuals alone could do.
- *It can result in conflict with other groups* – the cohesion and tendency to prefer the in-group can lead to conflicts with other groups (out-groups).
- *Members are able to act in a unified manner* – through processes of conformity pressure, the group tends to act as one.
- *It provide a means of communication and developing shared knowledge* – a highly effective means of communicating because of the face-to-face relationships.

The potential benefits of group membership in providing a self-disciplining, mutuality supporting framework for guiding individual performance are at the root of the use of work teams, and autonomous and semi-autonomous work groups. Yet the social psychology of group influences means that all the positive and negative influences on behaviour are to be found in the workplace.

Key point 7.2

Individuals form primary groups, and these influence individual behaviour and help individuals feel secure. Primary groups require face-to-face relationships between members and are limited in size.

Group influences in work organizations can be derived from the existence of both formal or informal groups to which individuals belong. *Formal groups* are set up in an organization to achieve the organization's goals. *Informal groups* come about within and alongside the formal organization. They are based on the social interactions of individuals. They influence behaviour in ways that may both support and oppose organizational goals.

Informal groups are a natural consequence of people working together. These, too, can have both positive and negative effects. Informal group membership (Mullins, 2002) can provide mechanisms for mutual support and shared purpose which lead to high morale and commitment. At the same time, informal groups can result in norms of behaviour which restrict production and have a conflictual stance with management. Informal leaders can perform an important role in challenging the formal leader in work organizations.

Groups come into being for a number of reasons, largely as a result of social dynamics and the interactions between members. Wood (1994) suggests that both formal and informal groups will be formed as a consequence of interactions between members and provides a summary list of reasons:

- *Personal attraction* – even in formal group settings when people are required to work together, the strength and cohesion of the group will be determined by the extent that individuals find other members attractive.
- *Group activities* – having opportunities to interact with and take part in group activities is essential if people are to develop the sense of affiliation with others.
- *Group goals* – sharing a set of common objectives is important to building the sense of common purpose and the norms required for the maintenance of a sense of identity and they way the group differentiates itself.
- *Security and social affiliation* – groups enable individuals to develop their belonging needs. Apart from the need to feel 'loved', the group meets security needs as individuals feel protected by the group.
- *Status and self-esteem* – groups often develop a sense of worth and status that confers greater self-esteem on members. These feelings are enhanced if membership is perceived to be exclusive or difficult.
- *Power* – groups can exert more power when dealing with non-group members than the collection of individuals would be able to achieve. Trade union membership, for example, provides an opportunity for the employee group to both protect and promote employee interests.

Case study 7.1

Beauty therapists at the Fountain Health Spa often work to support and help each other by rearranging shifts and duty rosters to meet with individuals' domestic and social commitments. When the ownership of the spa changed, a new manager was appointed and he did not like these arrangements. He was of the view that, 'Managers manage, and staff work within the systems and procedures set up.' 'Beauty therapists who want to change duty times must ask my permission first,' he declared. After two months of the new arrangements the therapists were unhappy about the change because it was too rigid and the manager was too inflexible. They got together and elected one of their number to go and speak to the manager on their behalf. They told their representative to tell the manager that they would hold a 'smile strike' if he did not return to the previous arrangement.

Key point 7.3

Informal groups are created by the social dynamic of the individuals involved and may exist alongside and within formal group structures.

Reflective practice

1 How does group membership influence behaviour in Case study 7.1?
2 What benefits do the beauty therapists gain from group membership?
3 What could the new manager have done to avoid the conflict?

Huczynski and Buchanan (1985) suggest that formal groups are formed for an organizational purpose. Within leisure service organizations the production and delivery of service to customers require people to work in a group. People often work in the same group because they are working on similar tasks or points in the service delivery – reception, the gym, the pool, the restaurant, the bar. Formal groups are therefore formed as a consequence of the organization of tasks and the organization structure. Formal groups (ibid.: 167) have a number of common features. They:

- have a formal structure
- are task orientated
- tend to be permanent
- contribute directly to the organization's purpose
- are consciously organized.

Individual employees are members of the formal group structure that the organization sets up:

- departments within the unit
- occupational and job role differences
- different unit membership
- units in different brands within the group
- units in other companies, and so on.

However, primary groups exist within the structures created. Managers try to use these group memberships arising from the formal structure to develop a sense of common purpose and shared expectations. Thus, creating a sense of 'us and them' can give the workforce a sense of common purpose to see the unit succeed in comparison to other units in the group, or against competitors. At the same time the formal structure can create a climate in which people in different departments are in conflict with each other and form as a barrier to effective operation. For example, the traditional conflicts between kitchen and restaurant are a good example of the negative effects excessive conflict can produce.

Managers often recognize the influences of informal group membership on individual behaviour and attempt to work with informal leaders. Teamworking and autonomous work group membership provide techniques that managers adopt so as to benefit from group dynamics at work. Initiatives based on group membership include:

- working with group members to reduce staff turnover
- using groups to assist in problem-solving
- encouraging a sense of common purpose and shared objectives

- recognizing and incorporating unofficial leaders from their groups
- aiming incentives at group performance
- providing opportunities for effective group working to be established.

Key point 7.4

Formal groups are established to meet an organization's objective or purpose. They have a formal structure, purpose and remit.

Working in teams

Teamworking is now a well-established technique used within organizations so as to gain from the benefits of group influences on individual behaviour. Huczynski and Buchanan (2001) quote several studies in the UK and USA showing that large numbers of organizations use teamworking with some employees. In the leisure service sector, both Harvester Restaurants and TGI Fridays in the UK involve teamworking. The major benefits are:

- improved communications between all managers and employees ensures that the organization's objectives and goals are understood and shared by all team members
- there will be improved commitment through a greater sense of ownership
- better suggestions and ideas
- more creative ideas available
- people learn from each other
- improved morale and motivation because people are included
- communication is improved by being involved in the decision.

Types of teams

Working with the management team will involve each individual team member having specific areas of responsibility. In many leisure service sector units, junior managers will have responsibility for a specific area of the operations – kitchen, bar, restaurant, accommodation, reception, gym, beauty therapy, and so on. These *functional* departments have to work towards common goals and it is up to the unit manager, as team leader, to ensure that all sections work in a co-operative way. A common problem in many operations is that these divisions based on departments can produce an 'us and them' culture with a lack of co-operation, or even conflict, between teams. Building a strong management team across the unit is an essential feature of effective management.

Setting up *multifunctional teams* is another way of developing the culture of co-operation and reducing tensions between teams. Often these are based round the identification and resolution of common problems – service quality improvement, employee satisfaction improvement, reduced wastage and improved operating procedures are examples of multifunctional teams. Some of these teams are permanent features of the unit's organization; other teams are set up to deal with specific issues.

Stages in team development

As the team is established and begins to develop, it goes through a number of phases. An experienced team leader aids the team through the various phases and recognizes the danger of inaction and cynicism which can occur if team members feel their efforts are not valued (Ellis and Dick, 2000).

1 *Searching stage*: team members in new teams often feel a thrill of enthusiasm as the team is first created. Particularly where team members are unused to being consulted, the team may experience a high level of commitment to the team and its goals. The team leader is required to recognize the benefits of this enthusiasm, but ensure that team members do not develop an overoptimistic expectation of outcomes.

   Team members are also searching for a shared definition of the objectives during this phase. An effective team leader will either provide the team with clear objectives or facilitate the team in developing the shared objectives necessary for effective performance. Most effective team leaders avoid 'telling' team members what they must do; 'asking' is much more effective. The tendency to underestimate the degree of disagreement cannot be overly stressed. The enthusiasm felt by members often leads those members to assume they all share the same objectives, but do not want to argue them out.

2 *Exploring stage*: once the team have agreed the broad objectives, they have to spend some time raising questions, making suggestions, evaluating alternatives and deciding on the appropriate course(s) of action. This stage will involve conflict as different team members suggest different courses of action. Disagreements will occur and team members may form into subgroups as team members come together round different suggested courses of action.

   Team leaders need to be aware that this is a necessary phase through which the group must travel. They help the team to establish mutual understanding and a healthy respect for the creative tension that the group needs to be most effective. Clearly, negative conflict can be harmful because it can prevent innovation and the working out of agreed paths. However, too much conformity or conflict avoidance can be equally damaging, because disagreements are never resolved. The team never formulates a consensus of action plans and priorities.

3 *Alliance stage*: the team eventually reaches a point where the members share both an understanding of the objectives and what needs to be done. Each member understands not only their role, but also the role of other group members. There is also a shared understanding of the strengths and weaknesses of all team members. The team has a uniformity of purpose; they are committed to the outcomes, but respect the diversity within the group, recognizing that different views and interests are essential for the team to work effectively.

   The team leader needs to help and enable the team to keep working towards the goals and outcomes identified. They need to encourage the team constantly to review objectives and action plans. There is a great danger of the team developing 'frozen thinking' at this stage. That is, the team, having decided on a course of action, continues to support the action, even when circumstances change and the action is no longer relevant.

   Any disruption to the dynamics of the team may cause the team to slip out of the alliance phase into the earlier stages – the loss of a member, a new team leader, new members or changes in the focus of the problem or purpose of the team. In these cases, the team will drop back to the earlier phases and work through the searching and exploring stages.

Threats to team development

Effective teams develop as the product of group bonds set up between specific individuals. In these circumstances, individual behaviour is influenced by a combination of individual and group motivations. The following are some of the key causes of team failure:

- high levels of instability due to staff turnover or movement around the organization
- limited opportunities for the team to meet and work through the stages
- limited support from more senior organization members
- restrictions placed on the team's ability to resolve the problem
- poor morale or inter-group conflict.

Roles in teams ● ● ●

Belbin's (1993) work suggests that groups made up of people with the same characteristics rarely succeed. Problem-solving work teams need to include a range of roles undertaken by the various members. Belbin claims that the most effect groups need nine types of contribution to be most effective in work team situations. He defines these team roles as a pattern of behaviour, characteristics in the way a team members relates to the rest of the team. Each role contributes to the way the team progresses towards achieving the tasks set.

Effective teams are said to require access to all these team roles. The most consistently successful creative teams had access to these nine roles. In some cases individuals could change roles or had a backup role. Belbin's *self-perception inventory* identifies an individual's primary role preference and the role they might have as 'backup'. Belbin's team role characteristics and contributions are

- *plant*: creative, imaginative, unorthodox, solves difficult problems
- *resource investigator*: extrovert, enthusiastic, communicative, explores opportunities and develops contacts
- *co-ordinator*: mature, confident, a good chairperson, clarifies goals, promotes decision-making, delegates well
- *shaper*: challenging, dynamic, thrives on pressure, has drive and courage to overcome obstacles
- *monitor-evaluator*: sober, strategic and discerning, judges accurately
- *team worker*: co-operative, mild, perceptive and diplomatic, listens, averts friction, calms waters
- *implementer*: disciplined, reliable, conservative and efficient, turns ideas into practical actions
- *completer*: painstaking, conscientious, anxious, searches out errors and omissions, delivers on time
- *specialist*: single-minded, self-sharing, dedicated, provides knowledge and skills in rare supply.

Belbin's model has been used by some leisure service organizations as a technique for building teams, particularly among problem-solving and management teams. The technique is less used when setting autonomous work groups within the workforce.

Benefits of working in teams

Clearly, the reasons why teams have been set up differ and the benefits which team working can generate will also vary, but there are some general benefits to be gained by the individuals involved, the unit management and the organization (Table 7.1).

Benefits of teams to individual members	• Increased job satisfaction • Personal development and growth • Career planning • Reduced fear of risk-taking • More involvement in decision-making • Increased recognition for their contribution
Benefits to unit management	• Decisions made by people most closely involved • Managers share the workload with others • All are focused on the same objectives • Improved commitment and support for decisions • More flexibility among team members
Benefits to the leisure service organization	• Improved quality of products and services • Creates a culture of continuous improvement • Improved trust and openness • Better communications reduces misunderstandings • Reduced duplication • Improved working relationships • Improved customer satisfaction • Increased opportunities to achieve or beat performance targets • Improved employee satisfaction • Reduced staff turnover • Improved sales and profit performance

Table 7.1 The benefits of teamworking
Source: Lashley (2000a).

Key point 7.5

Leisure service organizations attempt to gain from the benefits of group influences by the setting up of formal primary groups in the form of teams and autonomous work groups.

Different types of teams will deliver different clusters of benefits. Thus, team briefing sessions prior to the shift or occasional briefings to the staff will deliver different benefits to team structures based on autonomous work teams. In each of these examples the relationship between the team leader and team members is different. The amount of discretion allowed to the team is different and the extent to which they can make decisions is also different. In some cases team members merely receive information, while in others they are actively managing their own work and tasks. Clearly, the impact that these different arrangements have on team members is also influenced by the nature of the team members.

Reflective practice

1 Read the Case studies 7.2 and 7.3 and identify which is consultative and which participative.
2 What benefits flow from each?
3 Which would you prefer to work in and why?
4 What are the key benefits of each to the organization?

Case study 7.2

All staff at Harvester Restaurants are organized in three autonomous teams – bars, restaurants and kitchens. They have no immediate supervisor, section head or manager. They make decisions that in many more traditional organizations would be made by managers. Each team has team responsibilities and is left to get on with achieving its tasks without immediate management guidance. The teams deal with customer complaints, order stock, receive goods inwards, cash-up tills, hold the keys to the stock cupboard and organize repairs to broken equipment when needed. The company claims that these arrangements have resulted in improved service quality, fewer customer complaints, lower staff turnover, improved satisfaction, reduced stock levels and improved profits.

Case study 7.3

Team briefings are held before each of the two main shift periods – morning and evening. Front-of-house staff and back-of-house staff meet as two separate teams. The team meetings are organized by a senior team member, though managers have a major influence on the issues to be raised. The meetings enable team members to be briefed on objectives, priorities and targets for the day. They can raise issues of concern or problems that they have encountered. Team members can make suggestions and provide managers with insights into customer comments and reactions to products. Managers make all decisions and there is a manager for both of the key areas – front and back of house. During service the managers make all decisions – deal with customer complaints, check stock in, order equipment repairs, and so on.

Leadership

Groups of all kinds typically develop a leadership structure. In leisure service organizations the formal group structure involves appointed managers who traditionally manage the group through planning and control. In recent years organizations have evolved more flexible styles of working, and new structures such as empowerment discussed in Chapter 9. In these cases organizations are looking for the qualities of leadership – inspiring, influencing and empowering rather than enforcing required behaviour. Ellis and Dick (2000: 103) provide a useful table comparing the skills and behaviour of managers and leaders (see Table 7.2).

Management skills and behaviour	Leadership skills and behaviour
Planning	Inspiring
Controlling	Monitoring
Communicating	Envisioning
Evaluating	Behaviour modelling
Monitoring	Empowering
Teamworking	Promoting learning
Directing	Team building

Source: adapted from Ellis and Dick (2000).

Table 7.2 Management versus leadership

One aspect of the leader's style relates to the way he or she relates socially to team members. As stated earlier, the relationship is personal and involves social relationships with each member. Does the team leader remain psychologically aloof, or try be one of the boys/girls? Many formal leaders find this aspect most difficult to judge, particularly when they first take up a responsible post. An aloof and distant relationship can be perceived as cold and uncaring. The distance between the team leader and the team can create a barrier that cuts the manager as team leader off from the team and thereby prevents effective communication. However, an overly friendly manner can be misunderstood and can lead to disciplinary difficulties.

Hospitality, Leisure & Tourism Series

Key point 7.6

The skills needed of leaders in leisure organizations are different to those of more traditional managers. Leaders connect with group members as people rather than as functions.

In many ways the sociability style adopted by the team leader will be determined by a combination of his or her personality and experience, and the context in which the team is working. Some managers are by nature closer or more distant from subordinates. In these cases, it is difficult to suppress their personality traits and, all things being equal, they perform to their natural inclination. Table 7.3 shows the benefits and limitations of closeness and distance.

Psychological distance	Psychological closeness
Benefits	*Benefits*
• Disciplinary action easier	• Leader has better knowledge of team members
• Formality better matched to formal situations	• Good communications with team members
• Disciplined working methods	• Better knowledge of the immediate situation
• People 'know their place'	• Better able to build strong group bonds
	• Better able to tap the creativity of the team
Limitations	*Limitations*
• Distance acts as barrier to good communication	• Disciplinary difficulties
• Remoteness can breed misunderstanding	• Team member behaviour inappropriate in formal settings
• Team members fearful and hide the facts	• Sloppy working methods
• Leads to conflict with the group	• Poor follow through on instructions

Table 7.3 Benefits and limitations of distance and closeness

More experienced managers tend to have the confidence to be relaxed and informal with employees. Many new managers believe that it is easier to be formal first and more relaxed later. Some service situations require a formal service situation, particularly in front of house. In other cases, informality is required.

In addition to the differences in the degree of closeness and distance of leaders, it is also possible to distinguish differences in the priorities that leaders give to their work, particularly the priority they give to people or tasks. While some register a balance

Mainly technical/task priority	Mainly people priority
• Priority for task, systems, solutions, planning or action related to systems, operational methods, rules and procedures • Priority to monitoring and measuring task and the work of others • Priority to things focus – finance, strategy, planning, control, work study • Enjoys paper work and systems • Can have a problem with understanding people	• Focusing on the personal needs or problems of others, decisions, solutions, planning or actions related to morale, conflict and motivation problems • Priority to people-related activities – interviewing, selecting staff, appraisal, counselling • Enjoys communicating with individuals and groups • Can find figures and systems difficult

Table 7.4 Leadership task and people priorities

between the concerns for people and concerns for task, most leaders are prone to prioritize either people or tasks (Table 7.4).

Blake and McCanse (1991) provide a means of assessing the degree of concern for both task and production, and the degree of concern for people. They work on a quadrant that compares these two factors against high and low concerns to produce five leadership priority styles. The 'leadership grid' is reproduced in Figure 7.1.

The leadership grid shows how the balance between concern for production and people can vary between managers. These positions are likely to have different impacts upon subordinates and the team's morale:

- *Impoverished management*: people low, production low. Register a fairly neutral position with little concern for either dimension. The team leader is not sociable, tends to abdicate decisions, and involves minimal communications with the team. Subordinates are likely to react in an equally negative manner, many will move to a corresponding low concern for both people and task, morale will be low and staff turnover will be high.
- *Country-club management*: people high, production low. The team leader would be concerned with maintaining social relationships. A sociable team leader, less formal. Close to team, though avoids conflict and places production and tasks as a second priority. Subordinates are likely to be committed to the individual manager. A happy atmosphere to work in, but low output. Conflict within the team is stifled rather than resolved. May stifle creativity. *Pulse turnover* when the manager or other key team members leave.
- *Authority-obedience management*: people low, production high. The team leader prioritizes production, output levels and tasks. Low sociability and more directive styles of decision-making are typical. More comfortable with systems and rules – sets standards for team to work to. Subordinates are likely to react unfavourably to the manager's assumptions that they cannot be trusted. Low commitment is typical.

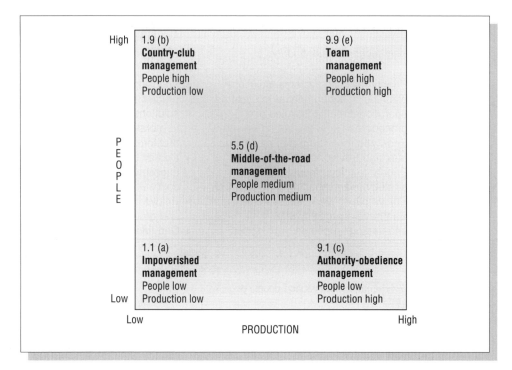

Figure 7.1 The leadership grid
Source: Blake and McCanse (1991).

Team members often work steadily when the team leader is there but they slack off when not being directly supervised. Conflict generated – may be individual or organized in collective forms.

- *Middle of the road management*: moderate people, moderate production. Priorities are balanced between concerns for people and concerns for production, but not strongly prioritized. Moderately sociable and decision-making will tend to be a mix of directive and consultative – tell and sell, tell and test. Subordinates are likely to be more instrumental – not too much effort, enough to satisfy the leader. Not outstanding quality of work or output. Standards not as good as they might be. Conflicts are never fully resolved.
- *Team management*: high people, high production. A high priority is placed on both production and the team. The team leader recognizes the significant role team members play in achieving high levels of high-quality output. The leader is sociable and adopts more participative styles of leadership and decision-making. Subordinates are highly motivated; staff turnover levels are lower. Conflict is low and the employees are committed to service and production goals. Quality of work is good and both employee and customer satisfaction are high.

According to the Blake and McCanse model, team management is the most effective style. The nature of the service encounter in leisure services does suggest that the management of organization members has a key significance (Lashley, 2001). In fact, it is possible to argue that these priorities are not an either/or choice. People are the key means by which leisure services are delivered, so people leadership is an integral part of organization management.

Chapter 9 explores some of the issues to do with the relationships between managers, as team leaders and team members, through the use of empowerment. One of the key points is that different applications of empowerment involve and empower employees in different ways. These variations in employee involvement in empowerment link to variations in the way leaders and team members make decisions. In principle there are only three basic approaches (see also Figure 7.2):

1 *Directive* – managers make the decisions with little input from employees who merely act on instructions.
2 *Consultative* – managers make the decisions but with suggestions or information provided from employees.
3 *Participative* – managers involve employees in making decisions jointly or delegate decision making to them.

	DIRECTIVE		CONSULTATIVE		PARTICIPATIVE		NONE
Style	Tell	Tell and sell	Tell and test	Seek	Joint problem-solving	Delegate	Abdicates
Manager involvement	Makes decisions and instructs	Makes decisions and instructs with reasons	Makes decisions but reviews after seeking views	Defines problem and seeks employees' view before deciding	Defines problem and makes decision jointly with employees	Defines scope of decision-making authority – monitors decisions	Provides limited direction or support to employees
Employee involvement	Acts on instructions	Acts on instructions and explanation given	Gives views of boss's proposed decision	Discusses alternatives and makes suggestions	Joins in the decision making process	Makes decisions within boundaries set by boss	Employees decide for themselves and react to events

Figure 7.2 Making decisions

The initiatives discussed in Chapter 9 suggest that there are broadly consistent approaches to empowering employees at an organizational and strategic level. In practice, however, the day-to-day management of a leisure service organization may involve leaders using a combination of styles, though one may be more dominant. In each case there are limitations and benefits to an overuse of each style, particularly if the style is at odds with the setting and the people who are being managed:

1 *Directive*

(a) Benefits: the directive style works best where there are few options to the tasks to be done – 'one best way', standardized, limited discretion, safety, high-risk situations, where a task has to be done now.

(b) Limitations: the directive style discourages personal initiative, often results in poor morale and poor communications. Can be inflexible and unresponsive to change. Frequently output levels are high under direct supervision, but drop when the manager is not present.

2 *Consultative*

(a) Benefits: the consultative style works best where managers want to gain from the knowledge and immediate experiences of the workforce. The manager retains control of decisions. Can be useful for overcoming service quality problems or making suggestions for achieving goals.

(b) Limitations: the consultative style is limited where managers continue to make decisions with little or no reference to employee suggestions. Manager control of decisions can be demotivating. The processes of consultation can be time consuming and directly costly, and the benefits more difficult to cost financially.

3 *Participative*

(a) Benefits: the participative style works best where managers need to allow employees to make immediate operational decisions, or where employees have better knowledge and experience. Can be useful for gaining employee commitment to service quality, customer and other business goals. Employees have a better sense of 'ownership' if they make the decisions.

(b) Limitations: the participative style is difficult for many managers because it involves letting employees make decisions and can represent a loss of control. If employees make decisions, they may make decisions which managers do not like. The processes of participation can be time-consuming and directly costly. The benefits may be difficult to cost financially.

The nature of the services being offered by leisure organizations may have to fit with the most appropriate leadership style. For example, high-uniformity dependant services (Lashley, 2000b) are usually based on systemized operating systems that involve 'one best way' methods of working. In these circumstances, it is likely that leadership styles will be mostly directive because service workers exercise limited discretion in their work. In the case of a relationship-dependant service offer (ibid.) frontline service staff are required personally to respond to customer service needs, and more participative leadership styles are more consistent. This is consistent with Fiedler's (1967) contingency theory of leadership that suggests that leadership styles should change when circumstances change (Ellis and Dick, 2000: 111).

Key point 7.7

Approaches to leadership vary in dimension including psychological closeness, task/people priorities and decision-making styles. Group leaders have to pay attention to the setting and context in which the group operates, so as to provide the leadership required.

Reflective practice

1 Identify the likely reactions of group members to leaders who are distant, task orientated and directive in their style of leadership.
2 Are there circumstances where these styles might be appropriate? If so, suggest the circumstances in which these approaches might be appropriate.
3 Describe a situation where you have either been a group member or a group leader. Consider the influence of both group membership and the leader.

Sources of leadership power

Group leaders are in a position to influence the behaviour of other group members. They are said to have power. In some circumstances this is because they are in a formal position appointed by senior organization members. They have power associated with this formal role that is based on an ability to reward or punish other individuals. In other circumstances, leaders exercise power through their relationship and standing with group members or their personality, expertise or standing as an individual selected by the group. Table 7.5 lists the various forms of power that are traditionally seen as the sources of leadership power.

Legitimate power	Power stemming from a formal position in the organization and from the authority attached to it
Reward power	Power associated with the leader's ability to give rewards
Coercive power	Power to punish or recommend punishment
Expert power	Power resulting from leader's expertise and knowledge about the group tasks involved
Referent power	Power based on respect and personal standing with members
Elected power	Power based on the election of the leader by members
Resource power	Power to allow the use of scarce resources

Source: adapted from Ellis and Dick (2000).

Table 7.5 Typical sources of leadership power

'The wicked leader is he who the people despise, the good leader is he who the people revere, the great leader is he who the people say, "We did it ourselves" (Lao Tsu 570–490 BC). Lao Tsu's famous observation suggest that the most effective leadership goes beyond the power to influence and make individual group members behave in a desired way. Empowering leadership involves an approach that enables, enthuses, encourages and empowers group members. Empowering leadership ultimately is aware of and builds the emotional state of empowerment (Lashley, 2001). Chapters 6 and 9 suggest that the emotional dimensions of organizations in general, and the emotions of empowerment in particular, are important considerations in leisure service organizations. Empowering leaders have an understanding of, and empathy with, the emotions of group members. By definition they transfer and spread power through the work group or team.

The feeling of power is fundamental to understanding the concept of empowerment and variations in its form and application. Most definitions of the state, rather than the form, of empowerment stress the need for the individual to feel in control (Conger, 1989), have a sense of personal power together with the freedom to use that power (van Oudtshoorn and Thomas, 1993) and a sense of personal efficacy and self determination (Alpander, 1991). 'People have to decide that they have power and can make a difference. They have to decide that they have choices and can exercise their choice' (Johnson, 1993: 5).

Feelings of disempowerment (van Oudtshoorn and Thomas, 1993) or powerlessness, stem from a lack of autonomy, authority and control (Johnson, 1993), or from lacking the capability, resources and discretion (Conger, 1989). The sense of powerlessness is responsible for a whole host of organizational and social problems. Low productivity, poor quality, sabotage, labour turnover, absenteeism, alcoholism, and job stress are all organizational consequences of employees who feel powerless (Johnson, 1993). The complaints of the Accor group (Barbee and Bott, 1991) or the observations of Wood (1992) suggest that many workers work in leisure service organizations which engender feelings of powerlessness in the workforce.

Key point 7.8

Leaders exercise power within organizations. They are able to influence the behaviour of other group members through a number of sources. Most importantly, however, empowering leaders widen the access to power and increase the feeling of power in empowered members.

Conclusion

All social life, by definition, involves group dimensions. People belong to groups to which they refer for a sense of personal identity. They help people define who they are, and who they are not. Group membership, even in groups where members are not known to each other, exercise influence over individuals. They suggest norms of behaviour and of values attitudes and beliefs. Individuals referring to groups for a sense of identity tend to conform to the norms of the group. Organizations are groups and employers frequently attempt to use these aspects of group membership to build a sense of organization loyalty and commitment to shared norms.

Primary groups are different to these large groups that operate on a grand scale. Group members know each other and have face-to-face relationships. They are smaller and typically emerge from the social dynamics of people who are in regular contact with each other. Organizations increasingly organize working relationships using group membership in formal groups through teamworking and autonomous work groups. Here the benefits of the social dynamics of the group are being put to use to meet organizational objectives.

One of the features of group life is that leaders emerge. Leaders may be formally appointed by the organization and have formally defined roles, authority and responsibility. Their approach to the group through emotional closeness, people or task centredness, or in their decision-making style has an impact on group members. In other cases, leaders emerge from the dynamics of the group. Nevertheless, leaders influence group members. In both cases, leaders will exercise some power over other group members in their ability to shape the behaviour of individual members. The power or the degree of strength of influence they can exert has a number of sources. Fundamentally, however, the power of leaders is dependent on the willingness of group members to be led.

Reflective practice

1 Explain the fundamentals of group formation and function in organizations.
2 Define leadership.
3 Critically discuss leadership through behavioural models.
4 Explain leadership power bases.

CHAPTER 8

Organizational culture: context for leisure services

- define organizational cultures

- understand how organizational cultures become established and maintained

- identify key organizational structures and their impacts (positive and negative) on organizational members in leisure services

- identify and explain the structural characteristics of leisure service organizations giving rise to occupational communities.

If you were asked to explain the meaning of culture, your first thoughts would probably be about the characteristics of nationality (other than your own). In part, this is because 'observable' national characteristics are often stereotyped and constantly presented naively or amusingly to us by the mass media. When seeking to illustrate your national culture there may be some difficulty because perceptions of self (or a group to which you belong) often differ from those of others.

Possibly you will then try to explain your culture by comparing and contrasting with characteristics you believe present in that of others. In any event, the outcome of the whole process is likely to contain inaccuracies and be difficult to express. In addition, by focusing exclusively on nationality you will have ignored other key pieces of the cultural jigsaw such as gender, religion, education, socioeconomic group, income and so on.

Understanding culture

Culture is a concept that is notoriously difficult to define accurately. Mullins (1996) suggests that this is partially because often we think only of:

- emergent issues (or 'whats') rather than considering why certain nationalities are labelled as 'polite', 'bombastic' or 'pragmatic' for example
- organizational culture which, similarly, is an incredibly elusive notion and tricky to explain.

The following extract from an interview with a hospitality manager helps give a feel for its almost esoteric nature:

> What is it? – I don't know; it's sometimes so obvious that I can almost taste it but equally it's difficult to button down. I guess it's like when you hear a certain song or notice a particular smell; you immediately travel to a special place or time in your life. For that instant, you remember everything as clearly as if it were only yesterday; then it's gone just as quickly. When you try and recall what you've just experienced in words, you just can't do it. Trying to explain organizational culture is a bit like that. It's all around you and at times you really feel its presence; at other times it's damn near invisible.

Researchers have sought to understand organizational culture by identifying and applying features of society to structural features of organizations. This perspective holds that organizations are merely a reflection of society at large. Clearly, the study of society is a distinct discipline in its own right but the overarching tenets are still valuable in an organizational behaviour context.

Welford and Prescott (1994) consider that a focus on salient societal features gives us some insight into the way cultures operate in organizations. There is some strong evidence to support the idea that national culture is effective in shaping that of organizations and the pioneering work of Hofstede (1980), conducted across IBM's international units for example, is based on this assumption. He considers culture to be a form of 'collective programming' which affects behaviour and may be understood according to its relative position along the following dimensions:

1 *Power distance* – willingness of employees to disagree with managers (high – Australia and Britain; low – Hong Kong and Iran).
2 *Uncertainty avoidance* – extent members feel threatened by unusual situations (high – Germany and Latin America; low – Australia and Britain).
3 *Individualism* – individualistic (high – Britain and USA; low – Hong Kong and India).
4 *Masculinity* – concerns stereotypical masculine and feminine traits, for example the former would include assertiveness ad competitiveness, while the latter comprise caring (high – Britain and USA; low – Netherlands).
5 *Confucian dynamism* – added in 1991 (seeks to address the Western bias of the original questionnaire): long termist or short termist (former stresses perseverance, judicious use of resources, accumulation of savings – China and Japan; short-termist organizations overspend for reasons of 'fashion' and expect quick results – Britain and Canada).

Hosftede's work has been criticized for reasons ranging from poor research design to his oversimplified notion of culture. For example, it is inappropriate to suggest that everyone in a nation state shares similar values and beliefs. Consider the cultural differences between indigenous and white Australians. In addition, it is clear that, despite contemporary efforts to redress the balance, there are still differences in the way men and women are socialized. Furthermore, educational and religious differences continue between social classes and increasingly in Western nations, citizens have diverse ethnic backgrounds.

However, let us not dismiss Hofstede's pioneering work too quickly. His typology is reasonable and has provided insight stimulating further study. For example, Mars and Nicod (1984) divide cultures into a grid/group structure. Simply, this views societies along two continua indicating the extent to which they prefer the security of, or identify strongly with, groups (extended family) and whether they prefer the presence of formal rules and regulations.

Similarly, Trompenaars (1993) links facets of culture with organizational behaviour incorporating alternative dimensions of diffuseness (whether holistic relationships need to be held with individuals rather than simply contractual); open displays of emotions; status through achievement; perspective of time (historical or contemporary); and achievement through own effort or environmental uncontrollable variables.

Reflective practice

1 In groups of four, write down some key words which you feel help explain or define your culture; do not reveal the results.
2 Get other members of the group to note what they believe your culture to be using key words.
3 Compare the results in an open discussion format.

National culture is particularly important for our purpose because hospitality, tourism and leisure organizations have always had a significant international appeal with people wanting to experience diverse and unique products.

Some commentators such as Naisbitt (1993) consider that host societies of tourist destinations and organizations therein will strive to maintain their uniqueness and culture to maximize competitive advantage. Alternatively, Tribe (1995) suggests that the increasing effect of globalization will result in a standardization of cosmopolitanism or a homogenization of leisure service products. Neither of these views is mutually exclusive and Dalen (1989) predicts that demand will remain constant for both uniqueness and standardization. Ritchie (1991) agrees and suggests reasonably, but ironically, that cultural diversity will probably survive in a sea of homogenization.

Clearly these arguments are more orientated towards products than organizational culture. Nevertheless, evidence suggests that broader societal values play a role in the formation and nature of organizational culture. For example, Johns, Chan and Yeung (2002) found that national cultural values were an important feature in this respect. In their study of 400 employees in twenty-seven Hong Kong food service outlets, variables of 'face', 'conservatism' and 'repayment of good/evil' affected their attitudes towards customers.

Similarly, in Joiner's (2001) study of seventy-eight Greek organizations, key societal cultural values were found present and linked with the job stress of managers. Pheng and Yuquan's (2002) comparative study of Singaporean and Chinese construction companies once again confirms the significant effect of broader societal values on organizational cultures.

It would therefore be unwise for international leisure companies to ignore the impact of national culture in the workplace; and these key questions must be addressed:

- How do national cultures impact on these firms and what do managers need to know to achieve and maintain organizational success?
- Can multinational firms impose their 'domestic' cultural values successfully in host nation organizations?

The answer to the first question is 'yes' and national cultural traits must be factored into organizational structures but with additional company-related elements. The answer to the second question is equivocal; in terms of product reliability it is understandable that corporations standardize delivery because in some respects, demand dictates that this is so. In terms of the overriding organizational culture, however, things may be different. Some leisure service organizations (mainly North American) have tried to impose a Western-style culture in this way and made notorious blunders.

Huyton and Ingold (1995) remind us of the problems experienced by the international Ritz-Carlton group when they tried to introduce a Western-style total quality management programme in their Hong Kong unit. In brief, the programme was fraught with difficulties because of strong Chinese cultural values summarized as 'Guanxi' relationships:

- respect for authority – employees always do what they are told
- informal group formation – strong propensity to form social groups within organizations (we will return to a Western form of this later in the chapter)
- power of relationships – essential and usually deferential
- authority without responsibility – achievement is important but achievers pass authority 'upwards'

- face – unwillingness to be honest about weaknesses
- unwillingness to share information – giving out all information is seen as a weakness.

Key point 8.1

National cultural characteristics have an important role to play in the formation of organizational culture.

The remainder of this chapter discusses the importance, nature and role of organizational culture, which is defined and some major contributions to the field are introduced. The establishment, maintenance and shaping of organization culture are explained together with an outline of formal and informal structures. Finally, an important informal cultural phenomenon known as an 'occupational community' is introduced and its key role and impact on hospitality, leisure and tourism organizations is discussed.

Organizational culture

Case study 8.1

Mason Edwards had recently applied for the job of waiter in a medium-sized, three-star seaside resort hotel. Over the next few days he was called for interview. The subsequent meeting between Mason and the hotel owner only lasted five minutes. Mason considered most of the host's questions irrelevant. For example, he was asked the correct way to serve fresh asparagus with butter when the item did not appear on the menu. Furthermore, the owner failed to enquire about his qualifications or experience. In addition, Mason's question about basic food service protocol was countered with, 'We've got a great team in the restaurant, they'll soon show you the way we do things around here'.

The owner then proceeded to tell Mason of his own experiences as a former chef and to emphasize how important the food production is. After a short time, the interview ended with Mason being told the job was his if he wanted it (beginning at 6 p.m. on that same day) but he would have to supply his own uniform. Luckily for the applicant, he already possessed some black trousers and a few white shirts.

From what Mason could gather, this hotel used a plate-service style so it would not cause him too many problems because his experience was in 'silver-service' at the luxury end of the market. Later that day Mason arrived at the hotel eager to start his new job. As he expected, plate service was no problem and compared to his former jobs, this one was straightforward and easy. During the first week, the other food servers seemed quite friendly and easygoing; they did not need to teach Mason much and so did not bother for long. Over time, Mason proved very popular with hotel customers and was rewarded handsomely for his efforts through tipping, despite being allocated tables which were located in unfavourable parts of the restaurant, for example, next to the kitchen, near to draughty windows and doors.

After a while, interpersonal relationships with other food servers seemed to take a turn for the worse. Increasingly, they ignored, criticized or verbally attacked him; sometimes in front of customers. Interestingly, the criticisms were not job-based but were personal and petty. For example, Mason's appearance, speech and general manner were openly ridiculed. He complained to the owner about the team's behaviour but soon realized nothing was being done about the situation. Eventually after five weeks, Mason decided to quit his job.

Reflective practice

1 What would you have done about this situation as owner of the hotel?
2 Who is in 'control' in this organization?
3 What does this case reveal about organizational culture and its establishment and maintenance?

Given the importance of overarching societal values and beliefs on organizations, described in the early part of this chapter, you would be tempted to think that culture is uniform and differentiated by nation states only; this is only partially the case. Other issues also have a key role to play in the formation of organizational culture.

In this respect Mullins's (1996) definition of generic culture is helpful because it acknowledges that smaller pockets or subcultures exist within a broader societal structure. If you consider organizations as broadly equivalent to Mullins's subgroups, his notion begins to make sense in an OB context: '[Culture is] a distinctive pattern of values and beliefs which are characteristic of a particular society or sub-group within that society ... [with] values and beliefs likely to have been transmitted by previous generations through socialization such as family and formal eductation' (ibid.: 18).

Mullins sheds light on what culture is (value and belief systems) and how it is communicated and thus maintained. For example, he suggests that culture is learned from school, parents, community, experience, media and so on. He continues by giving us a sense that cultural information is shared by a group of people with similar backgrounds but each culture has the chance of being different (subgroup) in the same way that individuals are all unique. The overused adage that 'birds of a feather flock together' seems appropriate here. Robbins's (2001) notion of organizational culture provides further clarification: 'A common perception held by the organization's members; a system of shared meaning' (ibid.: 510).

If indeed, organizational culture is a conglomerate of shared values, beliefs and perceptions, how do we unravel and understand it? Furthermore, if each system has a chance of being different, which factors cause these divergences? Mullins (1996) identifies several influences upon the development of organizational culture; see Figure 8.1.

This provides a useful framework from which to begin to unravel the cultural complexity of organizations. We can also begin to appreciate how organizational culture is established and sustained. Robbins's (2001) perspective helps to clarify this situation and is shown in Figure 8.2:

Hospitality, Leisure & Tourism Series

History – reason and manner in which organizations form, values and philosophy of first senior managers, can be used as effective induction tool for new members

Primary function and technology – includes range and quality of products/ service delivery, affect organizational structure

Location – rural or urban, may influence customer and staff types, also nature of service in terms of 'boundary' and distinctive entity

Environment – response rates to changes, organic/mechanistic (see Chapter 4)

Goals and objectives – focus on long-term survival, growth or development; attention to broader social issues; risk and uncertainty avoidance?

Size – large organizations have greater specialization and more geographical sites, may cause communication difficulties, misunderstanding and rivalries

Management and staffing – top executives have major impact and help sustain by behaving appropriately, staff too, some may only pay lip service to management philosophy though

Figure 8.1 Influences on the development of organizational culture

- Philosophy of founders – early culture formation when firm first established; founder's vision easily imparted to all members; for example, original Forte and Marriott groups union-busting and paternalistic culture is a philosophy of both Charles Forte and Bill Marriott; founders able to influence 'espoused' or formal culture but not actual/informal or 'culture-in-practice' (we shall return to the idea of competing and complimentary cultures later in this chapter).
- Selection criteria – staff hired in founders' image; other human resource practices such as training and reward systems linked similarly.
- Top management – behave in a manner which supports original philosophy; rituals and physical symbols which reinforce key values, norms and goals.

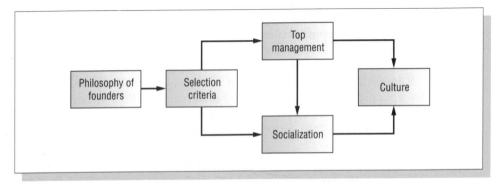

Figure 8.2 Key elements affecting the formation of organizational culture
Source: adapted from Robbins (2001: 523).

- Socialization – to founders' mindset, success perceived as linked directly with founding philosophy; self-perpetuating, sustained by legends of how firm began which justifies present behaviour or culture in the past, for example, Conrad Hilton, Richard Branson; use of company 'language', for example, in many UK hotels staff from different departments are often referred to by use of acronyms or other terms (KPs – kitchen porters or stewards; food service staff may be labelled, rather disparagingly, as 'plate carriers' by chefs).

Reflective practice

1 Think of three organizations in the hospitality, leisure and tourism industry with which you are familiar or have background information on.
2 Research and map each one separately, according to the categories shown in Figures 8.1 and 8.2.
3 Which is the most useful model?
4 Give your impression or characterize the likely culture of each organization according to your favoured model

Robbins (2001) uses the term 'primary characteristics' to capture the essence of organization culture. These characteristics appear in Figure 8.3.

Key point 8.2

Organizational cultures are established and sustained by founders, top management and human resource policies.

Based on the earlier work of Harrison (1972), Handy (1993) divides organizational culture into four distinct (but not mutually exclusive) parts:

- power – found in small entrepreneurial organizations based on trust, empathy and personal communications, controlled centrally, few rules and regulations
- role – bureaucratic, organizational specialists, strong control protocol, jobs take precedence over people, position is main seat of power
- task – project or 'matrix' orientated, power rooted in job or task expertise
- person – individual is central and has complete autonomy, control only possible by personal mutual consent.

It is likely that organizations will exhibit symptoms of several of the above cultures. For example, directors of an international hospitality chain comprising hotels, nightclubs, bars and so on, may operate primarily as a 'role' culture. Equally, the pervading culture among individual units of the corporation could function as 'person' or a 'power' structure.

Deal and Kennedy (1982) prefer their own typology of corporate cultures which is shown in Table 8.1.

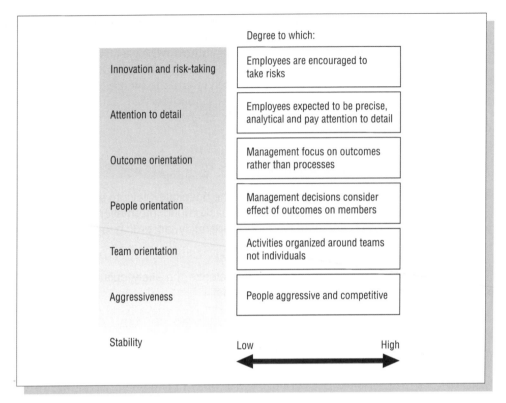

Figure 8.3 Primary characteristics of organizational culture
Source: adapted from Robbins (2001: 510–11).

Culture type	Characteristics
Macho	Comprising individuals prepared to take high risks, intensely pressurized working environment, members experience frequent 'burnout', high levels of labour turnover; examples include the entertainment industry and emergency services
Work hard/play hard	Action with few risks and swift feedback, dynamic with focus on customer needs, much team spirit; examples include retail, fast-food outlets and hospitality franchises
Bet-your-company	Key high-risk decisions with slow feedback, focus on future, hierarchical decision-making, innovative but slow moving; examples include oil companies and large-scale manufacturers of oxygen and carbon dioxide
Process	Low risk with slow unreliable feedback, bureaucratic 'self-preservation' approach to work, much time spent on minor detail; examples include insurance and civil service

Table 8.1 Generic corporate cultures

On a cynical note, the 'play hard/work hard' metaphor is sometimes a key focus of staff recruitment drives. In hospitality, leisure and tourism organizations it is often used as a euphemism for poor pay, disadvantaged working conditions and a cultural anticipation that members should expect to work lengthy and unsociable hours.

Key point 8.3

Organizational culture can be represented by any one of a number of metaphors, each of which helps us to understand its overarching character.

Neither Mullins's, Robbins's, Handy's or Deal and Kennedy's characterizations bear close scrutiny; for example, they do not fully explain values, beliefs or the subjectivity of perceptions (see Chapter 4). In other words, they provide us with meaningful content without process.

However, they are all useful as metaphors from which we can at least grasp an intuitive notion of organizational culture. Issues of meaning, systems and processes of social interaction is the focus of Schein's (1985) typology. His processual approach, shown in Figure 8.4, explains them as artefacts, norms and values and basic assumptions.

Artefacts appear at the first or superficial level of culture. For example, the physical design of an Australian Hungry Jack's restaurant, Novotel or Warner Brothers theme park is a manifestation of their respective cultures. Consider, too, the dress code used

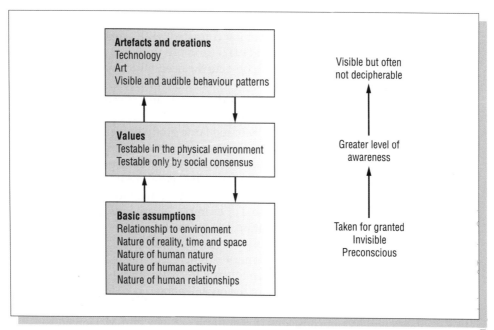

Figure 8.4 Levels of culture and their interaction
Source: Schein (1985).

by teaching staff at your college or university. Hospitality, leisure and tourism management staff typically will have a different 'uniform' to their social or natural science colleagues.

Each department is saying something about itself to its students and the wider community using these artefacts. Others include physical office design, technology, behaviour patterns and official documents. In addition, communication, presence of rituals and 'ceremonies' and adherence rules also feature at the superficial or manifestation level of Schein's model.

The reasons for group behaviour are contained at the second, or values, level. Essentially, they are explained as shared norms and values. Simply, norms are the rules governing behaviour or the way we think we should behave. Values concern beliefs about what is 'good and right' or ideals for which we strive. For example, is it acceptable to be on first-name terms with management or establish personal relationships with work colleagues?

The norms and values that pervade or dominate the organization are known as 'core'. The extent to which members hold these core values and norms as unquestionable determines whether the organizational culture is 'strong' or 'weak'. Inculcation of these values and norms is explained below.

Factors present at Schein's (1985) level three, concern basic and tacit assumptions that determine how members perceive, think and feel. This stage represents that which is taken for granted by the group or that which is so deeply rooted it enters the unconscious. If a strong culture is to be established and sustained successfully by managers, this is the level at which training and socialization procedures should focus. Intuitively, therefore, you would reason that a strong culture gives rise to strict adherence to formally established norms for the benefit of members and the organization. Moreover, these norms are a powerful alternative to strict management control procedures, and increased member cohesiveness, loyalty and a reduction of labour turnover should result.

However, is the above reasoning consistent with what actually happens in the real world? Peters and Waterman (1982) certainly think so, claiming that strong cultures have positive outcomes which obviate the need for formal protocol because everyone knows exactly what needs to be done. Conversely, Legge (1995: 203) argues that strong cultures give rise to 'inward-looking' and complacent organizations, where 'rigidity' and 'group-think' are rife.

Indeed, the demise of the UK-based Forte group in the 1990s is an excellent example of the damaging impact that strong power/role cultures may have on organizations. In this case, Forte failed to observe how anachronistic and uncompetitive it had become and to recognize the predatory behaviour of its eventual nemesis (Granada).

In addition, some cultural values may not have any positive effects on organizational performance in any case. For example, 'shared meanings' may be a potent way to engender member integration but is not linked to performance; indeed, it may actually prevent the firm's ability to learn and adapt.

However, based on the former extremely dubious notion, there are a number of management techniques which attempt to create strong cultures in the belief that this will have positive outcomes for the organization. These approaches effectively manipulate employees by imparting habitual responses designed eventually to pass into their collective unconscious (for example, Disney and McDonald's).

Such procedures are deemed particularly important for new recruits because they are arguably easier to manipulate than existing staff who may hold core values and norms which are not company orientated. However, they are not totally exclusive. Older and existing individuals may also be subjected to similar developmental and induction or 'socialization' programmes whereby company culture is communicated, established and sustained by a variety of methods (language, rules, stories and traditions).

Although this is used commonly, the practice raises some serious ethical dilemmas which should be addressed. A model of socialization is shown in Figure 8.5.

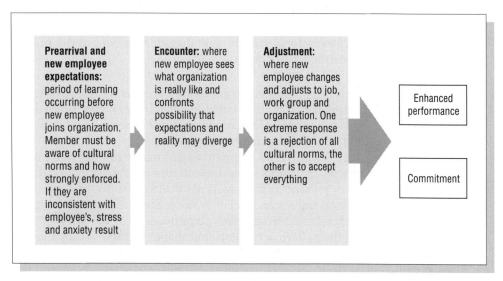

Figure 8.5 The socialization process
Source: adapted from Harvey and Brown (1996: 12).

So far we have presented and discussed the origins, maintenance and nature of organizational culture from one perspective, assuming that only one kind exists which is based on the philosophy of founders or top managers (sometimes known as 'espoused culture'). This is a somewhat incomplete view, especially of the hospitality, tourism and leisure sector. The following section discusses informal culture emphasizing the key role it plays within the organizational context.

Key point 8.4

New recruits are employed in accordance with the organization's formal value and belief system so that espoused culture is sustained.

Organizational subcultures

According to Legge (1995), organizational culture may be viewed from two perspectives, that is, whether organizations 'have' it or whether organizations actually 'are' it. The former is expressible as 'the way we do things around here' and is consistent with

Hospitality, Leisure & Tourism Series

Deal and Kennedy's (1982) structural view. The second holds that culture is separate from any framework imposed by management and is best described as a 'root metaphor' or system of meanings (Gregory, 1983).

If culture is, in fact:

- an objective embodiment of top management vision, or a summation of organizational values, language and rituals, it becomes something which is manageable
- on the other hand, if culture is something an organization simply just 'is' as an outcome of social interaction, active interpretation and transformation, then at best it can only be described or interpreted. This is not to say that management has no impact on organizational culture, just that all members of the organization have their own constructions of reality.

Thus, the diverse organizational community becomes more important in the development and maintenance of culture than management. Roper, Brookes and Hampton (1997) use the metaphor of 'kaleidoscope' to express the existence of many sub-groups in their cultural study of international hotels.

If culture truly is a powerful alternative to formal organizational protocol, as many researchers believe, managers should spend time trying to understand the impact of informal cultures present in their workplace. Attempts to eradicate them totally by imposing espoused values and belief systems are likely to fail. Morgan (1988: 207) provides an understandable summary in terms of a surfing analogy: 'the best surfer can understand the pattern of currents that shape the waves. They may then use them to stay upright and steer but this is not the same as changing the rhythms of the ocean'.

The reality of the situation is that both espoused and 'culture-in-practice' exist alongside each other. The formal one, on the face of it, is easier to manage than the informal one. However, espoused culture is impossible to direct effectively without an understanding of how both interact with each other. For example, Wood (1994) and Guerrier (1999) remind us that even when staff training schemes aim to inculcate members with espoused culture at Schein's (1985) 'basic assumption' level (see Figure 8.4), members may only pay 'lip service' to the idea.

Furthermore, leading service companies using such regimented socialization programmes, perpetuate the myth that strong espoused culture is consistent with organizational success. Wood (1994) is deeply critical of this credo and rightly insists that increasing productivity and profitability in companies such as Disney is more to do with tightly controlled human resource strategies and technology than espoused culture.

Key point 8.5

Both formal and informal organizational cultures coexist and impact upon each other. They also represent a powerful alternative to formal control protocols.

In Chapter 2 we classified labour markets as either core or peripheral. It would therefore seem reasonable to advance the argument that at least two cultures exist in leisure service organizations. The second of these may be further divided into non-exclusive notional categories characterized by individuals who are:

- unskilled
- enjoy widely differing salary packages and working conditions
- temporary or part time with reduced benefits and working conditions
- ethnically diverse
- perceive a job in this sector as a chance to enjoy a 'working holiday'
- have the propensity for undertaking temporary work only
- retrenched from 'traditional' male-orientated industries.

Individuals belonging to one or more of the above categories are also likely to have diverse backgrounds and motivations. Even without knowledge of each group's beliefs and values, intuitively one realizes that they will probably be dissimilar. It would be naive to assume that creating and sustaining an espoused culture in these circumstances produces an embracing manageable framework, because it does not account for nor empathize with other cultures-in-practice.

It is no understatement to say that effective management of this complex situation is difficult. Indeed, prevailing practice gives the impression that managers have either given up trying or use an autocratic style accepting of members paying only lip service to espoused values and beliefs. This is probably explained by the nature of the service product, the frenetic pace at which it is necessarily delivered and the competing demands this places on managers.

There are a number of other structural characteristics of the hospitality, tourism and leisure industry which impact upon cultures-in-practice:

- job tenure – mainly seasonal, part time, temporary or casual with an over-reliance on 'tipping', unofficial remuneration and other non-pecuniary benefits (HCTC, 1994; Leinster, 1985; Mars and Mitchell, 1976; Mars and Nicod, 1984; McGregor and Sproull, 1992; Taylor, 1983)
- high levels of labour turnover (Elliot, 1969; HCTB, 1988; Johnson, 1980; LCAT, 1990)
- low pay (Byrne, 1986)
- provision of accommodation on the premises which is often used to justify low pay and to provide a supply of workers at short notice to cope with fluctuating patterns of demand
- despotic and non-supportive management style (Guerrier, 1987; Jameson, 1987)
- virtual absence of trade unions (Byrne, 1986).

It is almost impossible to arrange the above in order of priority but much research consistently confirms the presence of some or all of these characteristics. Collectively they give rise to informal organizational cultures that operate alongside espoused organizational values and beliefs. While the complexity is difficult to unravel, these informal cultures may be partially explained by viewing them as 'occupational communities'. Thus, once managers are familiar with the basic causes and their characteristics, they can begin to understand the values and belief systems of their workers.

Salaman (1974: 19) defines an occupational community as: 'People who are members of the same occupation, or who work together, have some sort of common life together, and are, to some extent, separate from the rest of society'. A similar view is expressed by Van Maanen and Barley (1992: 281):

A group of people who consider themselves to be engaged in the same sort of work; whose identity is drawn from the work; who share with one another a set of values, norms and perspectives that apply to but extend beyond work-related matters, and whose social relationships meld work and leisure.

Contrary to the traditional way of viewing work (that is, from an organizational perspective), the occupational approach views the meaning of work to the person who is doing it. Furthermore, communities may take either a 'cosmopolitan' form, where members undertake the same occupation but work in different geographical areas, or a 'local' form where the community is comprised of people who work at the same job in the same place. Both of these definitions are consistent with the nature of work in the leisure sector, especially in hospitality organizations.

Table 8.2 expresses the above definitions of Salaman and Van Maanen and Barley as characteristics of occupational communities.

Characteristic	Explanation
The job	Pervasive and sets norms for activities outside workplace
The tasks	Set limits over non-work activities influencing friendship patterns, non-work norms and values
Non-job activities	Organization controls activities outside work directly like sleeping, eating and recreation
Job duration	Jobs of short duration may cause cultural norms and values to be constructed outside workplace and 'imported'
Skills – procedural and cognition – maintain the 'mystery' of certain jobs	It is one thing knowing what to do (knowledge, facts, descriptions), it is another knowing how to do it (know-how)
Self-control	Reliance on ill-defined procedures and techniques to maintain self-control. Once tasks are understood and codified, self-control is reduced
Work-based friends, interests and hobbies	Members discuss work outside the organization, read work-related literature, have work-related hobbies, join work-related clubs, and their friends are also members of the occupational community

Table 8.2 Major characteristics of occupational communities

If we now link the above with the structural characteristics of hospitality, tourism and leisure organizations presented just after Key point 8.5, it is not difficult to see why these communities exist.

Reflective practice

1 Think of a hospitality, leisure or tourism organization with which you are familiar or have background information on.
2 What would be an effective way to identify the presence of occupational communities?
3 Identify as many characteristics of occupational communities as you can but understand that not all will be present.
4 What kind of management style is used?
5 Discuss whether this style is likely to allow occupational communities to flourish.

Occupational communities were found to be present in Lee-Ross's (1996) seven-year study of seasonal hotel workers in the UK. Excepting a few minor points, most of the characteristics outlined in Table 8.2 existed among workers in all hotels studied.

In sum, employees fell into four variations of occupational community which were classified according to their job tenure preference and whether they lived on the hotel premises or not. Some subgroups established their values and beliefs outside the workplace. Moreover, the pivot for most of these groups was not the work itself but the opportunity hotel work allowed for a collective focus on issues external to the workplace.

The main findings are summarized in Figure 8.6 where the four groups are presented and positioned along two continua. The horizontal axis shows the extent to which groups accepted key characteristics of an espoused culture whereas the vertical axis shows similar for culture-in-practice or occupational community formation.

Figure 8.6 shows that the seasonal live-in subgroup are characterized more by occupational community criteria than those of espoused culture. Conversely, the culture of the year-round live-out subgroup are explained by formal organizational values and beliefs.

It would seem reasonable to think of occupational communities as social frameworks that create and sustain unique work cultures. One type may be organization based and the other, job based. Both have identifiable characteristics which include task rituals, standards for acceptable behaviour, work codes surrounding routine practices, rituals, standards, codes, occupational self-control and a fusion of work and non-work life.

Key point 8.6

Occupational communities do not view work from an organizational perspective but instead consider what it means to the person or group undertaking it.

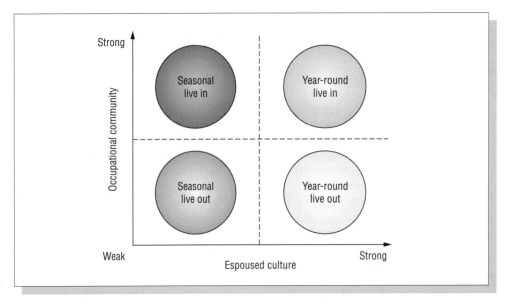

Figure 8.6 Propensity of hotel workers to adopt espoused culture or form occupational communities

Conclusion

Organizational culture is a tricky concept to define adequately and accurately, although there can be no doubt that it impacts on the way we view things. Various attempts have been made to identify its sources and major components, including that of nationality. Indeed, studies have shown that national culture impacts significantly on organizational culture. So, while it is important for managers of hospitality, leisure and tourism services to establish a consistent quality standard, members' cultural diversity must also be accounted for.

Clearly, organizational culture exists and is sourced from multiple origins. It is viewed by managers as a better alternative to formal organizational control protocols. Contemporary thinking recommends the establishment of strong cultures for this reason. However, evidence suggests that in some cases this results in organizations which fail to learn from experience, are introspective and resistant to change, for example, the UK-based Forte company succumbed to a hostile takeover bid from Granada due to the strength of its culture (much to the chagrin of Rocco Forte who had been trying in vain to temper the extant dominant set of values and beliefs).

Culture may be considered from two perspectives. The first regards it as something objective which organizations have and is therefore controllable. This espoused culture can be actively established, sustained and managed by founders, top managers and human resource policies. Consistent with this view, a number of researchers have attempted to classify organizations according to the overarching culture present or desired. Examples include 'macho', 'work hard/play hard', 'bet-your-company' and 'process' but there are plenty of others.

Schein's (1985) processual typology offers valuable insight into the artefacts, values and assumptions of which organizational culture is comprised. This is helpful because it suggests that another set of values and beliefs exist alongside the formal ones. The 'second' view considers culture to be a property and sum of social interaction and processes which ensue in organizations.

In other words, it suggests that management do not have a monopoly on organizational culture. Instead, organizational culture is the property of all members and may differ considerably from the espoused view. This informal culture, or culture-in-practice, is difficult for managers to control and some argue that it may only be described or at best manipulated. The key is therefore to recognize its presence and to acknowledge that it impacts upon the nature of formal organizational culture.

Usually, certain conditions need to be present for the development and sustainance of informal cultures. The leisure services sector, especially seasonal organizations, provide the appropriate structural characteristics for this to be so. Despite the potential for several informal cultures or subgroups to exist, they are best explained using a notion of occupational communities.

Essentially, these groups are social frameworks that establish and sustain work cultures. The construct allows informal cultures to be positioned along two scales. The first shows the extent to which subgroups resonate with espoused values and beliefs and the second shows the same for informal or culture-in-practice.

Reflective practice

1 Define culture and comment on its formation and sustainance in organizations.
2 List four metaphors of organizations and discuss whether they assist in the understanding of culture.
3 Choose two organizations from the hospitality, leisure and tourism sector and discuss their likely culture using Handy's constructs.
4 Explain how Schein's typology alerts us to the existence of cultures-in-practice.
5 Discuss the structural characteristics of the hospitality sector which give rise to occupational communities.
6 Comment on how useful you believe the occupational community model to be in describing the culture of your organization or one with which you are familiar.

The empowered leisure service organization

- define empowerment and service quality
- understand the psychology of empowerment
- understand relational empowerment
- critically discuss empowerment and the conditions needed for effective introduction.

Empowerment: what does it mean?

Empowerment is a somewhat enigmatic concept meaning different things to different writers (Potterfield, 1999). One of the aims of a good higher education is to create empowered students, and we aim to create empowered readers through this book.

Reflective practice

1 Define what empowerment means for you.
2 Think of occasions when you have felt empowered or disempowered?
3 Write a brief note to a sceptical relative making the case for the empowering nature of a higher education.

For us, the definition of empowerment used through this book is about helping develop a sense of personal autonomy, effectiveness, and control. This study of organizational behaviour aims to provide you with a set of concepts and controls that helps you have more control of what you do and when, and to give you more choices in your actions. While your development as empowered learners is an important aim of the text, we are specifically going to focus on empowerment as a management technique used in leisure service organizations.

In the employment field in particular, examples of empowerment in practice indicate that empowerment is a systematic attempt to manage people that takes on a range of forms encompassing participatory, consultative and directive styles of management (Lashley, 1997). That said, one of the defining features of empowerment, and a core feature of any claim to be different from involvement and participation, is the attention to how employees feel as a result of being empowered.

Empowered employees are supposed to feel in greater control (Conger, 1989), have a greater sense of personal power together with the freedom to use that power (van Oudtshoorn and Thomas, 1993), a sense of personal efficacy and self-determination (Alpander, 1991). They have to feel that they have power and can make a difference. They have choices and can exercise choice (Johnson 1993). Unlike disempowered or powerless employees, empowerment provides employees with a sense of autonomy, authority and control (ibid.) together with the abilities, resources and discretion to make decisions.

Key point 9.1

Empowerment, therefore, claims to produce an emotional state in employees from which additional commitment and effort stem.

Case study 9.1

The creaking door

The Crown Hotel is a small family run hotel in a small town that has a bustling tourism and conference trade. The hotel has fifty rooms in a traditional setting with many features of the original Elizabethan building. The owners, Mr and Mrs Pudd, are expecting a mystery visit from the representative of an American tour company which is attracted by the hotel's intimate historical character, location close to 'Shakespeare' country and potential for inclusion in the company's 'cultural heritage tour'. Mr and Mrs Pudd like to run a 'tight ship' and have increased the profits since they took control of the hotel two years ago. All work is allocated by them or their supervisors and staff are expected to act on instructions given. The owners are particularly keen to deal with all customer complaints personally; they believed that the personal touch is valued by customers.

Three months before the incident one of the room attendants on the third floor complained to one of her friends about the noise being made by the fire door on the third-floor corridor. She said, 'That door is so noisy, every time someone goes through it. It is driving me mad. I can't understand why Fred doesn't do anything about it'. At about the same time, Fred the maintenance man, said to his assistant, 'Blimey, that door is making a right row, why don't housekeeping ask me to fix it?'

The American representative arrived on a wonderful June day, the countryside was in full bloom, and she could see how the hotel and its setting were ideal for her clients. They would really enjoy the 'heritage setting'. The hotel with its beamed ceilings and ivy-clad walls was everyone's idea of 'Merry Old England'. Although everything looked ideal she recommended that her company did not use the hotel. Talking to a colleague later she said, 'I was really disappointed, the hotel looked great and it was in such a lovely spot. The staff seemed OK and the owners were very keen to please, but the room I was allocated was right next to a creaking door. Every time someone came through it the noise was awful. I didn't get a wink of sleep all night'.

Reflective practice

1 Suggest why the tour company representative did not recommend using the hotel?
2 What could have been done to prevent it?
3 How did Mr and Mrs Pudd contribute to the problem?

Relational empowerment

Changes in working arrangements that claim to be empowering for employees vary in form and experience for the empowered. At the operational level empowerment can be said to be a management 'rhetoric' that labels a variety of changes as being universally beneficial. Empowerment is described as producing a 'win-win' situation in which employees and managers gain. In reality, the different forms of empowerment represent quite different experiences for the empowered because empowerment covers directive, consultative and participative relationships between employers and managers. Some of these different forms are listed in Table 9.1. The effectiveness of a particular initiative in producing the necessary changes in employee feelings and work performance will largely be dependant on the experiences of the empowered by creating the 'state of empowerment'; that is, the extent that particular initiatives generate feelings of personal efficacy and control over situations in which the empowered can make a difference.

Your involvement in decisions	*How you feel about it*
You act on instructions given	
You act on instructions after an explanation is given	
You express your views on proposed decisions but you do not make the decision	
You discuss alternatives and make suggestions but you do not make the decision	
You join in the decision-making process	
Make decisions within boundaries set by those in authority	

Table 9.1 Decision-making questionnaire

Marchington et al. (1992: 7) provide a useful four-dimensional matrix through which to 'deconstruct the different components of employee involvement'. This can be helpful when analysing initiatives that claim to be empowering. They suggest that various techniques can be located against the dimensions that cover *degree* of involvement; the *form* which involvement takes; plus the *level* in the organization hierarchy in which involvement takes place; and the *range* of subjects dealt with under the arrangements. This four-dimensional model is a useful starting point and one that helps to establish similarities and differences between initiatives called employee empowerment, employee involvement and industrial democracy.

Degree of involvement

The degree of involvement refers to the extent that employees are able to influence decisions made within the organization. Several writers have produced continua of involvement of employees in decision-making. Poole (1986: 18) distinguishes between schemes via which 'workers influence decisions but are not responsible for them', and those where 'workers have actual control and authority over particular decisions' (ibid.). Earlier, Tannenbaum and Schmidt (1973) identified a continuum of employee involvement in managerial decisions which involves three broad relationships.

Reflective practice

1 Based on experiences at work, at school or at home, identify your feelings about being involved in decision-making in different styles and enter them in Table 9.1.

Marchington *et al.* use a model fashioned in the form of an escalator with employee self-control (autonomy or workers' control) as the 'upper stage'. Figure 9.1 reproduces this 'escalator model' because it assists in developing an understanding that different forms of employee involvement involve different relational dimensions.

In this model *information* involves providing employees with information in an essentially 'top-down' direction – company magazines and some forms of team briefing are examples. *Communication* includes schemes which involve two-way processes. Extended forms of team briefing that allow questions to be asked and clarification sought are examples – perhaps close to tell and test. Schemes that aim to gain from employees' ideas and experiences are described as *consultation*. Managers continue to make the ultimate decisions but quality circles, suggestion schemes and joint consultative committees assist in making decisions with inputs from employees. *Codetermination* involves schemes whereby employees and managers may jointly make decisions. Works councils and employee directors are examples, but issues of relative numbers are important. For example, in the German system of codetermination, employee directors have nominal parity with owner directors, but in practice can be outvoted by the casting vote of the chairman.

Employee-owned organizations occupy the top step on the escalator. *Control* involves those organizations in which employees retain ultimate decision-making powers, usually in the form of workers' co-operatives. The Mondragon co-operatives in Spain are some of the most successful examples. In this case employees own the organization and vote in the management and make key strategic decisions.

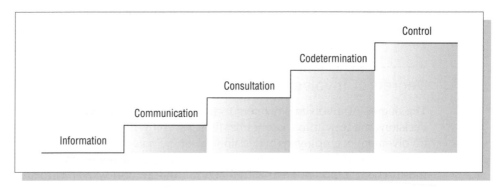

Figure 9.1 The escalator of employee participation in decision-making
Source: Marchington et al. (1992).

Key point 9.2

Most of the initiatives under discussion here, as being applied in leisure services, are not concerned with these democratic intents; they are driven by a management defined agenda to meet management defined problems.

Form of involvement

The second dimension identified by Marchington *et al.*, relates to the *form of involvement* in a particular initiative. They identified three forms through which individuals are involved – direct, indirect and financial.

In the *direct form* individual employees are themselves personally involved. Usually all employees in an organization, unit or department take part. Work organization through autonomous work groups, say, as in Harvester Restaurants (Ashness and Lashley, 1995) involved employees directly in team organization. Other initiatives involve team briefings, house journals, suggestion schemes or similar arrangements for downward information-giving and upward problem-solving which involve direct communications between managers and individual employees.

The *indirect forms* of involvement are where individuals are represented in the involving process. Usually, one or more individuals are elected, volunteered or appointed by managers to represent employees. Quality circles rarely involve all departmental employees and usually involve representatives who participate on behalf of the workforce as a whole. Works councils, employee directors and various forms of joint consultation committees involve representative involvement. The experiences of those involved in representing the workforce as a whole are likely to be different from the workforce. That is, the experiences and feelings of involvement will vary between those actively involved in the initiative and those of the bulk of employees for whom the initiative represents a conduit for involvement.

The third form of involvement is the *financial form*, which links employees having some economic benefit to the performance of the organization or their performance within it. A model favoured by the British Conservative government in the 1980s and early 1990s was the use of share ownership and profit-sharing schemes. In most cases the proportion of total income that came from these sources was relatively small and in many organizations was difficult to link to individual performance. Thus, in many schemes individuals found it hard to link their own performance with an immediate material benefit. In many service industries it is difficult to identify the individual contribution and many profit-related pay schemes are based on annual performance. In the case of TGI Fridays, total pay is made up from two principal sources: a 'commission' on sales paid by the company and 'tips' paid by customers. For food and drink service employees, commission is directly related to personal sales, while for the kitchen staff, the group on duty share a commission based on total food sales. Restaurant and bar staff receive tips from customers but kitchen staff do not (Lashley, 2000a).

Level of involvement

The level of involvement relates to the point in the organization in which employees are involved in decisions. Employees may be involved in task-level activities that may be individual, say, as Marriott Hotels or in autonomous work groups found at Harvester Restaurants. The key point with both these is that in both cases 'workers have some rights to organize his or her activities within some discretionary limits' (Poole, 1986: 16). Involvement may be at the level of the department or unit, say, in quality circles or team briefings. More widely seen in mainland Europe, works councils may operate at unit or corporate level. Employee directors are involved at board level. Collective bargaining may span task, department, unit or company, and in some cases spans all four levels. Financial involvement in share ownership and company profit-sharing schemes occur at company level, though bonus schemes based on personal sales occur at task level while other forms of financial involvement may be based on departmental or unit level.

Range of subjects

The fourth dimension identified by Marchington *et al.* is the range of subjects covered by involvement. In some cases, the range of topics being covered is limited to aspects of the tasks or interpretation of service delivery. In many service firms the employee is constrained in what he or she can do with tangible aspects of the business, but may be encouraged to interpret the service delivery as he or she sees fit. In some firms, employees may be involved in decisions about the general conditions of the employment relationship, involving negotiations over pay and conditions of employment. In other firms decisions may well take on a more strategic nature and thereby incorporate decisions which affect the business as a whole. Pret à Manger, the UK-based sandwich bar and snack business, involves employees making recruitment decisions. All new recruits work a probationary shift with their would-be workmates who then vote, at the end of the shift, as to whether the recruit should be employed. There are few other aspects of the organization's decisions that involve employees in the same way.

Power

A fifth dimension, not covered by the Marchington *et al.* model needs to be added to aid our understanding of the nature of this range of initiatives and to assist in distinguishing between them. The power dimension, needs to be added. Without wishing to enter the numerous debates about power in work organizations, it is necessary to comment on the power of the employees, on the one hand, and managers, on the other, to make decisions stick. 'Who makes the final decision?' has to be a key question. Is involvement constrained by limits placed on the authority which has been delegated, and who has decided what those limits should be? In whose interests has the proposal been initiated – managers and owners, or employees? To what extent has the proposer been able to impose the initiative without opposition, or to what extent have processes of consultation and negotiation ameliorated and amended the proposal? To what extent are employees, or employers, able to resist proposals or decisions made by the other party?

Key point 9.3

The way people are managed and involved, empowered or disempowered in an organization can be analysed by asking a series of questions about how employees are involved in decisions, the form of involvement, the level at which the involvement takes place, the range of items covered and the power to make their decisions stick.

Initiatives that claim to be empowering can be analysed in a similar way. Table 9.2 provides some examples of forms of empowerment from case study organizations. They are based on a variety of approaches where the degree of involvement and the form of involvement, level and range of subjects vary. Perhaps not surprisingly, the power involved in empowerment also varies.

Company	Initiative
Accor Group	Quality circles
McDonald's Restaurants	Suggestion schemes
Harvester Restaurants	Autonomous work groups
Marriott Hotels	Whatever it takes training
Hilton Hotels	Team briefings

Table 9.2 Some forms of empowerment in service operations

It has also been suggested (Lashley 1995; Lockwood, 1996) that, depending on the nature of the service encounter, managers may require employees to exercise varying degrees of discretion in the service encounter. In turn, these intentions will shape the form of empowerment included. Table 9.3 provides an overview of managerial intentions for empowerment and suggests appropriate forms that empowerment might take.

Managers introduce different forms of empowerment as an attempt to meet a variety of perceived needs. In particular, there is likely to be different approaches to empowering people in different service contexts and delivering different service needs. As Table 9.3 shows three of the initiatives are aimed at empowering employees in contexts that are participative, consultative and more directive. In both empowerment through participation and empowerment through involvement, empowerment is aimed at altering the *relationship* between managers and employees.

Empowerment through participation involves employees in making decisions that might have been made by a supervisor or manager in the past, or jointly making decisions with supervisors or managers. This might typically involve leisure service employees being allowed to deal personally with customer complaints, or with unusual requests from customers. In Case study 9.1, the room attendant might have been allowed to request maintenance staff to fix the door; the maintenance

Managerial meaning	Initiatives used
Empowerment through participation	Autonomous work groups Whatever it takes training Job enrichment Works council
Empowerment through involvement	Employee directors Quality circles Team briefings Suggestion schemes
Empowerment through commitment	Employee share ownership Profit sharing and bonus schemes Quality of working life programmes – job rotation, job enlargement
Empowerment through delayering	Job redesign Retraining Autonomous work groups Job enrichment Profit sharing and bonus schemes

Table 9.3 Managerial meanings of empowerment

man might have been empowered to do whatever it takes to keep the hotel running smoothly. 'Whatever it takes training', practised at Marriott Hotels, is an approach that includes all staff being trained in customer care skills and being empowered to deal personally with customer needs.

Autonomous work groups is again a direct form of empowerment where groups of service workers work in teams without immediate supervision. Works councils are representative in form because not all employees are members of the council. These work councils are found in many mainland European leisure companies and have legal rights to information and consultation. In Germany, for example, employees have a legal right to set up a works council where there are five or more employees. Many leisure service organizations would have a works council in each of its units.

Empowerment through involvement describes arrangements that are essentially consultative. Empowerment is supposed to develop through employees having an input before decisions are made. These initiatives assume that employees will have more of a sense of ownership of the decisions made, and the decisions will be better informed by the experiences of employees at the point of service. Team briefing sessions before or after service periods are an example of a direct form of empowerment through involvement because all staff are included in the sessions. Quality circles involve representatives of employees meeting with managers to discuss service quality improvement. These approaches are widely held in leisure service organizations. TGI Fridays and Hilton Hotels both use some form of team briefing sessions, and quality circles are used in hotels groups such as Accor in France, and many hotels in the USA (Comen, 1989).

Empowerment through commitment is more motivational in intent. While empowerment through participation and empowerment through involvement aim to create a sense of empowerment by altering the relationship between managers and employees, empowerment through commitment is concerned to alter the way employees feel about their work. Even in traditionally command and control situations, where there are limited opportunities to be consulted about decisions or to share in them, initiatives can be aimed at empowering individuals. In some cases, these initiatives are aimed at individual employees as they are developed through a training programme and given increased responsibility and authority. McDonald's Restaurants' crew and manager development programme is an example of a scheme aimed at empowering individuals in this way. In other cases, initiatives are concerned with changing job design so as to include more skill or personal judgement.

Empowerment through delayering is concerned with reducing the number of levels in the hierarchy of the organization structure. This is a particular problem for leisure retail organizations that are controlling hundreds or thousands of units. There often are many levels of managers between frontline service staff in the units and senior managers at head office. Senior managers can seem remote and information flows can become distorted. One way of dealing with these problems is to 'delayer' the structure and empower junior managers to make more of the decisions that might have been the responsibility of more senior managers in the past. McDonald's Restaurants in the UK made similar adjustments when they removed the role of area supervisors and empowered restaurant managers to work with more autonomy.

Key point 9.4

Empowerment in leisure service organizations can take a variety of forms to meet a variety of managerial concerns and intentions. One of the key questions when studying empowerment is what do managers intend when they introduce an initiative?

Reflective practice

1 In a work organization known to you, consider the following questions.
2 Is it your impression that the employees are empowered or disempowered?
3 If they are empowered, describe the form using the concepts outlined above.
4 If they are disempowered, how might empowerment deal with some of the problems being experienced in the organization?

The psychology of empowerment

Aspirations for empowerment include a change in employees' feelings of personal power and control, together with more positive attitudes to the organization and increased commitment to its policies and goals.

- It is hoped that empowered employees will be confident to do whatever is necessary to meet customer service needs in leisure service organizations.
- They will understand and manage potential tensions between organizational commitments to customer service quality, brand rigidities and profits, and will be loyal employees who will 'pay back' training costs by remaining with the organization.

Much of the more simplistic literature takes these benefits as read and does not foresee difficulties. Empowerment of employees will result in the desired outcomes (Barry, 1993; Johnson and Redmond, 1999). There is little by way of an explanation of how these changes in working relationships will result in changes in feelings, attitudes and behaviour.

Conger and Kanungo (1988: 471) do, however, attempt to provide some explanations of the 'empowerment process' and signal up those contextual factors which are likely to influence the development of feelings of powerlessness and feelings of empowerment in organizational life. First, they draw a distinction between concepts of empowerment which are *relational* and those which are *motivational*. Relational constructs stress the power relationships between managers and employees. Conger and Kanungo state that this focus has led to the development of approaches to the relationship between employees which equate, even out or redistribute power between managers and employees. Techniques that involve more employee participation and involvement are responsible for the merging of terms where empowerment is identified as meaning the same as participation and involvement (Johnson and Redmond, 1999). The key problem, they suggest, is that these meanings do not address the experiences of empowered employees. As we have seen, empowerment can be used as an operational term to cover quite different degrees of involvement, forms, levels, ranges of issues to be covered and power to influence decisions.

Empowerment as a motivational construct relies more for an understanding of empowerment through an individual's internal needs for power and control (McClelland, 1975) and feelings of personal efficacy (Bandura, 1986). Using this model, individuals perceive themselves as having power when they are able to control events or situations and deal effectively with the environments and situations that they encounter. Conversely, individuals are likely to feel powerless in situations which they cannot influence or where they do not have the time, resources or skills to be effective. From a motivational perspective, power is intrinsic based on a need for self-determination, and managers should adopt techniques which strengthen employees' needs for self-determination and personal efficacy. Sparrowe (1994) adds that to be effective in generating feelings of empowerment, the empowered have to both value that which they have been empowered to do, and feel that their empowerment encompasses meaningful actions.

Under this motivational construct of empowerment, employees are enabled through the development of personal efficacy. This means that employee perceptions are paramount. They have to believe in their ability to cope in situations where they value success, and can exercise a range of judgements and skills. The link between having choice about what is done, and when, are powerful.

Effective management needs to be aware that heightened motivation to complete organizational tasks and aspire to greater organizational goals, such as increased customer satisfaction, will be achieved through the development of a 'strong sense of personal efficacy' (Conger and Kanungo, 1988: 474). Using the motivational construct, Conger and Kanungo define empowerment, 'as a process of enhancing feelings of self-efficacy among organizational members through the identification of conditions that foster powerlessness and through their removal by both formal organizational practices and informal techniques of providing efficacy information' (ibid.: 474).

For Conger and Kanungo, relational models of empowerment, may or may not, provide necessary conditions for the empowerment of employees. Thus a redistribution of power over organizational resources with more participative forms of empowerment or the ability to influences decisions via empowerment through involvement may provide an environment in which employees develop a sense of personal efficacy, they are not guarantees of feelings of empowerment in themselves.

Conger and Kanungo (1988) identify feelings of powerlessness as they key target of initiatives designed to empower employees. Although this may be an important motive, and one consistent with the suggestion that empowerment is a necessary ingredient to the management of organizations in modern internationally competitive economies, it is not the only motive. Service organizations have a particularly urgent need to engage employees on an emotional level. The nature of service requires that employees are committed to delighting the customer and this requires the display of the appropriate emotions of welcome, care and concern for customer needs. To be most effective, employees need to both believe in their own efficacy and central significance in making the service encounter a success and in summoning up the appropriate feelings required of the interaction. The empowering process has a key role in developing feelings of efficacy and in managing the feelings required.

Conger and Kanungo suggest five stages in the process of empowerment. Figure 9.2 reproduces Conger and Kanungo's model; of the stages that need to be gone through in moving an employee from being disempowered to being empowered. Command and control organization structures often rely on directive styles of decision-making and people feel excluded from decisions. Case study 9.1 involves this situation. Mr and Mrs Pudd aimed to control their employees to the point that the employees felt only involved in their immediate task, so problems detected were someone else's problem.

Conger and Kanungo's approach suggests a gradual increase of employee involvement and sense of person efficacy.

This model can be criticized because it fails to recognize some of the contradictions inherent in the empowerment of employees, particularly in branded leisure service organizations. For example, many organizations in the sector have introduced employee empowerment and have done so in circumstances where the organization is making a tightly defined branded offer to its customers. In these cases, employees may be encouraged to 'delight the customer' by meeting customer service needs as they arise, but they may not do anything 'out of brand', where customers might become confused because they are getting different experiences in different establishments. In these situations, empowered employees are in a difficult position and have to manage the tension inherent in their relationships with both customers and the organization. If tips, or commission, are also elements in these relationships, the positive benefits of employee empowerment and the associated sense of personal efficacy may be counterbalanced by negative feelings of pressure and stress. Thus, managers may be constrained by the nature of the service offer being made to customers in the extent that they can manipulate job design and rewards so as to generate feelings of personal efficacy.

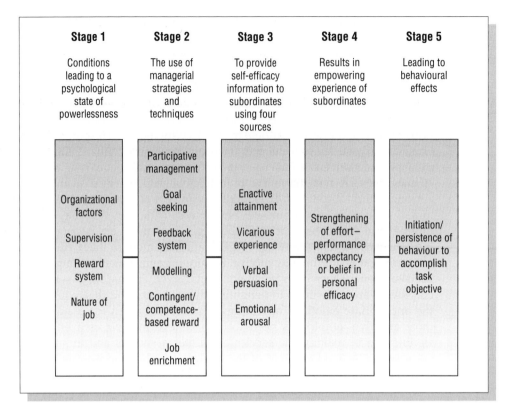

Figure 9.2 The empowerment process
Source: Conger and Kanungo (1988).

A further difficulty with the general sweep of Conger and Kanungo's model is that it fails to recognize the complexity of the chain that they are attempting to build. There is no consideration of the contextual factors that may restrain managers in their analysis of the benefits of empowering employees; labour market conditions, business strategy and the nature of the service offer to customers are likely to influence the way managers perceive empowerment and the benefits supposedly generated.

Similarly, some of the linkages are not foregone conclusions whereby one step leads naturally to another. For example, managers introduce a form of empowerment which changes working practices, but employee experiences of these many not result in the development of a sense of personal efficacy. Even if employees do develop this sense of personal efficacy and permanently change their work behaviour, as in stage 5, there is no guarantee that organizational effectiveness will be increased, because there may be factors internally or externally which are more influential in determining the organization's success.

These reservations limit the overall utility of their observations, but Conger and Kanungo do provide a model for understanding how personal efficacy might be developed at an individual level. While recognizing the significance of content, theorists suggesting that discomfort with disempowerment may stem from inner need states – the need for power (McClelland, 1975) and the need for self-actualization (Maslow, 1954), for example – look to process theory for explanations of how variations in the strengths of these needs might occur. Lawler's (1973) expectancy theory and Bandura's (1977; 1986) self-efficacy theory suggest the feelings of empowerment will develop through employees' evaluations of the situations in which they find themselves. Put simply, this assumes a two-stage process of empowerment to result in changes in employee behaviour. First, the employee has to believe that their efforts will result in an improvement in their performance and, second, that their improved performance will produce valued outcomes.

Thomas and Velthouse (1990) also suggest that employee expectancies are likely to be key to the development of feelings of empowerment. They suggest a four-dimensional model based on a cognitive assessment of their own *competence* to operate effectively in the situation. They go on to consider the *impact* that they as individual employees can make to effective performance, as well as the *meaningfulness* which they attach to the tasks which they undertake as empowered employees, and the *choice* which they can exercise. The emotional state of empowerment is, therefore, likely to be a consequence of the individual's assessment of their ability to be effective. They need to feel they can make a difference in a task which they perceive as worthwhile, and that they have some degree of freedom to act as they see fit in the situation.

Key point 9.5

By definition, initiatives that claim to be empowering will only be empowering if they create the psychological state of being empowered.

A second model borrowed from an industrial relations context suggests that attitude change, whereby managers and subordinates develop shared understanding and attitudes, can be developed though a series of activities that involve increasing amounts of inter-group contact. Figure 9.2 suggests that there are three pathways. Using models from social psychology, Kelly and Kelly (1990) suggest that the development of 'us and them' attitudes can be located in the relationships between group membership to which individuals belong. In most organizational contexts, operatives and managers belong to different groups. Any individual belongs to an 'in-group' and through group membership develops attitudes to individuals who belong to other groups – 'out-groups'. Attitudes are likely to become more conflictual in situations where there appear to be differences in status and rewards and competition over scarce resources. Kelly and Kelly examine the conditions necessary to bring about change in these circumstances using the discipline of social psychology and attitude change in inter-group contexts.

Figure 9.3 highlights three possible routes to the change of attitudes which would reduce notions of 'us and them', and thereby the development of shared goals and commitment to the organization. The *first route* suggests that increased worker management contact might help to shift attitudes away from stereotypes and produce more positive attitudes between inter-group memberships. Some initiatives which claim to be empowering do involve staff and managers working together in quality circles or in teams.

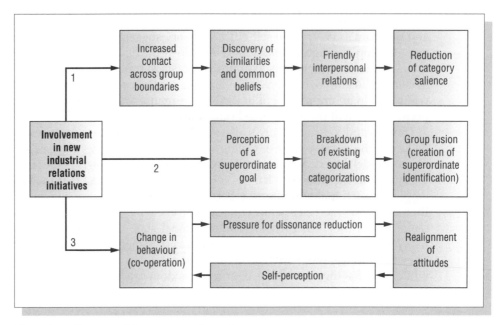

Figure 9.3 Three possible routes to attitude change
Source: Kelly and Kelly (1990).

The *second route* suggests that attitudes between conflicting groups will change if they are both faced with a challenge, or goal, which is common to both groups and which neither can overcome, or achieve, on their own. Clearly, appeals to common competitors, nationally or internationally, are attempting to persuade employees that they have a common goal and threat.

The *third route* to attitude change suggests that changes in behaviour lead to changes in attitudes. Thus, more participatory management techniques which involve working co-operatively between managers and employees may result in changes in attitudes, because it is difficult to maintain attitudes which are in conflict with behaviour. Empowered employees might, therefore, develop more positive attitudes to the organization through the experience of working co-operatively with managers in work groups, work teams and quality circles. That said, attitude change is unlikely to occur if individuals feel they have no freedom of choice in the behaviour.

Managers at all levels, play a crucial role in developing the context in which empowerment can be developed. As discussed earlier, the provision of training, communication processes and a culture of trust are some of the necessary ingredients for the psychological state of empowerment to be created. Furthermore, Figure 9.4 highlights a process that can be used to bring on the individual to reach a state of empowerment by successively taking individuals through a series of stages that alter the relationship and build confidence. The key point here is that this process can be aimed at individual employees and can therefore be helpful in a traditional command and control structure. It is taken and adapted from a model promoted in the McDonald's Restaurants management development programme.

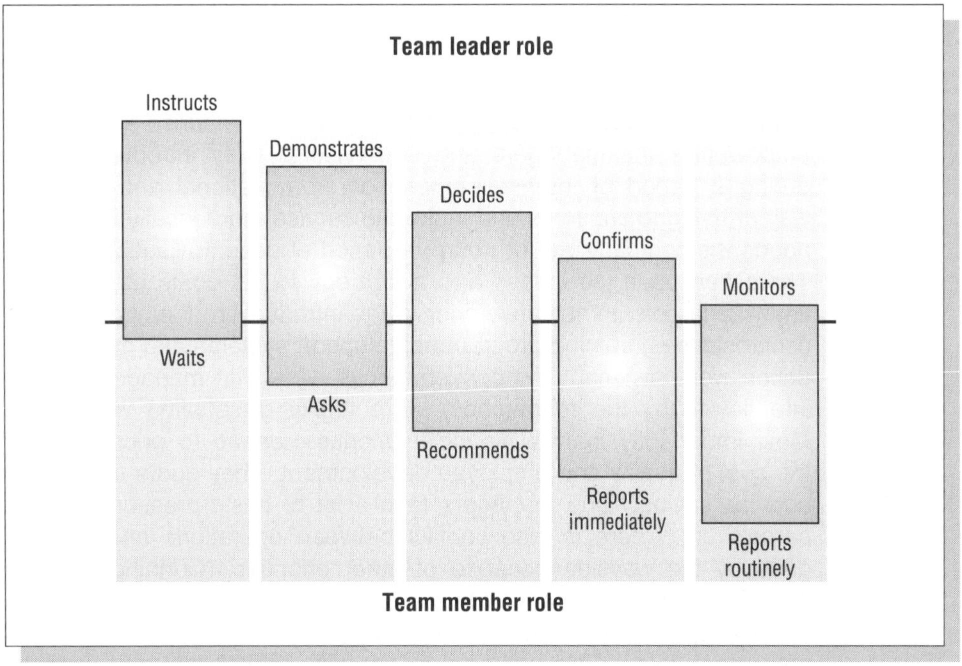

Figure 9.4   Building empowerment

The approach does not necessarily change the relationship between managers and employees, but it does show that individuals can be developed to take on more responsibility and be given more authority for specific projects or aspects of the business. Careful scrutiny shows that the stages move through directive, consultative and participative. The main point that is reflected in this and other chapters is that managers need to consider carefully the state of empowerment and how it will be created. All the case study evidence suggests that this is the key to success or failure.

Key point 9.6

Organizations can develop this sense of personal efficacy in employees if there is an organizational commitment to identifying those policies and practices which create barriers to its development, changes are made so as to overcome the barriers and employees are encouraged to monitor their own development.

Reflective practice

1 Critically evaluate Case studies 9.2 and 9.3, and suggest why the initiatives either failed or succeeded.

Case study 9.2

Parcelco

Parcelco, a national parcel distribution service, introduced an initiative aimed at empowering line managers and supervisors. They introduced empowerment during a period of intense competition from national and local firms. As a way of trying to cut costs and make the service more locally sensitive to service needs the company went through a period of decentralization and cost-cutting. There had been job losses and a strategy to cut costs as a way of meeting financial targets immediately prior to the introduction of empowerment. In these circumstances, training programmes, support systems and monitoring and evaluation were minimal. The consequences were that managers and employees interviewed by the researchers were highly dissatisfied with empowerment. Most importantly, narrow financial priorities tended to prioritize operations at the cost of quality and employee development. They quote the personnel manager as saying, 'Line managers face a lot of basic pressures like getting the parcels out. There is also conflict between operations and training. IiP had gone by the wayside because of other priorities' (Cunningham and Hyman, 1999: 201). A line manager interviewed also reinforced this view. He is reported as saying, 'I have to get the job done as easily and cheaply with as little resources' (ibid.). This pressure to prioritize operational and financial goals is a barrier to the success of empowerment because resources are not made available to ensure success.

Case study 9.3

Harvester Restaurants

Harvester Restaurants is a chain of eighty-nine restaurants branded round a British country pub and farmhouse theme. Most of the units employ forty staff who are organized in three autonomous work teams – bars, restaurant and kitchen. These teams work without immediate supervision. Each unit involves the team manager (unit manager) and a team coach (responsible for training). Supervision at department and unit level is provided by team members. Each team works to an agreed set of team accountabilities. Weekly meetings inform and monitor progress. There are just three levels between frontline staff and the senior management because, prior to introducing empowerment in the restaurants, the structure was delayered and the middle management team was empowered.

Interviews with employees and managers who have been supposedly empowered provide some interesting insights into the potential impacts on employees' sense of personal efficacy, attitudes to the organization and feelings generated. One kitchen team member at Harvester Restaurants said, 'The flat structure gives us our own responsibilities, we don't have to run to management, we can sort things out ourselves'.

Being able to resolve problems as they arise and a sense of personal efficacy comes out strongly from these interviews. The communication process was also seen as beneficial because it gave people information about progress. One team member summed up the feelings of several employees when she said of the team meetings, 'The meetings are good because you get to know how the business is doing, you see the figures and you try to improve on your performance each week'. Others provided examples of how these meetings help to resolve tensions between shifts or between departments. For example, one restaurant member said, 'We had this problem with the night-time shift. They kept leaving the table layout as it had been for their shift and we had to spend fifteen minutes each morning rearranging the tables. We brought it up at the team meeting. Now they move the tables and we can spend another fifteen minutes in the morning cleaning the restaurant'.

The need to be informed also extended to part-time staff who work only a small number of shifts. One restaurant team member commenting on part-timers said, 'Yes there are some people who want to come to work, do their shift and go home, but even they will read the minute book which reports on our weekly meetings'.

Conclusion

Empowerment is one of those terms that sounds positive but has been applied across a wide range of contexts and situations. Certainly, the authors of this book are committed to students being empowered as individuals through education and the pursuit of knowledge. That said, this text is primarily concerned with creating a critical understanding of leisure service organizations. Hence, we are concerned with empowerment in work organizations which provide leisure services.

Empowerment has been attractive as a management technique in leisure service organizations because it seems to provide a strategy for managing the service encounter in a more effective manner. Empowered employees are said to be more committed to making happy customers. Managerial motives for introducing empowerment vary and, as a consequence, empowerment takes a variety of forms across leisure service organizations. In these circumstances it is important to adopt a framework for analysing empowerment.

Empowerment involves both the objective facts of what a person is empowered to do and the subjective feelings which the individual experiences as a result. Initiatives introduced by management will, therefore, be tested against the experience of being empowered and the sense of personal efficacy created. No matter which form empowerment may take, initiatives entitled 'empowerment' will be exposed as empty rhetoric if they do not produce in the recipients feelings of being empowered. Thus the 'boundaries set for the empowered' (van Oudtshoorn and Thomas, 1993), the organizational processes in which the empowered work and the management of those processes become crucial factors in the development of personal efficacy and empowerment.

Reflective practice

1 Return to your notes at the beginning of the chapter and critically review your definition in the light of reading this chapter.

2 Relational empowerment takes a number of forms. Identify the basic types and how the empowered employee and empowering managers have different relations under these basic forms.

3 Critically discuss the suggestion that the defining feature of empowerment is that the empowered feel empowered.

4 Critically discuss empowerment and the factors needed to introduce it so that both employees and managers gain from the initiative.

5 Write a fifty-word note to a sceptical senior manager about the benefits of empowering the workforce in a leisure service organization known to you.

Effective communication in leisure service organizations

- understand the communication process
- define effective communication in leisure service organizations
- identify steps needed for improving communications
- critically discuss the contribution that effective communications makes to organization performance.

Effective communication: what does it mean?

We all spend large parts of our day communicating, yet so often we do it in such a way as to cause confusion and misunderstanding. If communication can be difficult on an interpersonal level, then large work organizations such as those that dominate much leisure service provision have some real difficulties. These large organizations often have to co-ordinate communication among thousands of organization members and hundreds of outlets. Before we explore the communication processes found in leisure service organizations, it is necessary to lay down some general principles about communications.

Reflective practice

1 What proportion of your day do you spend communicating with others?
2 List some of the forms that communications take.
3 Provide some examples of how you alter the style and type of communication depending on the person(s) with whom you communicate.
4 Provide an example of a situation where you have misunderstood the message communicated by another person, and an example where another person misunderstood a communication from you.
5 Why did these problems occur?

Thomson (1998) makes an important distinction between *communications* and *communication*:

- Communications are concerned with the activities, methods and processes of communication – speaking, posters, e-mail, text messaging and so on.
- Communication only takes place when the message transmitted by the communicator has been received and understood by the target communicatee(s).

This distinction is important because it reminds us that the purpose of communicating is to communicate, and we must not forget the need to ensure that the person(s) receiving the message understand it as it was intended. A common problem is often that the message sender assumes that communication has occurred because he or she sent the message. Bazzett (1999: 3), commenting on effective communication, says, 'Most of us become proficient in communicating our basic needs, but unfortunately when dealing with complex issues we often fail to develop communication skills that are equal to the complexity of the issues we are trying to communicate'.

Kikoski (1993) claims that managers spend more of their day on communicating than on any other activity. He estimates that managers spend approximately 75 per cent of their day listening, reading, writing and speaking with subordinates, colleagues and job superiors. Brownell (1991) detects problems with all these forms of communication because they do not match with the needs of the message or the needs of the receivers of the message.

Kikoski (1993) is particularly critical of the quality of interpersonal communication. He is concerned that activity in which most managers spend most time is poorly conducted and their preparation for this important aspect of their work is rarely adequate. Furthermore, the quality and problems associated with poor communication are rarely address in a systematic way in organizations, neither is communication the subject the focus of much academic work.

Key point 10.1

To better inform communicating processes, and thereby improve effective communication, it is important to understand the basic models of communication that have been developed.

Figure 10.1 outlines one of the oldest and most basic of these models. The Shannon and Weaver (1949/1963) model assumes a somewhat linear and mechanistic model that involves four elements – a sender, a channel, a message and a receiver.

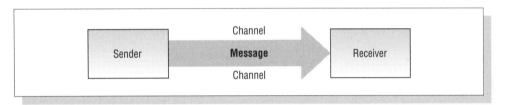

Figure 10.1 The Shannon–Weaver model of interpersonal communication
Source: Kikoski (1993).

A manager of leisure services is typically regarded as the sender; though, given the need to learn from employee performance, the employee might be the sender. Most typically the communication is face to face, but there may be other forms where the parties do not meet when communicating (for example, e-mail, memo, phone).

Figure 10.2 explores the possibility that the channel can be verbal and/or non-verbal, and can be visual and non-visual. In each case there are benefits and limitations.

Face-to-face communications with employees have the potential benefit of allowing clarification and an assumed clarity. Although there is evidence that people think they are better at this form of communication and trust it more: 'We know what we are trying to communicate, however, we don't always understand that what our audience is hearing may not be the message we think we are communicating' (Bazzett, 1999: 3).

Written forms of communication introduce the potential dimension of permanence, record and formality. Thus they can overcome some potential problems of the face-to-face communication where individuals in organizations frequently have conversations involving 'I thought I told you to . . .' followed by 'I thought you said that . . .' (Kikoski, 1993: 85). Written forms of communication allow for checking

	Verbal	**Non-verbal**
V I S U A L	**Visual/verbal** Written forms of communication Face-to-face communication Language	**Visual non-verbal** Cartoons Pictures Body language Facial expressions
N O N / V I S U A L	**Verbal/non-visual** Recorded messages Announcements Telephone	**Non-verbal/non-visual** Alarms Music at work or in customer contexts – shops, bars, hotels, leisure clubs Tone of voice

Figure 10.2 Some examples of channels of communication

back and confirming the message, though again they are not immune from the problems outlined above.

Permanent messages in both verbal and non-verbal, and visual and non-visual forms have the benefit of being low-cost ways of communicating messages. They can, however, be so general that the receiver does not engage with them. Messages need to have the attention of the receiver; the receiver needs to be motivated to receive the message (Biddle and Evenden, 1980). Notice boards, staff newsletters, suggestion schemes and generalized e-mails often fail to communicate because they become part of the environment that individuals accept without recognition of the messages being directed at them.

According to the Shannon and Weaver model, communication only takes place when the receiver has received the message intended. Effective communication has only taken place when the message has been received and understood; 'Communication, therefore, is the act of communicating, with the act of understanding as well as being understood' (Kikoski: 1993: 67).

Key point 10.2

The effective communicator, according to the Shannon and Weaver model must be concerned not with the act of sending, but with the act of receiving.

A second attempt to understand communication within organizations was developed from the Shannon and Weaver model by Berlo (1960). This model added an encoder stage for the sender and a decoder stage for the receiver.

- This allowed for the choice of words and language by the sender and the potential skills of the receiver being factors.
- People supposedly speaking the same language, say English, may have different skills and may use language differently.
- This can be a problem for communication within organizations, because managers and employees use the same words but attach different meanings to the words.

A manager might talk about the need to improve productivity, meaning the need to improve working methods, while employees might receive this message as meaning that they will be made to work harder.

- The encoder/decoder dimension also opens up the possibility of communications with people speaking different languages.
- This is an issue of particular relevance to leisure service organizations where customers, employees and managers may be of different national, cultural and ethnic backgrounds.

Even non-verbal communication can lead to difficulties. McDonald's Restaurants in Moscow experienced some early difficulties, because local Russian customers interpreted the ubiquitous 'Mac smile' as staff laughing at them.

Berlo's model, in Figure 10.3, also added a feedback loop to the Shannon and Weaver model. Feedback provides a useful dimension to the communication because it allows the process of communicating to include a device for ensuring that the receiver has understood the intended message sent by the sender.

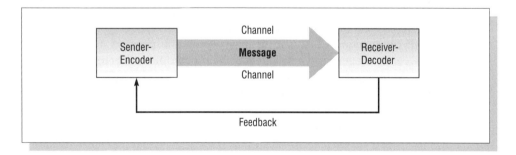

Figure 10.3 The Berlo model of interpersonal communication
Source: Kikoski (1993).

Key point 10.3

Berlo suggests that feedback is useful because it helps both the receiver and the sender confirm a shared understanding of the message.

Both models have been criticized (Kikoski, 1993) for being based on the dominant culture in the USA. Even allowing for the added coder/decoder dimension they fail to reflect the cultural diversity found in truly global business contexts, neither do they recognize the impact of multiculturalism in many countries.

Although writing about the need to build models that assist public sector managers in multicultural USA, the model developed can be helpful for managers in leisure service organizations. As organizations in leisure services both internationalize and recruit employees from diverse cultural backgrounds, every manager will need to understand cross-cultural management.

Kikoski reminds us that many African-Americans (and, incidentally, people from the West Indies) have developed cultural norms that require them to avoid eye contact when communicating with an authority figure, or with an older person. If managers, brought up in traditions where eye contact is interpreted as proof of interest and attentiveness, do not understand this, they might think that the employee is demotivated or not paying attention.

In other cultures there are strong objections to having performance corrected by managers in a public forum. Managers can create difficulties if they cause a 'loss of face' to individuals being corrected in front of their colleagues.

These cultural differences might even cover differences in gender, where some writers suggested 'that frictions arise because boys and girls grow up in what are essentially different cultures, so talk between men and women is cross cultural communication' (Kikoski, 1993: 91).

The Ivey model (Ivey, Ivey and Simek-Downing, 1987) developed for psychologists is potentially useful for leisure service organizations to understand communications in these cross-cultural contexts (whether ethnic or gender based). The model suggests four participants in communication in these settings: the manager; his or her cultural setting; the employee; and his or her cultural setting. Figure 10.4 suggests three possible ways that these four 'participants' might interact. Only model A with managers and employees being aware of each other as individuals and being aware of each other's cultural background will produce effective communication. In model B individuals attempt to communicate ignoring their historical/cultural background, thereby denying the impact of these factors. In model C the risk is that stereotyping interferes with the communication between individuals.

All these models are helpful in stressing the need to consider communications between managers and employees as being complex and requiring careful consideration. At root, effective communication takes place only when the receiver has understood the message being sent. The sender needs to consider the most appropriate channel through which to communicate, but also to consider the way the receiver may decode the message sent. In particular, effective communication needs a thorough consideration of the cultural and historical backgrounds of both the senders and the receivers involved in the communication process.

Key point 10.4

Effective communication only takes place when the receiver has received and understood the message sent by the sender. It is important that the effective communicator understands the needs of the receiver and selects the most appropriate means to communicate.

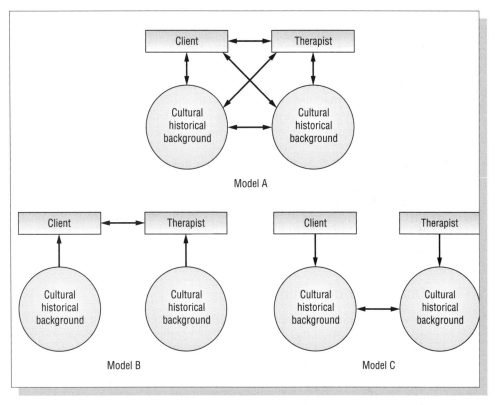

Figure 10.4 The Ivey model of communication (the four participants)
Source: Kikoski (1993).

Reflective practice

1 Go back to the communication difficulties you identified at the beginning of the chapter and consider how the problems might have been overcome with an understanding of the models outlined above.
2 How might these models be helpful in your studies?

Communication flows in leisure service organizations

A feature of all leisure service organizations is that they have both formal and informal means by which information is transferred round the organization (Brownell, 1991). Formal methods of communication are those set up within the organization structure through information flows and structured supposedly to meet the needs of the organization. Usually these are said to involve downward, upwards and lateral lines of communication (Mullins, 1992):

● Downwards communication involve messages being transmitted from a more senior to a more junior level in the organization.

Hospitality, Leisure & Tourism Series

- Upward communications flow from lower levels to more senior levels.
- Lateral communications involve messages being transmitted between individuals on the same level.

Informal communication flows exist in all organizations, and these can be powerful sources of information for organization members. Informal flows are those outside the direct control of the formal management structure. They may involve informal friendship groups covering people from different departments, or trade union networks.

It is important to remember that these formal and informal flows are part of the communicating environment. Each presents problems and difficulties for effective communications with employees, particularly in the light of the models discussed in the earlier section, they can represent quite different cultures between levels, departments or between formal and informal networks.

Downward communication

Downward communications stem ultimately from the most senior levels of management flows through the organization to frontline staff (Mullins, 1992). Messages are generally concerned with policies and procedures, creating rules making judgements and giving feedback on performance to the lower levels.

All organizations have potential communication difficulties with downwards communications, because messages may have to pass through various levels and be subject to variations in understanding. They sometimes become distorted because the many links in the communications chain distort the message. The 'Chinese whispers' effect results in small changes inserted by the individuals through whom the message passes. Thus, the final receiver actually receives a message that is considerably different from the original. This process is in part a natural consequence of having a long line through which messages pass; in part it may be that for 'tactical' reasons the message is distorted on purpose.

Leisure service organizations can also have added difficulties where services are being delivered through hundreds or thousands of local units, say in hotels, restaurants or bars. Messages starting at head office may have to pass through regional and area offices before they reach the unit manager and are passed on to staff. At each stage, geographical distance potentially compounds the hierarchical problems.

Upward communication

Upward communications involve passing messages regarding performance, results, sales, costs and changes in customer tastes, where appropriate (Mullins, 1992). Many similar problems are faced as with downward communication. Long lines of communication also create distortion as messages pass up the organization.

To some extent these are worsened if communications are conveying bad news. It is often the case that people want to soften the impact of bad news by making it seem less bad than it is for fear of reprisals (Brownell, 1991). Messages can get distorted to such an extent that senior managers can be making decisions based on imperfect information.

Lateral communications

Lateral communications occur between people at similar levels in the organization, say between departments or between units in the same company. Poor communications between staff in the restaurant and the kitchen is a well-established tradition among hospitality employees. The work of Mars and Mitchell (1976) suggests that this is based on competition, differences in skill levels, and status differences between those 'cooking' and those 'serving'.

If allowed to go unchecked communication problems between departments can cause inefficiency and conflict. Similarly, multi-unit organizations have difficulty passing information, say, best practice or new techniques, between units. So different practices emerge in different units or regions, and attempting to sustain consistency is a major problem for managers in these organizations.

In all cases, the problems discussed earlier may be at play in that managers, communicating with other managers at the same or different levels, and subordinates communicating with other employees or with managers, may be encoding and decoding messages in ways that create distortions. They may be communicating from quite different cultural and historical origins. These help distort the communication so the message received say by staff, or by senior managers, is different to the one intended.

These hierarchical communications flows that stem from the nature of large organizations that need to communicate across many hundreds or thousands of local units, and across boundaries and cultures, are further compounded by much management practice. Argenti (1998: 202) states, 'Top managers often isolate themselves physically and psychologically from other employees at the peril of effective communication'.

At root, effective communication stems from the communication between employees on a day-to-day basis. Managers at all levels must be made aware of the need to communicate effectively with employees in a way that genuinely creates understanding. Flowing from this, employees frequently complain that managers do not consult with them enough and do not involve them in decision-making (Argenti, 1998). Indeed, a commonly expressed joke among employees is that their firm practices the 'mushroom theory of communication', that is, 'We are kept in the dark and have manure thrown at us regularly'.

Key point 10.5

Formal organization communications flow downward, upward and laterally in most leisure service organizations. Effective communications need to take account of the nature of these flows and correct for difficulties.

Informal communications

The 'grapevine' is a feature of most work organizations. Informal networks of contacts exist within and alongside the formal organization structure (Go, Monachello and Baum, 1996). In some cases, the networks are created by the happenstance of personal contacts and friendships. In other cases, the networks are associated with geographical structures, say where particular units are somewhat isolated, the networks may be passed through links with employees in supply departments or transport staff. In yet other cases, the informal network is a consequence of a semi-formal network through trade union membership. Here the communications are not so much due to happenstance as through an organization that operates in relation to the formal organization and external to it (Salaman, 1974).

Informal networks can provide an alternative source of information for employees. Effective communication with employees requires an understanding of these informal networks and their credence as a source of information for employees. Generally, the less effective the formal information flows, the more value and credibility employees give to informal sources (Harcourt, Richardson and Wittier, 1991). Where formal communications are open and frank, and based on culture of trust, informal sources will be less significant.

The 'grapevine' is most effective when formal communications processes are limited or where there is a culture of conflict between managers and employees. In these cases, employees regarded management communications to be suspect and they look for sources of information that is seen by them to be more trustworthy (Salaman, 1979). For all these reasons, effective communication cannot be extracted from the general management style and culture of trust and co-operation between managers and employees.

Key point 10.6

Informal communication sources can be an important source of information in some organizations, particularly where formal communication flows are ineffective or where there is a culture of organizational conflict.

Reflective practice

1 Suggest some electronic forms of communication that might be used by multi-unit leisure organizations to enable communication flows within the organization.
2 Reflect on why these forms of communication can still be problematic in leisure service organizations.
3 What other forms of communication might be used to confront some of the problems faced by leisure service organizations?
4 Critically evaluate the workings of the 'grapevine' in an organization known to you. Is it usually your main source of information? How do you rate formal sources of communication?
5 Consider Case study 10.1 and make suggestions as to how the organization can improve the communication problems highlighted.

Case study 10.1

A willing pair of hands?

Karen is an undergraduate on a Leisure Management programme in a British university. She is close to the end of her course and has been considering her career after university.

Since joining the three-year course she has worked part time in one of the pubs in her university town. During vacation periods she increased the hours she worked in the pub, because this would help build up her savings for the next term. The pub is one of a branded chain of pubs run by a major licensed retail organization. During the three years she has worked for the organization, the licensed retail organization has not acknowledged that Karen is a student. In fact, the organization employs over 2000 students in its various brands yet has no record of who they are, or the courses on which they are enrolled.

The head office human resource management team is proud of their graduate development programme. Over recent years they have moved away from the 'one programme fits all' model and now they are able to create a programme that meets the individual needs of each graduate recruit. They aim to make their unit management team totally graduate driven within the next five years.

Although Karen has worked at the pub for three years, she has worked for three different pub managers, and has never met the area business manager or any other executive from the organization. The three managers who have been Karen's immediate line managers, have all expressed satisfaction with her work. Ted Smith the most recent pub manager has been in the pub for six months. Ted told his wife that, 'Karen is a real treasure, you can rely on her. She is quick to learn and flexible and great with customers. I wish they were all like her'. He is surprised one day when Karen tells him that she will be leaving in a couple of weeks when the course finishes.

She has enjoyed working for the pub to the extent that she has now secured a job on a graduate management training programme with a rival organization. She told her friend that she really wanted to build a career with the organization, 'I really liked working here, I understand the business and all my experience has given me lots of ideas for improvements. I thought if I became a manager I would be able to make some useful changes. I asked all my managers about how I could get on the graduate training programme, but none of them could help me. I even wrote to head office and just got a standard letter reply. Now I've secured a post with one of their rivals. It's a pity really'.

Effective communication in leisure service organizations

Organization management styles and culture will be set in a context that influences the dominant approach to communications within the organization. These were introduced in Chapter 9.

Command and control

Command and control organizations frequently involve dominant *tell* or *tell and sell* ways of communication. Instruction-giving involves mostly a downward flow of communication from managers at senior levels to frontline employees. Lateral communications will take place where managers or employees need to share information and upward communication will largely involve the flow of results. That said, the dominant flow is downward and 'one way'. It is these organizations that frequently experience communications difficulties and an appearance that they are 'faceless organizations with no soul' (Argenti, 1998: 202).

Consultation

Effective organization communication must be two-way and in a way that goes beyond merely passing on results. It is important that employees have opportunities to be consulted and to participate in some decisions. When managers consult with employees they will use various techniques to *tell and test* out possible solutions to problems or decisions, or *seek* employees' views before they make decisions. Even though managers continue to make the decisions, they will probably make more robust decisions once they have checked out the opinions and views of employees.

These consultative approaches using team briefing sessions, buzz groups or works councils (Lashley, 2001) have particular relevance to hospitality and tourism organizations where frontline employees are uniquely placed to inform management about customer responses to management policies or changes in customer taste.

A problem frequently identified by employees is that organizations do not encourage two-way communications. In some cases they operate a climate of fear that discourages the expression of views and opinions: 'Employees must feel secure enough in their position to ask questions and offer advice without the fear of reprisals from top management' (Argenti, 1998: 202).

The encouragement of effective two-way communications must begin with supervisors or frontline managers and their communications with employees. Several research projects in multi-unit leisure organizations demonstrate the key importance of unit managers in shaping the employment experiences and performance of frontline employees (Eaglen and Lashley, 2001; Eaglen, Lashley and Thomas, 1999; Lashley and Rowson, 2000). As with levels of training activity and staff turnover, effective communication will be enabled or hampered by the significance given to it and skills exercised by the immediate unit manager.

The quality of face-to-face communications is of much greater significance to employees than is any other form of communication. Unit manager training in effective communication is an essential ingredient of effective communication across the organization; 'Prior studies suggest that leaders can be trained to improve their language with significant positive impacts on subordinate outcomes' (Mayfield, Mayfield and Kopf, 1998: 236).

It is important that monitoring and management of unit manager performance also takes manager communication with employees into account.

Key point 10.7

As with other aspects of employee relations, managers will give priority to effective communication if they are made accountable for it.

The encouragement of more consultative approaches can be further reinforced by the use of meetings that bring together representatives of frontline staff and senior management:

- The works council approach widely practised in Germany and other mainland European countries provides an example of a device that creates a forum where employee views and suggestions are gathered (Lashley 2001).
- Less formal arrangements bring employees together with senior managers in such gatherings at dinners or lunches.
- Some organizations set up small groups of twelve or so randomly selected employees to meet with a senior executive (Argenti, 1998). The important point here is that the selection needs to be random and it must be clear that employees are free to speak frankly.

As with all forms of communication in organizations, employees soon get the message if the reality of management behaviour is at odds with the rhetoric of consultation and two-way communications; in other words, where consultation is just a public relations exercise and employees feel that managers are not listening to what they say.

Print media can provide a valuable form of employee communication, though their potential is rarely realized. Argenti (1998: 203) states, 'Unfortunately, a random sample of such publications turns up some very boring publications'. Often they communicate a public relations agenda that appears bland and unconnected to the reading material that most employees read in the newspapers. The secret is to give the organizational newsletter a newspaper feel, and to encourage some genuine debate with employees.

An honest debate that celebrates diversity suggests a maturity that can reinforce the willingness to learn from employees. Publications also play an important role in correcting rumours and misinformation that can be a feature of the 'grapevine'. They become essential in a crisis, because they provide a source of information that employees will treat as reliable if prior experience has confirmed that it can be relied upon.

In addition to newsletters, management can communicate with employees through memos and letters. Regular use of suggestion schemes can establish personal links between the organization and the employee. It is likely that employees will feel personally committed to reading the message, and the formality with which written messages are received helps 'the employee to feel more of an insider' (Argenti, 1998: 204).

Finally, visual communication made possible through information technology can provide opportunities for, say, video conferencing and for people in diverse locations to talk to senior managers. Some companies are using information technology to provide training support through their diverse organization structures, but few hospitality, leisure and tourism employers have used it to gather suggestions and ideas from the workforce.

Key point 10.8

Many leisure service organizations still see wisdom as solely located in senior management. This chapter argues that such organizations need to come up with communication strategies that tap into the collective wisdom of the organization as a whole.

Participation

A second grievance often expressed by employees in a variety of surveys (Lashley, 2001; Rodwell, Kienzie and Shadur, 1998; Senge, 1990) suggests that employees feel that they are not included enough in decision-making within the organization. Leisure service organizations faced with a need to gain competitive advantage have looked to techniques such as 'total quality management' (Demming, 1986), 'flat organization structures' (Lashley, 2001) and other 'best practices' (Rodwell, Kienzie and Shadur, 1998) to help improve service quality.

In all these cases employer organizations have considered employee participation in decision-making as a means of improving employee performance. Although some of the literature describes these participative approaches as involvement, the employee communication includes both *joint decision-making* where managers and employees make the decisions together, or *delegation* of decision-making to employees. In the latter cases communication focuses on boundary-setting and accounting for decisions made in a non-blame setting. Cotton (1993) found that direct forms of involvement were more powerful in their impacts on employee attitudes and performance than those that had a more representative nature.

Rodwell, Kienzie and Shadur (1998) suggest that teamworking, communication, and participation in decision-making are important components in improving employee performance, but these are mediated by levels of employee commitment, job satisfaction and stress. 'Teams in their many forms, have been found to create a broad set of positive changes in organizations. These benefits have included increased communication, increased innovation that can drive continuous improvement and increased work satisfaction' (Rodwell, Kienzie and Shadur, 1998: 279).

- Teamworking in the form of autonomous or semi-autonomous work groups can provide both mutual support and encouragement for team members.
- Communication is positively related to job performance though this can be mediated by communication overload.
- Communication is most effective when it is timely and appropriate, and enables the employee to develop a clear understanding of what is required of the job. Involvement in decision-making by lower-level employees can have a positive impact on service quality in leisure service organizations because frontline employees can quickly respond to customer service requests (Lashley, 2001).
- Decision-making involvement can also have a positive impact on employee satisfaction levels.

That said, the relationship between employee satisfaction and improved business performance is complex and may be impaired by work factors outside the control of the individual.

Key point 10.9

Leisure service organizations could benefit from forms of communication that allow the ideas and experiences of frontline staff to be made available to the organization as a whole.

The importance of line manager communications

Most employee–manager communications are likely to involve a range of different styles of communications. Managers need to be able to assess the nature of the styles of communication that they engage in with employees, and ensure that they are not locked into a style that is inappropriate for the context in which they work. Johlke and Duhan (2000) stress the fundamental importance of the effectiveness of these employee–manager communications. They suggest that, 'one of the most powerful and pervasive supervisory behaviours are the communications practices a supervisor uses with employees' (ibid.: 154). While this quotation, and their research, refers specifically to quality of communications between employees and their supervisor, it is important to recognize this as being concerned with employee and manager communication, the supervisor being the first-line manager.

Johlke and Duhan (2000) are particularly concerned with the impact of these communications in service firms where frontline employees are delivering the service to customers. They say that in industries such as leisure services manager interactions with employee, 'are able to directly affect employee job outcomes and therefore customers' service experience' (ibid.: 154). Specifically they suggest that supervisor and employee communications can have both positive or negative impacts on employee role ambiguity, employee satisfaction and job performance.

- Their research found that the frequency of supervisor communications had a positive impact on employee satisfactions, though not with employee job performance, though they quote other research where relationships have been found.
- Several studies (Marrett, Hage and Aiken, 1975; Mayfield, Mayfield and Kopf, 1998; Muchinsky, 1977; Orpen, 1997) found that the mode of communication in the form of informal, impromptu verbal and face-to-face communications had a positive impact on job satisfaction and job performance if it was associated with coaching in fast changing situations.
- The Johlke and Duhan (2000) study was unable to confirm this relationship, though service context is likely to be in important factor in so far as service interactions can be predicted and staff know what is expected of them.
- Where services are 'standardized' there may be less need for supervisor inputs because employees know what customers expect and how to meet their expectations.

- Clampitt and Downs (1993) also suggest that where employees 'know the job' frequency of contact between employees and supervisors has less significant impact on productivity, than where there is a high degree of variability in the work undertaken by employees.

Two-way communications between the employee and the supervisor is positively related to employee performance and satisfaction. Where employees are able to work and communicate with managers they are able to register more job satisfaction and effectiveness in the service encounter: 'Therefore supervisors may emphasize this particular communication practice by providing feedback to their employees and by seeking out, valuing, and (when feasible) acting on information and suggestions provided by service employees' (Johlke and Duhan, 2000: 161).

This links back to the issues discussed in the styles of communication discussed above. The research also confirmed that where service roles are somewhat ambiguous, both employee job performance and job satisfaction suffer. Following from this the researchers also suggest, 'an additional (albeit indirect) positive outcome of reduced ambiguity regarding customers may be decreased employee turnover' (Johlke and Duhan, 2000: 161).

Other research suggests a two-way relationship, that is, well-trained and satisfied staff are less likely to leave, and where turnover is high employees do not stay long enough to be trained (Eaglen, Lashley and Thomas, 1999).

Ultimately, the Johlke and Duhan (2000) research confirms that manager (supervisor) and employee communication does have an impact on employee satisfaction and job performance.

Frequent and informal, two-way communications reduce employee role ambiguity, increase employee awareness of customer and employer service expectations, improve employee understanding of promotion routes and sensitize them to the ethical issues related to their tasks. They conclude, 'Therefore, service oriented firms may wish to familiarize their managers with these different communications practices, to train them to use these practices effectively, and to evaluate and reward them on their ability and willingness to do so' (Johlke and Duhan, 2000: 162).

This latter point is important, because evaluation and reward of desirable managerial behaviour is fundamental to ensuring effective practice (Eaglen, Lashley and Thomas, 1999). Brownell (1991) draws similar conclusions, suggesting three steps:

1 Communicate detailed information as well as the big picture.
2 Talk with other managers – communicate horizontally.
3 Foster openness and trust.

Although conceptualized slightly differently, these authors are stressing the central importance of communications between managers and employees in service businesses such as those in leisure service organizations. Managers need to understand the need for, and limitations of, information flows upwards, downwards and laterally in their organizations. They need to adopt communications strategies that will ensure all organization members share information and communicate effectively across the whole organization.

Key point 10.10

Effective communication between managers and employees adopts a range of styles so that they are able to develop communications practices that improve employee satisfaction, encourage two-way dialogue, foster openness and trust, and reduce employee role ambiguity.

Communication and leisure service organization performance

The evaluation of organization of performance needs to consider a 'balanced score card' approach if it is to capture the benefits that effective communication can contribute. The balanced score card recognizes that the evaluation of organization performance needs to be viewed from the perspectives of different organization stakeholders. These are usually defined as customers, employees, shareholders and, sometimes, local communities. The balanced score card typically measures the organization from the perspectives of the three key stakeholders – customers, employees and shareholders (Table 10.1).

Stakeholders	Score card measures
Customers	Customer complaints received Praise received Mystery customer scores Internal customer audits Customer repeats
Employees	Employee satisfaction scores Retention rates Staff turnover rates
Shareholders	Increased productivity Reduced costs Increased sales Increased profit measures

Table 10.1   Organization stakeholders and balanced score card measures

Increasing numbers of leisure service organizations are using the balanced score card to evaluate organization performance (Eaglen, Lashley and Thomas, 1999). They recognize the integrity of factors that are likely to impact on business performance. Primarily, the success of the organization from a shareholder perspective is dependent on customer satisfaction and repeat custom, and this is dependent on employee performance and customer satisfaction. Effective communication in leisure service organizations is primarily likely to impact on employee performance, though effective communication with customers is an increasingly sophisticated activity.

Two examples:

1 Based on electronic analysis of customer purchase profiles, Tesco the UK retail chain, are able to produce 5000 different promotional leaflets that are sent to customers' homes. Through this technique they are able to target special offers at customers most likely to respond to the promotion.
2 It's A Scream is a chain of thirty British bars aimed primarily at students and young people gains access to customers' mobile phone numbers through a customer loyalty programme. Text messages are sent out every night inviting customers to come to the bar so as to gain entry to a prize draw where the top prize is £100.

The impact on individual employees will vary according to their 'involvement' in the work. Employee involvement in, and commitment to, alternative management styles such as empowerment vary depending on their commitment to the work and reasons for being in their job (Ashness and Lashley, 1995); that is, according to the significance of their jobs to them as individuals.

Frone and Major (1988) found that variations in responses to communications from nurse managers were dependent on their attitudes to their jobs. The more positive their attitudes to their jobs, the more likely they were to react positively or negatively to the quality of communications.

The model used by Clampitt and Downs (1993) allows for employees to register different levels of satisfaction across eight dimensions. Employees may, therefore, register different degrees of satisfaction or dissatisfaction with these different dimensions. Clearly, individuals may well vary in their assessment of these different dimensions, and it is likely that the most personal dimensions will register the greatest significance.

Clampitt and Downs's eight dimensions are listed in Table 10.2. The list includes items that relate to the general climate of communication in the organization, through to those aspects of communication that impact immediately on the employee's close working relationships such as with supervision and with co-workers.

The second issue flowing from the Eaglen, Lashley and Thomas research is that there is likely to be a two-step impact when considering the impact of management practice. That is, management improvements to communications with employees may not directly result in improvements to organizational performance, because the impact is directly on employees. Hopefully they change their behaviour and this leads to organizational benefits.

Figure 10.5 is developed from the model relating to training interventions but identifies communication issues that are likely to impact on employee behaviour. The factors are those broadly identified by Clampitt and Downs (1993). Any assessment of the communications environment considers the quality of communications through the array of factors discussed earlier.

- The quality of communications, in so far as these are assessed by employees individually, primarily have an impact on their levels of satisfaction and thereby with the way they work.
- It is important to remember that changes in employee work behaviour are likely to encompass an array of issues stemming from improved job satisfaction due to more effective communications.

Communications climate	Extent that communications environment stimulates employees and the general attitudes to communication
Supervisory communication	Upwards and downwards communications with job superiors – consulting and participative styles
Organization integration	The extent that individuals receive feedback about the immediate work environment
Media quality	Meetings well organized, written communications clear and succinct – volume at level needed
Co-worker communication	Lateral communication is accurate and free flowing – includes the working of informal channels
Corporate information	Broadest kind of information about the organization – overall policies and goals, and progress
Personal feedback	How employees are being judged and how their performance is being appraised
Subordinate communication	Upwards and downwards communications in so far as they impact on those in managerial positions – non-managerial employees no do not respond to these questions

Source: Clampitt and Downs (1993)

Table 10.2   Dimension of communication satisfaction

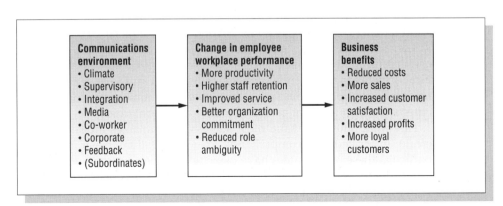

Figure 10.5   Communications impacts on business performance
Source: adapted from Eaglen and Lashley (2001).

- A reduction in staff turnover has important cost implications. Research by Lashley and Rowson (2000) demonstrates that staff turnover costs some leisure service organizations huge sums, though few firms in the sector account for it in financial terms. Similarly, a reduction in absenteeism of employees reduces the need to take on agency staff at inflated hourly rates, and has cost reduction implications.
- The work of Clampitt and Downs (1993) suggests that their interviews confirmed that employees believe that communications have an above average impact on productivity, though the quality of immediate communication processes are most powerful.
- The personal feedback factor has a significant impact on productivity in Clampitt and Downs's (1993) study. In addition, they comment on the relative importance of formal communications processes. They conclude, 'While employees in both companies indicate that they receive some useful communication from these sources, they suggest that other sources, such as the supervisor, were more critical communication concerns' (ibid.: 19). They add that in service sector organizations, these relational aspects of communication have greater impacts on productivity. They suggest that, 'The service industry demands that employees be more sensitive to customer needs because that is the measure of effectiveness' (ibid.: 22).
- The impact of dissatisfaction with particular dimensions of communications may also be a product of job design and employees' ability to self-evaluate performance.

Once an individual is experienced, he or she may need less feedback from supervisors, because they are able to evaluate their own performance in the job role. The significance of even these important communications dimensions may vary between employees, jobs and service being delivered.

Service contexts in which employees are meeting unusual or difficult to predict service needs may need more empowered approaches that require effective feedback after the event (Lashley, 2001). Chapter 9 deals with empowerment in more depth.

Gilsdorf (1998: 197) reported in her study that communications failures can have marked impacts on organizational profitability: 'At the high end of the cost scale, the incident narrated led to one medium-size company's having to cease doing business. One very large company saw an entire department collapse'.

This link between communication and the bottom line is being seen by many forward-looking companies as going beyond cost avoidance. Sanchez's (1999) study of 913 organizations suggests that there is an observable link between communications and organization success: 'Over the past four years, companies that identify communication skills as a core employee competence had an 18 per cent greater shareholder return. Furthermore, companies that have communication skills as a promotional criteria had a 24 per cent greater shareholder return' (ibid.: 13).

This work shows that the most successful companies are increasingly ones that create 'integrated and comprehensive communications programmes' (ibid.: 15). In particular these programmes have to include dimensions that incorporate individual, group and mass communications. Fundamentally, the conclusion is, 'In organizations with successful communications programs, senior management clearly has taken the time to articulate and support communications philosophies and strategies that flow from organizational values' (ibid.: 15).

Key point 10.11

There is wide range of evidence that effective communication improves organization performance, but effective communication impacts primarily on organization members and it is changes in work performance that ultimately impact on organizational performance.

Conclusion

Effective employee communication is an important feature of organization life. Employees report that they feel more satisfied when they have the information needed to be effective. Studies also seem to show that organizations that have clear, well planned and managed communications strategies tend to outperform their competitors. That said, it is important to start from a clear understanding of the principles of effective communication. At root, communication has only taken place when the subject has received and understood the message intended by the sender. Being aware of different ways of using language between sender and receiver, and how these may create barriers in large organizations, is vital for effective employee communication. The chapter suggested an important link between the approach to passing messages and the use of feedback, and the need to be aware of cultural differences with the workforce and management.

The chapter also suggests that organizations must look to the patterns of communications flows in the organization. Large organizations can suffer communications difficulties because of problems arising from formal communications flows moving upwards, downwards and laterally. Each can produce distortion if not carefully attended. In some cases, employees put more trust in unofficial sources of information such as the 'grapevine'. The grapevine is likely to be most highly regarded and widely used where official sources are less reliable. Several studies seemed to show that employee satisfaction and performance were linked to the quality of employee/manager communications. The immediate communication relationship between the employee and his or her manager seemed particularly important sources of employee satisfaction or dissatisfaction. That said, there are a variety of techniques that firms can apply to improve the general quality of communications. Most importantly, techniques that addressed employees' needs to be consulted and to be involved in decision-making were likely to increase employee satisfaction.

At an organization level, the general quality of communications has an important impact on performance in leisure service organizations. Employee performance has an immediate and direct linkage to customer satisfaction because frontline employees directly deliver the service to customers. In these circumstances, it is vital to understand the need to communicate effectively with employees. In particular, having a communications strategy that encompasses all levels of the organization, and that provides both training and incentives for managers are important ingredients that seem to give organizations a competitive advantage over other firms in their sector. Indeed, firms with systematic approaches to managing employee communications seem to outperform competitors in their sector.

Reflective practice

1 Define the communication process to ensure effective communication.
2 Identify the differences between communicating and effective communication in leisure service organizations.
3 Identify steps needed for improving communications.
4 Critically discuss the contribution that effective communications makes to organization performance.

Diversity management in organizations

After working through this chapter you should be able to:

- understand discrimination in the workplace
- define the barriers to organizational diversity
- identify approaches to diversity management
- critically discuss the ways organizations can prevent discrimination and encourage diversity.

Leisure service organizations employ more diverse workforces than traditional manufacturing plants of old. The emergence of service economies has changed the nature of work and the nature of those who work in service sector organizations. Leisure service organizations are more likely to employee large numbers of women, young people and members of ethnic minorities. Some leisure service organizations are renowned for poorly paid, low-skilled jobs with few career prospects (HtF, 2002). In some countries these organizations are likely to employ people who work part-time or on a casual basis to satisfy variations in demand for leisure services. In many ways they have been described as 'secondary labour market employers'. In other words, they recruit people whose labour skill base is low, plentiful and cheap, and who belong to groups in society which are perceived as having low value. This chapter will explore some of the issues related to prejudices that value some people's labour as having less value than others, and the implications this has for employing organizations.

Reflective practice

1 Reflect on some of the words that you have used to describe yourself in Chapter 7, and comment on how society and employer organizations are likely to assess the worth of your labour.
2 Consider a leisure service organization known to you and describe the most senior managers in terms of their group membership.
3 Highlight similarities and differences between the two lists.

Diversity in the sense that we are examining it here means differences between organization members and the impact that these differences might have on their experiences of work. Initially, we are therefore looking at differences on the basis of gender, ethnicity, colour, sexual orientation, religion, disability, age, education, personality, skills, trade union membership and work orientation. Increasingly, mature democratic governments are attempting to regulate the way that people in different groups are managed because there have been many examples of discriminatory practice, that is, consciously or unconsciously treating people differently because of the perceived variation in the value of their contribution to the organization. In the UK, for example, the Sex Discrimination Act 1975 and 1986, the Race Relations Act 1976, and the Disability Discrimination Act 1995 prohibit unequal treatment on the basis of gender, race or disability. Earlier the Equal Pay Act 1970 made it illegal to pay people doing the same job different rates of pay on the basis of gender.

Case study 11.1

Pauline was the first black receptionist appointed in a five-star London hotel. She told her friend about the assumptions that were made about her when she first started her industrial placement.

'Of course all the chamber maids are black, or the majority of them are black, and you know a couple of them said to me "Oh you're going to be our new housekeeper", so I said "No, actually I am going to be working in reception". And they said "Oh god, how long has it taken". This prompted me to ask my manager "Is there any reason why you've never had a black receptionist before?" and she said she'd never thought about it to any degree. She went on to tell me that the whilst she wanted to appoint me straight away, the General Manager checked with other staff about their reaction if I was put to work on reception.'

(*Source*: Guerrier and Adib, 2000)

Case study 11.2

Jill was determined to work in a top restaurant kitchen, and become a chef as a career. She undertook all the appropriate qualifications and was awarded excellent grades. When she tried to get a trainee job in suitable restaurants and hotels she found no one would employ her. She was frequently told that the work was too hard and unsuitable for her. After many years working in a senior executive dinning room in the head office of an international bank, and securing the top chef qualification, she managed to get a job in a five-star hotel kitchen. During the first six months her life was hell. She was given the worst shift patterns with long split shifts. She was often asked to carry heavy loads upstairs from the basement store. One day the Second Chef threw a side of lamb in her direction and told her to catch it. At no point did the Head Chef speak to her during this period, and she was required even to take meal and tea breaks away from the other kitchen staff. She often complained to her friends about how badly she was being treated, but she was determined not to give in. 'I'll show them', she said. One morning after about six months she came into work to find a note in her knife drawer. The note was from the Second Chef. It said, 'Well done, you've made it'.

(*Source*: Lashley, 1985)

Reflective practice

1 Using Case studies 11.1 and 11.2 identify the problems that they reveal.
2 What could be done to overcome some of the difficulties
3 Highlight some ways that an organization could monitor fair employment practice.

Dickens (1997) states that service organizations employ higher than average numbers of women, but they tend to be concentrated at the lower levels of the organization and are underrepresented in managerial posts. Even in organizations which are almost exclusively female, it is not unusual to find the most senior jobs filled by men (Lashley, 1985). There is evidence to suggest that women face difficulties in career advancement because of hidden discrimination – the glass ceiling is said to present an invisible barrier to promotion. The same sorts of barriers are often faced by people from ethnic minorities, where both the glass ceiling and the workings of perceived prejudices of customers often limit the numbers gaining work experiences in frontline service jobs.

Thus, ethnic minority members are often employed in low-paid, low-status jobs behind the scenes in leisure service organizations.

Key point 11.1

Leisure service organizations include people with diverse backgrounds and this can be the basis for unequal treatment within the organization and in society at large. Diversity management involves approaches to managing people from different backgrounds in a way that ensures equality of treatment and opportunity.

Over recent years governments throughout the world have begun to introduce legislation making discrimination on the grounds of gender, ethnicity and other reasons of diversity illegal. This is partly owing to changing perceptions of social justice; people have begun to see this unfair treatment of people for superficial reasons as unacceptable in modern democracies. In part, this is due to a growing politicization of people in discriminated groups who press for changes in the law (Ellis and Dick, 2000).

Leisure service organizations have in the past been as prone to uneven and discriminatory practice as other organizations. In recent years a growing number of firms have begun to change their policies and management as they recognize the public relations benefits of diversity management. Particularly as firms begin to move to more quality focused competitive strategies, they prioritize labour retention, skill development and being an employer of first choice. Diversity management is consistent with that approach.

Discrimination in the workplace

It is not possible to understand discrimination in organizations or in society at large without reference to social psychology. By its very nature prejudice involves making assumptions about the supposedly common characteristics of whole groups of people. Discrimination involves making prejudgements about individuals because of their perceived group membership. Discrimination involves:

1 *Stereotypes*: assumptions are made that all people belonging to particular groups are the same in character, beliefs, values, abilities and so on. Mullins (2002: 406) provides some examples:

   (a) *National*: all Germans are orderly and industrious.
   (b) *Occupations*: all accountants are boring.
   (c) *Age*: all young people are unreliable; old people don't like change.
   (d) *Physical*: people with red hair have fiery tempers.
   (e) *Social*: all unemployed people are lazy, and so on.

2 *Prejudgements*: individuals are judged solely on the basis of group membership, not on the basis of the individual concerned:

(a) *The halo effect*: whereby favourable judgements about a person are made on the basis of a small number of factors. The person appears smart and orderly or has the right sort of accent and it is assumed they will be a good worker or manager.

(b) *The rusty halo effect*: general judgements about the person are formed on the basis of one negative characteristic.

(c) *Perceptual defence*: there is a tendency to ignore, or screen out, that which threatens or challenges their point of view, or preconceived ideas and beliefs.

(d) *Projection*: attributing one's own feelings, motives or characteristics on to others. This can offer stress undesirable traits in others that they fail to recognize in themselves.

3 *Unequal treatment*: on the basis of these stereotypes and prejudgements, people are treated differently and unfairly. Legislation in this field has recognized two forms of unequal treatment to be outlawed:

(a) *Direct discrimination* precludes some people from certain jobs, roles or positions in the organization, whilst

(b) *Indirect discrimination* creates conditions or requirements for certain jobs, roles or positions which in their effect make it unlikely that certain groups will be able to meet the requirements.

4 Usually comments are made about others on the basis of in-group and out-group positions:

(a) *In-group* is the term used by social psychologists to describe the groups to which an individual claims to belong. In the exercise at the beginning of Chapter 7 you listed your in-group memberships. Usually these groups influence individuals' behaviour through the establishment of norms and pressures to conform. They encourage views about the out-groups.

(b) *Out-groups* is the term used to describe the groups to which the individual does not belong. Out-group members typically are seen as less than human, as having lower social values and morals or as having less worth. Religious conflict involves obvious dimensions of this negative labelling, but all discrimination involves it to a greater or lesser degree.

The social psychology of discrimination that supports the assumptions that *we are good* and *they are not good* is given added impetus when there are limited contacts between groups in society, and when groups have different power and status in society. It is not accidental, for example, that discrimination is often directed at those who are in minority groups.

- In many cases discrimination is more an outcome of assumptions about those who lead or occupy the dominant positions in society or in an organization.
- In part, Jill's experiences in Case study 11.2 were a result of her not being a male when it was assumed that only men can be chefs – only men can take it. Her trials and tribulations were about testing her ability to 'take it'.
- Thus the more it is assumed that jobs are the natural preserve of some groups, the more other groups are likely to be excluded from them.
- It is not surprising that discrimination at work mirrors discrimination and stereotyped assumptions at large in society.

The role of organizational culture

Organizational culture sets the tone of the norms, values, beliefs and attitudes expressed as the way 'we do things round here'. It is believed that organizational culture can create barriers to the equal treatment and advancement of all organizational members. In most European and US leisure service organizations the management is dominated by able-bodied, conventional, white middle-class males. Women, ethnic minority, gay and disabled people are excluded because they are not part of the dominant group (Ellis and Dick, 2000).

On one level this creates assumptions about who should be included in the powerful group. In other words, someone wishing to be promoted to the dominant group has to learn to act and behave like others in the group. But, fundamentally, they have to overcome the indirect prejudice that perceives them as different and not having the same worth. In addition, many women, ethnic minority members and others do not think of themselves in dominant positions because of the *demonstration effect*.

The demonstration effect is a by-product of the way people identify what people like them do. In other words, there are few, if any, people like me in dominant positions so people like me do not aspire to dominant positions.

Studies from around the world suggest that being promoted in many organizations is, in part, a function of networking with influential decision-makers. Networking occurs through having shared, educational backgrounds, social and/or recreational interests. For example, interests in golf or football can provide the basis for this networking that may exclude women and other groups because they do not have access to these opportunities to be included and to get noticed (Crompton and Jones, 1984).

It has been argued that the language of job roles and of organizational performance underpin and reinforce dominant group images. Thus, words like manager and manageress that stress the unusual female are examples of where the need to feminize a word implies the male norm. In recent years organizations have tried to move away from these terms. The language of competition and business is often couched in the words of warfare. It is not surprising the works of Machiavelli about the art of government and of Japanese Samurai on the arts of war have been used in recent decades as models for the instruction of organization managers. These images and language can be said to exclude women and others who do not relate to these aggressive and macho dimensions in organization culture.

According to Sheppard (1989), women managers find it hard to maintain a balance between maintaining their femininity and appearing competent and able to cope in this male culture. If they appear too feminine they may not be taken seriously, whereas overly male behaviour may create an impression of being of being too 'butch'. It is not unusual to find women managers heading up 'personnel' or HR departments while the operational or accounts departments are managed by men.

It has been said that the demands for more service-quality focused leisure service organizations will create the need for different forms of organization culture that will need to be more feminine. Competitive strategies based on improved service quality increase the perceived value of employees. Labour skill development, staff retention and an improved sense of commitment to the organization and its customers are likely to require more nurturing and participative styles of management. In these circumstances it is felt that women will progress quicker as their skills and characteristics are more valued within the dominant culture.

Socialization

Socialization is also seen as a cause of discrimination. Men and women, for example, are defined differently in the way they are socialized into their roles in society, and these are said to influence occupations that typically are perceived to be male and female. Thus men make up the majority of the workforce in manufacturing and craft jobs, whereas women are more likely to be found in nurturing and caring job roles such as nurses, cleaners or teachers. Organizations are being encouraged to attract men and women into non-traditional roles, but to some extent efforts are hampered by these socialization processes that begin in the home and in society prior to joining the leisure service organization.

Similarly, members of ethnic minority communities have a sense of self, that is, the person's identity beyond their psychological make-up. The way a person walks, talks, moves and looks all help shape a person's identity and create a sense of who they are and who they are not. Ethnic minority, social class, gender and sexual orientation differences, for example, involves aspects of these body language and identity features that influence the way individuals behave and the way others perceive them (Cassell, 1996). Furthermore, these influence how the people in roles, such as managers, are expected to look and dress and to appear at interview. Ellis and Dick (2000: 179) say, 'People do differ because of their gender, class, their religion or their ethnicity. These differences are not experienced in the same way by everybody, but as a group, minorities might find it hard to embody identities that they simply cannot assume'.

Apart from these classic examples of discrimination based largely on appearance or religious beliefs or sexual orientation, some leisure service organization members are discriminated against because of trade union membership. Those employees who choose to join a trade union and request that the trade union represents them can face unfair and unequal treatment. Patterns of trade union membership in leisure service organizations varies among countries and sectors. In the UK, for example, trade union membership across leisure services tends to be low compared with the national average (Lucas, 1995). Some sectors have higher than average trade union membership, while others are very much below average. Membership tends to be higher in leisure centres, canteens and school meals, and low in hotels, restaurants and pubs. In Germany trade union membership tends to be higher across the service sector than in the UK and there is an important legislative framework to support employee rights in all organizations.

Key point 11.2

Discrimination at work can be directed at people who are different to those who exercise power in an organization. Prejudging people on the basis of stereotypes can present barriers to equality of opportunity and limit chances of progression and career advancement.

Reflective practice

1 What problems does discrimination cause for an organization
2 List the reasons why organizations are increasingly concerned to promote equality of opportunity.
3 Highlight some ways that an organization could monitor fair employment practice.

Over recent years a number of factors have brought about increased concern that organizations address some of the discriminatory practices of the past:

1 Increased social awareness of the unfair treatment of people through discrimination has created a climate wherein firms are required to at least achieve some basic standards of social justice. Negative public relations effects are likely to ensue for a firm that is seen to practise discriminatory polices.
2 As a result of pressure group influence, firms involved in unacceptable practices have been targeted for campaigns aimed at damaging the business – product boycotts, leaflet campaigns and adverse publicity campaigns have all been used.
3 As a result of this increased public awareness and campaigns, governments across the world have introduced legislation that outlaws discrimination and requires organizations to practise equal opportunities.
4 Firms have increasingly recognized the links between investment profile and employment practice. Firms wanting to be seen as a good business investment have built a profile of a 'good practice' employer. A sound equal opportunities policy has been one of the cornerstones of this 'good employer' model.
5 As labour markets have tightened and employers have experienced recruitment problems many organizations have recognized that a range of 'minority' groups provide useful sources of recruits.
6 There has been a recognition that discriminatory practices may lead to a loss of talent to the organization because not all the available skills are being developed to the benefit of the organization.
7 Leisure service organizations aiming to build competitive advantage through service quality recognize and manage the contribution by all organization members. Developing the talents of the workforce is an important strand in quality competitive strategy.
8 Discriminatory employment practices can have a detrimental effect on employee commitment and morale, and can result in poor work commitment and conflict with the organization's employees.

This combination of 'push' and 'pull' factors has led to a number of approaches and variations in the degree that organizations have dealt with both discriminatory employment practice and equal opportunities practice.

Increasing workplace diversity

Approaches to promoting greater workforce diversity involve two broad strands. The first is concerned with steps to attract people into the organization from diverse backgrounds, and the second is about ensuring fair treatment of minority groups.

Recruitment strategies

One of the approaches to creating a more diverse workforce is by attracting people from the groups currently underrepresented in the workforce or in particular job categories. An organization attempting to have more women in management positions could undertake a number of steps to recruit more women into management jobs. Similarly, any other minority group can be targeted if it is felt that the current employment profile does not reflect the proportions required.

Positive discrimination ● ● ●

Positive discrimination is adopting an all-minority short list during interviews for the target jobs. In this way it is intended that the imbalances can be addressed quite quickly.

● This has been criticized as an approach because it can be counterproductive as existing organization members perceive the minority as having an easy entry to the posts concerned, which can stoke up negative feelings.
● If people are selected because they *are* members of the disadvantaged minority, is the approach any different from the discriminatory practice it attempts to correct?
● Positive discrimination has also been criticized where the person selected does not have the skills sufficient to perform effectively.

That said, in the right circumstances, where minorities have the required skills and organization members understand and accept the need for action to remove an injustice or to reflect more accurately the community in which the organization is located, positive discrimination can be effective. Ellis and Dick (2000) remind us that selection processes are not always rational and, despite all the justification, recruiters frequently select people whom they perceive to be like themselves.

Removing barriers to entry ● ● ●

Positive action to understand and then remove the obstacles that prevent under-represented groups from participating in the jobs or occupations under consideration is another approach the will result in more applicants and potentially more recruits.

● One of the problems faced by women with family responsibilities is that a break in service to have children often occurs at the age when a manager is building a profile for senior promotion. Many organizations (retailer Sainsbury's for example) now allow women to work in managerial positions on a part-time basis so that their skills are not lost and they are available for promotion when they pick up their career again. Other firms provide women with career breaks, but maintain contact and support skill development so that the manager is in touch with developments when she wishes to return to work.
● Flexible working practices aimed at meeting domestic responsibilities are another approach to assist employees with family responsibilities. This will allow fractional

contracts, or timetabling to meet school pick-up and holidays. In other cases, allowing time and space to attend regular prayer sessions, or other religious observance, can assist the recruitment of minority religious groups (Cooper and Lewis, 1989).

- In Germany annualized hours allow flexibility to meet responsibilities away from work within reasonable limits. They are required to work a set number of hours per year and can arrange to do these to suit personal circumstances.
- Home working for many employed in clerical or managerial roles in leisure service organizations is an option for many. The options made available by e-mail and other forms of computer based working mean that employees with family responsibilities can work from home and at times that suit them.
- Some firms have provided childcare facilities at the workplace. Nursery services are provided for employees' children. Although successful for head office staff, the provision of these services at all leisure service premises is regarded as costly and largely impractical.

Overcoming barriers to recruitment involves careful consideration of the needs of each group under investigation and the development of approaches that are tailored to the needs of each.

Equal opportunities policy ● ● ●

An equal opportunities policy is necessary as a statement of intent that may be helpful during recruitment and selection. The policy is a written statement of intent committing the organization to the eradication of discrimination and that also states the actions that can be taken by individuals who consider they have been discriminated against.

Where an organization is genuinely committed to making the policy effective it is likely to support the policy with a number of actions that involve monitoring, the recruitment and selections process, training and development within the organization, and minority profiles in roles, jobs and occupations throughout the organization.

Selection training ● ● ●

Selection training is concerned with raising awareness that the process can have discriminatory effects. Targeted at organization members typically involved in making recruitment and selection decisions, it involves raising awareness of direct and indirect discrimination when designing advertisements, selecting individuals and conducting interviews.

Minority monitoring ● ● ●

Minority monitoring involves a statistical check of minority membership across levels and jobs within an organization. This is particularly practised in large organizations in processes involved in recruiting, developing and managing minority members across the organization. For example, if it was found that only 5 per cent of Asians interviewed for jobs in the organizations were offered a permanent post compared with 40 per cent of white candidates, a need to scrutinize the selection process would be signalled.

Actively reviewing minority representation in different job roles is the first step in ensuring that recruitment and selection procedures do not prevent minority member recruitment in the short term, and it encourages more recruits in the long run.

Managing diversity

Increasing the diversity across the organization and aiming to end more overt acts of discrimination is only a starting point. The key issue is how to manage diversity within the organization. Interestingly, most of the literature about managing organizational diversity tends to come from North America, and a recent conference of European hospitality educators focused almost exclusively on diversity management with customers. These two observations reflect both the intensity of pressure group lobbying in the USA and the low level of awareness of these issues in Europe. Ellis and Dick (2000) suggest three broad approaches managing diversity:

- *Episodic approaches*: involve a one-off approach. Acts of racial discrimination are regarded as isolated incidents and down to individual actions. Managers may be sent on diversity seminars, but there is little integration of the approach into the culture of the organization. Training occurs but has little ongoing support through the organization.
- *Free-standing approaches*: the organization has an approach to managing diversity. It has policies and training programmes, perhaps policies include awareness-raising and steps that show how to deal with grievances over harassment or other discriminatory practices. The policies towards diversity management are not central to the organization or to its strategic direction. Diversity management is there but somewhat isolated from the organization and its objectives.
- *Systematic approaches*: these are likely to occur where there has been a high degree of external pressure for diversity management and the policy is central to the organization's strategy and mission.

Herriott and Pemberton (1995) suggest three culinary terms to describe different approaches to diversity management:

- *Vindaloo* involves companies recruiting people who are similar to those in the organization at present. Those who do not fit in leave. Ultimately, all organization members develop similar beliefs, attitudes and behaviours. Like the vindaloo, the ingredients start out differently but end up tasting the same.
- *Nouvelle cuisine* describes organizations that are keen to have minority members in prominent positions, but in reality minorities are underrepresented in the organization. Such organizations are often accused of tokenism. Like nouvelle cuisine, the appearance is more significant than the substance.
- *Sunday lunch* describes organizations that genuinely value diversity. Differences on the basis of different backgrounds and cultures or experiences and way of thinking

are seen as strengthening the organization. Like a British Sunday lunch, the ingredients are distinctive but contribute equally to the experience.

Key point 11.4

Managing diversity requires a strategic commitment to managing diversity in a systematic way that also recognizes that diversity of organization members adds strength the organization.

Reflective practice

1 Describe the difference between positive discrimination and diversity management.
2 Suggest some of the elements needed for successful diversity management.
3 How would you answer a senior colleague who suggested that customers are racists and prevent anti-discrimination employment practices?
4 Suggest a model for diversity management.

Kandola and Fullerton (1998) suggest an integrated approach that starts with an organization vision informing the organization; this has to include top management commitment. Flowing from this vision is an organizational audit of culture and needs to manage diversity which then inform the creation of clear objectives and targets. Accountability needs to be set and, importantly, reward systems need to reflect the management of diversity and achievement of targets. Effective communication based on empowerment and training ensure that all organization members understand the policy and targets. This requires co-ordinated effort and team approaches. Finally, the whole process is subject to evaluation and the management of the process.

Celebrating diversity

Given the models of thinking about organizations outlined in Chapter 1, organizations that recognize a plurality of interests are potentially able to benefit from this Sunday lunch model of organization diversity. A diversity of interests in the organization between people of different status in the hierarchy and of different skill sets will mean that different people may see the organization and its policies differently. Diversity management can assist organization managers to recognize the need to be a learning organization, that is, dedicated to learning across the organization as a whole.

The recognition of the different perceptions of frontline staff leads to consideration of more participative forms of organizational management and empowerment in leisure service organizations. In addition, the potential value of recognizing trade unions to represent organization members needs some brief discussion.

For leisure service organizations that operate the cost-driven employment strategies discussed in Chapter 1, trade union recognition has been seen as a threat to management control and the ability to treat labour as a resource to be bought and released as service demand required. Although the legislative framework for trade union recognition varies between countries, a dominant pattern in the UK and the USA has been to resist union membership where possible.

The following are perceptions of the union threat:

- a threat to management prerogatives
- increased costs through higher wages
- increased inflexibility as it is more difficult to sack unwanted staff
- more bureaucracy.

Although these views are likely to be held by organization managers with unitarist views that inform the cost-driven strategy, strategies that aim to build competitive advantage through service quality are likely to recognize a more pluralist, or even radical, perspective. That is, organization members are likely to hold differing, if not conflicting views. Organizations that recognize and learn from these differences are likely to be stronger and more able to survive.

As we have seen, a common problem faced in recruitment is that organization recruits can tend to select people like themselves. By implication this limits the challenge and debate that is essential in many leisure service organizations.

Trade unions in particular can provide a means of raising views and experiences of frontline organization members who may have insights that are not captured in some organizations.

Perceptions of union opportunity are that it:

- provides a means of raising issues and problems faced by organization members independent of the hierarchy
- is a vehicle for increasing organization democracy
- adds value through added workforce stability
- develops the skill base through improved stability
- improves service quality through participative culture.

The development of a culture dedicated to service quality improvement in a participative environment where diversity of views are seen as healthy and essential is a key feature of learning organizations. Diversity is thereby seen as a strength that builds business success.

Key point 11.5

Learning organizations celebrate diversity and encourage critical debate. Diversity management requires the development of a culture that supports critical debate.

The social psychology of togetherness

The social psychology of attitude change has recently been used to understand the shortcomings of the 'new industrial relations' (Kelly and Kelly, 1990) and to develop an understanding of the psychology of empowerment (Lashley, 2002). In these circumstances the link between inter-group attitudes within an organization, and the removal of divisive and discriminatory practice could be informed by an understanding of attitude change and behaviour.

Social psychologists have been interested in the processes involved in attitude change and the link to behaviour for a long time. Diversity management could explore changing attitudes of organization members through an understanding of these models of attitudinal change.

The workings of 'cognitive dissonance' mean that individuals find it difficult to hold attitudes that are in conflict with their behaviour. Social psychologists can help change the negative attitudes that people may have towards minorities, or between groups, through more co-operation.

Using models from social psychology, Kelly and Kelly suggest that the development of 'us and them' attitudes can be located in the relationships between group membership to which individuals belong. In most organizational contexts, operatives and managers belong to different groups. Any one individual belongs to an 'in-group' and through group membership develops attitudes to individuals who belong to other groups – 'out-groups'.

Attitudes are likely to become more conflictual in situations where there appear differences in status and rewards and in competition over scarce resources. Kelly and Kelly examine the conditions necessary to bring about change in these circumstances using the discipline of social psychology and attitude change in inter-group contexts.

Social psychologists highlight three possible routes to the change of attitudes which would reduce notions of 'us and them', and thereby the development of shared goals and commitment to the organization:

1 Increased inter-group (say worker–management) contact might help to shift attitudes away from stereotypes and produce more positive attitudes between inter-group memberships.
2 Attitudes between conflicting groups will change if the groups are both faced with a challenge or goal which is common to both groups and which neither group can overcome or achieve on its own. Clearly, appeals to common competitors, nationally or internationally, are attempting to persuade employees that they have a common goal and threat. These claims can be seen to be unconvincing in situations where the benefits and rewards of international success are perceived to be unequal or where employees have little choice in the initiative.
3 Changes in behaviour lead to changes in attitudes. Thus, more participatory management techniques which involve managers and employees working co-operatively may result in changes in attitudes, because it is difficult to maintain attitudes which are in conflict with behaviour. Thus cognitive dissonance theory suggests that when attitudes are in conflict with behaviour it is easier to amend attitudes to come into line with behaviour.

These three possible routes to attitude change are useful in showing how diversity management could help to change employees' attitudes to the organization, and thereby generate more employee commitment to the organization. They also suggest attempts to build more positive attitudes often fail due to the presence of several barriers to attitude change within the context in which these initiatives are introduced.

A *lack of choice* for employees about the adoption and form of the initiative, together with a lack of choice as to whether they are involved once the initiative is introduced, limits the power of persuasion. This lack of choice is unlikely to result in attitude change because cognitive dissonance mechanism will not come into play. Workers compelled to act in a certain way do not experience the psychological tension likely to result in attitude change. Thus, important ingredients in the successful introduction of discrimination management that results in attitude change have to be choice, negotiation and developing a sense of employee ownership of the changes.

Similarly, a *lack of trust* between the parties can be a considerable barrier to attitude change. Organizations that have experienced conflict between managers and the workforce, rapid organization change, say, via redundancies, or changes in working practices may find it difficult easily to overcome the hostility felt by members of different groups. Perceptions of the motives for the change are likely to be important. Thus, if one group, say, operatives, perceives the change as being brought in because the other group (management) genuinely want to improve relations and share benefits with employees, attitude change is likely to ensue. If employees feel that diversity management is being introduced as an underhand way of making them work harder or reducing costs, attitude change is less likely.

Unequal status in outcomes is a barrier to a change in attitudes. If employees perceive themselves and managers as having unequal status in the outcomes and management of diversity, employees are less likely to change attitudes. Similarly, if their perceptions of either the inputs in effort or benefits resulting from the initiative are unequal, attitude change is less likely to occur.

Lack of institutional support is also identified as presenting a barrier to attitudinal change. To be successful in generating positive attitudes and commitment to the organization, diversity management needs to be part of an established and long-term approach to the management of people.

This section has argued that for initiatives which claim to be about diversity management to result in employees changing their attitudes, social psychology provides a means of explaining how these processes might occur and identifies the obstacles which might prevent the desired changes taking place. That said, this is a somewhat mono-causal explanation of attitude development and behavioural change. It is possible to criticize the approach for having a simplistic view of organizational life and the conflicting pressures on managers. Hochschild (1993) criticizes social psychology for studying employee attitudes and job satisfaction while leaving employee emotions untouched. Yet the management of emotions and emotional labour is 'a large part of what trainers train and supervisors supervise' (ibid.: xii). It is true of organizational life in general, 'but is far more true in the rapidly expanding service sector – department stores, airports, hotels, leisure worlds, hospitals, welfare office and schools' (ibid.).

Key point 11.6

One of the aspirations for diversity management is that organization members develop positive attitudes and behaviours to other organization members. Those attempting to manage these changes needs to understand the means by which attitude change might take places as well as understand the barriers that might prevent attitude change.

Conclusion

Some leisure service organizations have, in the past, operated in a way that involved discriminatory employment practices. The use of cheaper and low-skilled, secondary labour market employees was consistent with cost-driven employment strategies that dominated some leisure service sector organizations. Poor development and the operation of internal labour markets that condemned some minorities to low-status, low-skilled and low-paid jobs was a consequence of this approach.

Societies around the world increasingly have recognized the discriminatory treatment of minority and low-status groups as unacceptable and have introduced legislation that prohibits discriminatory treatment at work. A legislative framework that makes discriminatory practice illegal on the basis of gender, ethnicity, religion and disability has brought about some imposed requirements for organizations to address recruitment and selection, and employment practice in general.

In addition, leisure service organizations have increasingly recognized diversity management as one means of building improved service quality through improved employment practice. Organizations that recognize uneven chances of promotion and development among sections of the workforce are deemed counterproductive in the long run.

As with other employment practices, diversity management will be most effective when it is recognized and managed as a core business activity. Senior managers need to put in place the necessary policies that manage and monitor diversity management. Essentially, the approach has to be systematic and based on a recognition that diversity of views, beliefs, attitudes and way of working provide opportunities for organization learning and growth.

Reflective practice

1 Define discrimination in the workplace and provide examples of groups most affected in an organization known to you.
2 What are the main causes of discrimination at work and what are the main barriers to be overcome when attempting diversity management.
3 Diversity management can be approached in a number of ways. Critically evaluate these.
4 Critically discuss the ways organizations can prevent discrimination and build diversity.

Management practice in leisure service organizations

- identify the key classical principles of management
- discuss the practical realities of management
- identify the predominant style of management in hospitality, leisure and tourism organizations
- discuss how the alleged 'uniqueness' of sector specific characteristics affects this management style.

A question we are often asked as educators is whether managers are born or made (which itself is similar to enquiring whether management is an art or a science). There is, of course, no simple answer although the very presence of management subjects in university and college *curricula* suggests that management can be learned. It may be useful to clarify our position using a musical metaphor.

Consider individuals who are described as having an 'ear' for music. This actually means that they have an innate ability to 'connect' with the subject matter and can often play instruments and compose without possessing any theoretical musical knowledge whatsoever. On the other hand, there are those who study first, and play and compose music subsequently. Both will become adept musicians eventually because each benefits from an understanding of underpinning musical theory.

The study of management is like this, with everyone benefiting from a knowledge of theoretical principles. However, there is no doubt that some 'successful' managers are mavericks, have little management training and delight in telling us so. The 'self-made man', often synonymous with the term 'entrepreneur', is a popular idea and we are often seduced into believing all we need for success is a raw willingness to work hard. Sometimes this may be the case but, in the main, our efforts need to be channelled and sound management training provides this focus.

Nonetheless, the fact that some individuals can succeed without formal training reveals the complex nature of management in practice. Indeed, attempts to find the 'Holy Grail' or a singular best way of managing organizations have proved ineffective. One only has to consider the sheer number of theories, texts and so-called management gurus (all white, Western and middle-class males of course) emerging over the most recent 100 years to realize the difficulties involved.

Using medicine as an analogy, compare a serious disease with a simple one; there are always more remedies and potions available for conditions which cannot be cured than those which can. Management is like this; there is no single 'cure' because the variables involved are overwhelming, complex and dynamic. However, a few principles of management have been identified (or at least advocated) but their effectiveness arguably depends on context.

In terms of management practice, additional complexity has been added to the situation due to the erosion of some traditional managerial roles. For example, recent changes and increasing competition have resulted in a virtual eradication of middle managers in many organizations. In this respect, operatives are filling this void and becoming newly empowered, enjoying involvement in organization-wide planning, decision-making and monitoring.

Global competition, economic downturns and specific events have also had significant and drastic effects on hospitality, leisure and tourism organizations. For example, there has been an unprecedented number of strategic alliances, mergers and acquisitions (see Chapter 5) creating an increasingly diverse workforce. While there is no consensus on the impact that globalization will have for those involved (Wahab and Cooper, 2001), managers can expect intra-cultural, attitudinal and aspirational differences amongst employees to be a major concern in an OB context.

Increasing productivity and enhancing competitiveness in this new frenetic trading environment means organizations must consider new ways to manage the dynamics of chaos and constant innovation. Many service firms now realize an effective way to establish competitive advantage is through their workers because they play a key role in differentiating the product. Indeed, it may be argued that frontline workers actually become the product given the emphasis on the intangible service element during delivery.

These so-called learning organizations tend to have flat structures, (see Chapter 2) are small in size and consider their employees as assets rather than costs. In this context, modern management must be adaptable and effective in problem diagnosis and implementing change programmes. Many enlightened (or third wave) organizations are currently addressing these challenges by adopting newer philosophies, including total quality management and organizational development.

While the various schools of management thinking have made significant contributions to the field, many are additions or augmentations of their predecessors. As such, to give you a real feel for management practice we introduce and compare an earlier or classical approach with a more contemporary perspective. Issues of future strategies as a response to globalization are also considered, including management of modern organizational structures.

In addition, some writers consider a number of unique characteristics to have had a key impact on the practice of management in the hospitality, leisure and tourism sector. Whether these factors are peculiar to this area is a matter of debate. Indeed, we contend that they are not but believe the argument sufficiently important to include them in this chapter.

Reflective practice

1 In groups of four, organize a debate around the question: 'Management: common sense or common myth?' Two of you should play the roles advocating the first or second of these positions.

What do managers actually do?

The *Collins English Dictionary and Thesaurus* defines a manager as someone who is an 'Administrator, boss, controller, organiser, supervisor'. Although this provides clues about managerial activities, it is cryptic and does not explain how they are best implemented or undertaken. However, most writers agree that managers are hired for what they know rather than what they do. In other words, managers realize the aims of the organizations through other people. Thus, the somewhat glib adage about 'not having a dog and barking yourself' may actually be a fairly accurate way to summarize the role of effective management (although the saying reveals a somewhat unfortunate view of workers).

So what does this mean in a practical sense? Mullins's (1996: 398) idea of management is helpful and contends that management may be regarded as:

- taking place within a structured organizational setting and with prescribed roles
- directed towards the attainment of aims and objectives
- achieved through the efforts of other people
- using systems and procedures.

Once again for our purposes this is helpful, but a more complete understanding of management is required.

Bartol et al. (2001) say much the same as Mullins but usefully divide it into categories. They regard management as the process of achieving organizational goals by engaging in the four major functions of planning, organizing, leading and controlling (ibid.: 5):

- planning is defined as the process of setting goals and deciding how to achieve them
- organizing is essentially the process of allocating and arranging human and other resources so that plans can be carried out successfully
- leading is explained as the process of influencing others to engage in the work behaviours necessary to reach organization goals (see Chapter 7)
- controlling is the process of regulating activities so that performance conforms to expected organizational standards and goals.

Reflective practice

1 You are the new manager of a local sandwich bar and are thinking about the activities you will be performing. It is clear that the activities will fall under one or other of the four major management functions discussed in this chapter. There is a list of some activities in Table 12.1; indicate which ones you believe are either planning, organizing, leading or controlling functions.

Both Mullins's (1996) and Bartol *et al*'s. (2001) notions are alike and expressed in terms similar to those used by the classical or scientific view of management. This perspective was first conceptualized in the early part of the twentieth century by Fayol (1949) and classifies management activity as forecasting, planning, organizing, commanding and co-ordinating.

Other writers have since contributed similar typologies but, from the 1960s onwards, people questioned whether managers were actually logical and scientific in their attitudes and behaviours. With hindsight it is probably fair to say that the classical approach was more an expression of idealism rather than practical reality. Mintzberg's (1973) significant contribution along with others including Kotter (1982), contends that in contrast to the classical view, managerial work may almost be considered random because of the unrelenting pace and pressure due to significant workloads.

Futhermore, he considers managerial work to contain variety, brevity and fragmentation where individuals only spend short amounts of time on any one issue and have little time for planning or thinking. Other factors identified in Mintzberg's (1973) study of chief executives include managers' preference for:

- current issues which are specific and non-routine, decision-making on an ad hoc basis
- verbal rather than written communication, solving problems face to face rather than via memos or reports
- spending time networking, and developing interpersonal relationships and political alliances.

Activity	Planning	Organizing	Leading	Controlling
1 Decide whether to open another sandwich bar				
2 Conduct a job analysis				
3 Check register slips to ensure correct prices are being charged				
4 Implement quality control procedures for raw materials				
5 Check that sandwiches are prepared on time				
6 Decide what new items to offer				
7 Hire experienced staff				
8 Determine profit margins for the next quarter				
9 Implement an employee incentive programme				
10 Prepare monthly staff rosters				

Source: adapted from Bartol *et al.* (2001: 28).

Table 12.1   Reflective practice activity

Key point 12.1

Management is the process of achieving organizational goals through others by engaging in functions of planning, organizing, leading and controlling.

Mintzberg's (1973) perspective of management 'under pressure' is certainly reflected in the situation in Case study 12.1. It shows an example of a manager's 'diary' to explain what this role entails in a medium-sized hotel.

Case study 12.1

A day in the life

8.30 a.m. – Arrived at work bleary-eyed due to the late finish of wedding party the night before – 3 a.m. – and made myself pot of tea and some toast.

9.00 – Cashed up bar takings from day before.

9.15 – Received phone call from local tourist officer to arrange meeting to discuss new resort brochure targeting conference market. Sharp intake of breath when discovered no government funding for any part of the project.

9.30 – Room attendants arrive (late again and only seven of ten employed) and await any special guest requirements from me.

9.45 – Breakfast over without many mishaps, tour guides speak with me about places to go during their stay.

10.00 – Receptionists arrive which frees me to do a 'tour of duty' around the hotel.

10.05 – Entered kitchen with hope of speaking with head chef about inventory for forthcoming week only to discover two trainee chefs had failed to turn into work on time on account of some vigorous socializing the night before. Result – slow production of meals in kitchen leading to misunderstandings and friction between kitchen and foodservice staff. Recommendation – written warning to absentee chefs – already happened before. How will this affect staffing profile if dismissed?

10.30 – Spoke with restaurant head about friction between two departments and requested all staff attend meeting scheduled for 5.00 p.m. today.

11.30 – Visited head bartender in public bar about previous night's activities. Two fights broke out, police were called, no serious injuries. Bar looks like a bomb's been dropped. Contact housekeeper to tidy up.

11.45 – Return to office to deal with first of many irate complaints about this morning's tardy breakfast service.

11.50 – Phone call from utility company offering cheaper gas and electric, provided I make an upfront payment of $1,500AUD

12 noon – Mended two upright vacuum cleaners after complaints from room attendants that they weren't powerful enough.

12.30 p.m. – Another complaint from guests about poor breakfast service.

12.45 – Visit from tour operator wishing to check the facilities, operations, etc. for inclusion in their brochure for next year. Walking tour of the hotel, sample menus, tariff.

12.50 – Another complaint about breakfast, all I need when discussing future business.

2.00 – Phone call from one of last night's wedding party to explain that they had slipped over in the ballroom because the floor was too highly polished. Intention to prosecute – will have to get some witnesses to refute claims (among other things).

2.30 – Message from elderly resident that husband isn't feeling too well, has a history of heart disease. Called doctor, spoke to a very rude medical secretary. Doctor arrives one hour later and pronounces man dead at 3.40 p.m. I sit with bereaved for as long as I can and try to make the appropriate noises. I contact relations who plan to arrive today to collect wife.

4.00 – Bank manager calls inviting me to meet to discuss my rationale for financial plan for construction of gymnasium and swimming pool in hotel.

5.00 – Sit and wait for chefs and foodservice staff to turn up to meeting. Only head chef and restaurant head show. Meeting abandoned after brief discussions – waste of my time.

6.30 – Dinner service begins. Walking tour to meet and speak with people, without interrupting the flow of operations too much.

7.00 – Called into kitchen because fight breaks out between two kitchen porters. Both walk out, I have to do some dishwashing for a while – the pleasures of management.

Consistent with Mintzberg, the above situation suggests that the reality of management is characterized by brevity and fragmentation. In an attempt to provide a robust classification system for the plethora of management activities, Mintzberg (1973) groups them under three overall roles. Figure 12.1 shows these classifications together with some associated behaviours.

Mintzberg concedes that these roles are:

- arbitrary
- difficult to isolate in practice
- only one of many ways to categorize the roles of management.

For example, a recent television broadcast of a tourism-orientated programme (*Passport to the Sun*, 2002) featured tour managers categorizing their jobs as

ROLE	DESCRIPTION
Interpersonal	
Figurehead	Performs symbolic duties of a legal and social nature
Leader	Builds relationships, communicates with, motivates and teaches subordinates
Liaison	Maintains networks outside workplace who provide help and information
Informational	
Monitor	Seeks internal and external information about issues affecting the organization
Disseminator	Transmits information obtained internally or externally
Spokesperson	Transmits information about the organization to outsiders
Decisional	
Entrepreneur	Acts as initiator, designer and encourager of change and innovation
Disturbance handler	Takes corrective action when organization faces important unexpected difficulties
Resource allocator	Distributes resources of all types
Negotiator	Represents the organization in major negotiations affecting the manager's area of responsibility

Figure 12.1 Mintzberg's ten managerial roles
Source: adapted from Mullins (1996: 415–16).

dynamic and alternating between 'social worker', 'minder', 'lawyer', 'doctor' and so on.

Similarly, this role flexibility is implicit in Stewart's (1982) model of managerial work and behaviour. Essentially, the construct provides a way of thinking about the nature of management jobs and the way in which they are undertaken. After reviewing evidence, Stewart (1983) concludes that far from planning, organizing, co-ordinating, motivating and controlling, management is a human 'whirlwind' of activity. His construct enables generalizations to be made about all managerial jobs according to three categories of demands:

- what must be done
- constraints – internal or external which limit what can be done
- choices – activities managers are free to do, that is, working differently than each other.

Bartol *et al.* (2001) contend that managers cope with the complex nature of their jobs by setting their own agendas which they describe as a loosely connected set of tentative goals concerning long- and short-run job responsibilities.

The practice of management, while not exactly haphazard, would appear to be a conglomerate of activities which may be broadly categorized using any number of appropriate role descriptors. Individuals can adopt any or more than one of these non-exclusive roles at any time.

This suggests that in practice, management is far from the convenient and neatly ordered model suggested by the classical school. There is no doubt that managers plan, organize, lead and control (co-ordinate and motivate) but do so under situational, operational and contextual constraints. Nonetheless, to gain further understanding of the management process we now focus on other issues, beginning with the organizational levels at which managers may be appointed.

Key point 12.2

The activities of managers are wide and varied and may be classified into arbitrary and non-exclusive roles of interpersonal, informational and decisional.

Management levels

Managerial jobs vary considerably in organizations, but common to all is job differentiation by hierarchy and scope of responsibility (see Chapter 2). Often these criteria depend on organizational size. 'Small' organizations have fewer levels of hierarchy and managers are responsible for virtually all aspects of the organization.

It is not difficult to imagine the vast number of roles occupied by the owner/manager of a small restaurant for example. Large organizations cannot be managed effectively by one individual, and the increasing complexity is divided into hierarchical and horizontal (or functional) sections.

Each level has a range of managerial jobs differentiated by responsibilities associated with each area. For example, in the hospitality, leisure and tourism sector the job of accommodation manager is at the same level in the vertical hierarchy as the food and beverage manager (functional).

The responsibilities of each will differ (horizontally) according to the specific requirements of providing accommodation or catering services. Figure 12.2 shows a typical hierarchy of managerial levels.

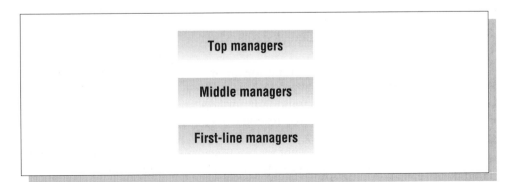

Figure 12.2 Managers by hierarchical level

Figure 12.2 is self-explanatory with 'Top managers' residing in the higher echelons of the organization structure. In short, these individuals have the responsibility for:

- making strategic or organization-wide decisions
- planning and working with upper layer of middle managers to implement and control organizational progress
- establishing policies and procedures and they have a range of titles depending on the organization in question. Usually these include 'general manager', 'director', 'president' and so on.

'Middle managers' occupy all levels of management between 'First-line' and 'Top'. These managers tend to be responsible for managers at lower levels of the organization. Middle managers recently have been removed from many organizations in an attempt to save costs and improve communications (Labich, 1995). Handy (1984) warned that that this would result in extra workloads for remaining individuals and the need to develop skills of delegation and team-building to manage newly empowered workers (who are effectively undertaking some middle management tasks themselves).

According to Bartol *et al.* (2001) there is now less distinction between managers and employees at this organizational level, with more emphasis on peer networking, increased access to information and empowerment. Middle management titles typically include 'manager', 'duty manager' and 'deputy head'.

'First-line managers', or supervisors, occupy the lowest organizational level and are responsible for:

- day-to-day job tasks
- other work procedures of operatives.

As with middle managers, the roles and responsibilities of supervisors are gradually being supplanted because of increased employee autonomy (Bartol *et al.*, 2001).

Is the management process different at each of these three hierarchical levels? The answer to this question is 'yes', and they can be traced to the functions of management we introduced earlier in this chapter. These functions are like those posited by the classicists and are, namely, planning, organizing, leading and controlling. Each hierarchical level responds and reacts to different environmental and organization pressures with each having a different function. Bartol *et al.* (2001) summarize the evidence and conclude the following:

- planning – more important for top managers because they determine the organization's overall direction
- organizing – more important for top and middle managers due to allocating and arranging resource responsibility (but can also be done by frontline managers)
- leading – more important for frontline managers since they are in charge of service production and rely more on communicating, motivation, directing and supporting than other levels (see Chapter 7)
- controlling – similar for all levels of management.

Key point 12.3

With the gradual erosion of organizational layers, remaining middle managers now have more responsibility and require proficiency in delegating responsibility, empowering workers, team-building and leadership.

Management skills

In order for managers at all levels to perform effectively they require appropriate knowledge and a number of key skills falling into three categories: technical, human and conceptual. Like the above management functions, each hierarchical level typically demands these skills in different proportions.

Technical skills reflect understanding and proficiency in a specialized field and are usually in demand by first-line managers. Until recently, most writers subscribed to the view that 'human skills' or the ability to work well with others was maximized at middle management level.

As we have seen, the demise of middle management has almost unified the need for these skills at all hierarchical levels of the organization. Indeed, it may be argued that this was always the case because all managers achieve their goals through other people; the contemporary business climate has simply added another dimension.

Finally, conceptual skills are also fundamental for managerial effectiveness and are normally required at top management level. These may be explained as an ability to identify relationships among component organizational parts, to visualize the organization 'holistically' and to understand how it fits into a wider industrial and global context.

Demand for the above skills is by no means prescriptive and it is almost certain that individual organizations (even within the same company) will prioritize them differently. For example, Case study 12.1 clearly shows that the general manager requires technical, human and conceptual skills, with an emphasis on the former two.

In addition, creativity among first-line and middle managers is also important. Some strategic decision-making should be delegated to lower levels for reasons other than simply empowerment.

First-line managers are often young and inexperienced and, therefore, have no historical precedents to restrict their decisions or ideas. Solutions are more likely to be novel and creative because the process is unencumbered by 'safe', proven or traditional solutions.

In the current global and competitive climate, innovative or entrepreneurial management thinking (more correctly known as intrapreneurial) is at a premium. Proactive organizations would be wise to actively seek participation and develop these creative skills among their managers. The innovative process typically involves individuals at various levels occupying three entrepreneurial roles of:

- 'idea champion' – a person who generates or believes in the value of a new idea and supports it despite potential obstacles
- 'sponsor' – a middle manager who recognizes the significance of an idea, helps secure resources for its development and implementation

- 'orchestrator' – a top manager who explains the need for innovation, provides funding and creates incentives, and protects 'new ideas people'.

Key point 12.4

'New' managers should be encouraged to participate in strategic decision-making and problem-solving because they are less encumbered by traditional or 'safe' historical ideas and solutions.

Reflective practice

1 The key difference between entrepreneurs and intrapreneurs is that the former are self-employed while the latter are paid company employees. Although the element of 'risk' is often greater for entrepreneurs, other characteristics are similar. The questionnaire in Table 12.2 is designed to see whether you have some of these entrepreneurial/intrapreneurial traits.

Count the number of 'Yes' answers and award one point for each. A score of 17 or more suggests you have the drive to become an entrepreneur – the desire, energy and adaptability to make a viable business venture successful. A score of between 13 and 17 suggests an absence of entrepreneurial drive. While you may have the ability, make sure you can accept all of the problems and headaches that accompany the joy of being your own boss. If you scored less than 13 you are unlikely to become an entrepreneur, although you might think about the possibility occasionally.

The whole area of innovation, change and organizational proactivity is fast becoming standard fare on business programmes in many universities. Essentially, this perspective holds organizations to be:

- dynamic
- in continuous interaction with external forces
- varying but all firms must have the capacity to adapt and consider 'new' ways to manage organizational change.

Moreover, in the future, hospitality, leisure and tourism firms will face increasing global competition with companies more likely to be operating overseas. For example, managers will be required to have a greater knowledge of global issues, including international market and human resource diversity.

In an OB sense, an understanding of increasing cultural diversity among workers is paramount for reasons of increasing productivity and organizational 'health' or employee wellbeing. In addition, managers with the ability to understand and anticipate employee attitudes and aspirations creates a self-perpetuating cycle of enhanced reputation, thereby improving attraction and retention of talented workers and minimizing the problem of high labour turnover in certain hospitality, leisure and tourism organizations.

Can you start a project and see it through to completion in spite of a myriad of obstacles?	Yes	No
Can you make a decision on a matter and then stick to the decision even when challenged?	Yes	No
Do you like to be in charge and be responsible?	Yes	No
Do other people you deal with respect and trust you?	Yes	No
Are you in good physical health?	Yes	No
Are you willing to work long hours with little immediate compensation?	Yes	No
Do you like meeting and dealing with people?	Yes	No
Can you communicate effectively and persuade people to go along with your dream?	Yes	No
Do others understand your ideas and concepts easily?	Yes	No
Have you had extensive experience in the type of business you wish to start?	Yes	No
Do you know the mechanics of forms and running a business (tax, payroll, income statements and balance sheets)?	Yes	No
Is there a need in your geographical area for the product or service you are intending to provide?	Yes	No
Do you have skills in marketing and finance?	Yes	No
Are other firms in your industrial classification doing well in your geographical region?	Yes	No
Do you have a location in mind for your operation?	Yes	No
Do you have enough money to fund the start of your business or have access to it through family and friends?	Yes	No
Do you know the necessary suppliers for your business to succeed?	Yes	No
Do you know people with the skills and talents you lack?	Yes	No
Do you really want to start this business more than anything else?	Yes	No

Source: adapted from Hisrich and Peters (1998: 32).

Table 12.2 Entrepreneurial assessment quiz

Many firms are adopting philosophies of

- 'total quality management' (TQM – see Chapter 9)
- 'organizational development' (OD)

to address the above issues. Briefly, OD may be explained as an organization-wide planned effort to deal with change and increase effectiveness and 'health' through planned interventions in organizational processes using behavioural science knowledge (Sanzgiri and Gottlieb, 1992).

In essence, both TQM and OD are not new and were advocated as early as the mid-1960s by 'open systems' or 'socio-technical' theorists. However, the novelty lies in the overall tacit acceptance of the need to change and renew for organizational survival. In a practical sense, Stewart (1993: 66) provides a useful summary of this imperative: 'Call it whatever you like ... re-engineering, restructuring, transformation, flattening, downsizing, rightsizing, a quest for global competitiveness . . . it's real, radical and it's arriving every day at a company near you.'

While recognizing the individual nature of organizations and thus management practice, Harvey and Brown (1996) consider successful firms of the future to share the characteristics shown in Figure 12.3.

'New' organizations
- Faster response to environmental shifts
- Quality conscious
- Employee involvement
- Customer orientated
- Smaller and more flexible

Figure 12.3 Changing organization of the twenty-first century
Source: adapted from Harvey and Brown (1996: 9).

Interestingly, it is not too difficult to identify some of these characteristics among hospitality, leisure and tourism organizations. Nevertheless, Williams's (1998) study of service quality in the UK leisure sector (theatres, art galleries, museums, leisure centres, golf courses and amusement parks) reveals an absence of the philosophy, especially among senior managers. Instead, compromise and a focus on short-term financial return tend to dominate organizational cultures.

On a positive note, Ridley's (1995) review of research into business cultures in hospitality, tourism and leisure organizations suggests they are seeking competitive advantage through service quality, customer orientation and through their employees. However, the extent to which they are implementing related policies and procedures is unclear.

Key point 12.5

For future organizational success, employees should be recognized as assets rather than costs and as playing a key role in establishing competitive advantage through practices of TQM and OD.

- Management in practice is about achieving organizational goals through others.
- It is a multidimensional activity which can be understood as a series of non-exclusive roles typified by high pressure and frenetic activity, and requiring a number of management skills. These include the ability to think creatively, to interact and deal effectively with people and an understanding of technical aspects of specialized fields.
- Until recently managers were defined as either top, middle or first-line. However, these roles are changing, with middle managers being eroded partly to increase

efficiency but also to improve effectiveness through better communication, more teamworking and increased employee autonomy.

- Increasingly, 'learning' service companies now recognize their workers as assets rather than costs and, consequently, seek competitive advantage through human resources.
- In an attempt to cope with an increasingly dynamic and competitive global environment, intrapreneurism and innovation should be encouraged among employees. According to Peters (1993) these measures are crucial, given the unpredictability of future trading environments. In addition, Peters comments that future organizational success depends on strategies characterized by quality, innovation and flexibility.

Interestingly, a key defining feature of many hospitality, leisure and tourism organizations is their ability to be flexible in response to cyclical demand patterns. Indeed, some writers consider this one of several unique features of the sector. This perspective contends that several 'special' characteristics influence management practice in these organizations. Whether they are unique or special is a matter of opinion, but the basic tenets are discussed below.

Reflective practice

1 Using organizations with which you are familiar, argue for or against the above 'uniqueness' thesis.

Unique characteristics?

Collective 'wisdom' holds the factors shown in Figure 12.4 to be unique and collectively responsible for producing a management style in hospitality, leisure and tourism organizations which is predominantly despotic and non-supportive.

Training, semi-skilled jobs and labour turnover

Some managers argue that training workers is not worthwhile because jobs are 'semi-skilled' and do not require lengthy and complex instruction. Moreover, even if employees are trained, their skills will benefit other employers due to high levels of labour turnover in the industry and because they are 'generalizable' (a standard set of skills applicable to similar jobs across a range of establishments).

One could reasonably argue that training is an expression of interest or investment in employees; if none is offered, employees may feel undervalued and quit in any case. Furthermore, pay is also an expression of reward for effort, competence and skill. If little training is required because jobs have been semi-skilled, pay will be correspondingly low. Paying low wages sends a negative message to workers, which in turn may cause them to quit their job.

Hospitality, Leisure & Tourism Series

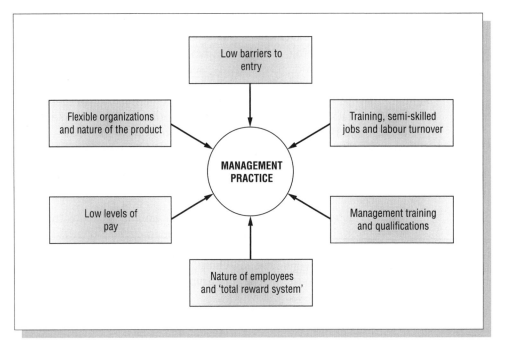

Figure 12.4 Factors influencing management practice

Nature of employees and total reward system

Some writers hold that employees in the hospitality, leisure and tourism sector (particularly in the former industry) are in some way marginal or different from other workers. They have been described as deviants, non-conformists and affected by dishonesty and delinquency, and are alleged to enjoy environments where transient relationships can be made (Mars, Bryant and Mitchell, 1979; Whyte, 1948). These depictions are linked to the alleged 'total reward system' said to exist in hospitality organizations. In short, Mars and Nicod (1984) contend that hospitality workers are dishonest and because of low wage levels, engage in clandestine activities to enable more appropriate rewards for their efforts. Both of the above situations could help explain high levels of labour turnover.

A less extreme, but consistent, perspective is adopted by Ball (1988). His UK-based study of tourism (and agricultural) employees suggests that both industries are dominated by a seasonal workforce which, in fact, prefers to work on a temporary or short-term basis. It seems likely that both employer and employee perspectives contain some 'truths' in the search for an explanation of labour turnover.

Flexible organizations and nature of the product

The way in which workers are scheduled or contracted to meet cyclical demand patterns for services eventuates in mass redundancies at the end of every busy trading period.

- The apparently seamless practice of 'hiring and firing' is perfectly legal and common in the hospitality, leisure and tourism sector.
- Employers argue that this enables them to remain viable during the quiet 'off' season.
- With effectively no employment protection (including no union representation) employers can terminate these contacts at any time.
- From the seasonal employee's perspective, it means job insecurity, low pay and poor working conditions, especially in comparison with year-round or core workers in the same organization.
- The usual justification for these impoverished conditions is that seasonal or peripheral workers undertake less important work than core employees and should be rewarded accordingly.

As we saw in Chapter 3, this is not the case in service organizations because many peripherals perform a crucial role at the frontline or customer interface. Thus, 'poor' seasonal employment contracts may fall significantly below the justifiable expectations of peripheral workers.

Management training and qualifications

Other factors said to affect management style in the hospitality, leisure and tourism sector include the:

- operational focus of organizations
- unique training and educational backgrounds of managers
- ease with which individuals can purchase and operate their own establishments.

Each of these factors is outlined below, beginning with operational bias.

Mars and Mitchell (1976) comment that managers roll up their sleeves and work alongside operatives in order to cope with fluctuating demand patterns for a perishable product. Guerrier and Lockwood (1989) make similar comments, as do Prais, Jarvis and Wagner (1989: 161): 'British hotel managers allow themselves to be preoccupied with routine duties and feel the need to be there in case of any problem.'

Guerrier (1999) points out that this situation prevents employees from solving their own problems. She also questions the rationale of the 'outmoded' European training tradition which requires managers to possess extensive craft skills as opposed to that of North America which does not (ascribing the latter system to its own tradition of service branding and standardization beginning in the 1950s).

A decade earlier Witt and Witt (1989) made similar comment. In an earlier study of hospitality managers, Guerrier (1987) also holds the 'craft-based' training perspective responsible for producing insularity among managers; with the consequence that hospitality managers are recruited from vocational courses rather than from the general graduate population. In addition, they belong to their own management association (the Hotel and Catering International Management Association) rather than to general management associations which prevents idea sharing and the proliferation of good practice. She comments: 'The notion of the manager as a "generalist organization man" seems to have been less successful in supplanting the notion of the manager as the superior craft specialist than in other industries' (ibid.: 130).

Some writers consider the requirement for separate development of hospitality managers (for example, see Nailon, 1982) necessary because of alleged industrial uniqueness. Proponents consider that the provision of accommodation and food and beverage away from home places distinct demands on managers.

The above is explained as the requirement to manage restaurants, reception and kitchens simultaneously while delivering a perishable product. It is therefore argued that managers need in-depth technical job knowledge to ensure the consistent delivery of a quality product. Levitt (1972: 41) argues against this and makes the following comment about service industries in general: 'Purveyors of service think that they and their problems are fundamentally different from other businesses ... these distinctions are spurious ... everyone is in service.'

Baum (1989) warns that overemphasis of these alleged unique characteristics may be at the expense of sound management principles. Moreover, Parsons and Cave (1991) maintain that the 'uniqueness' position may be damaging to the industry at large because it allows the performance of incompetent and 'amateur' managers to go unchallenged.

On a positive note, Gilbert and Guerrier (1997) looked at ways in which the perceived role of UK-based hospitality managers has changed and concluded that they are becoming more consistent with that of managers in other industries:

- working in delayered organizations with reduced hierarchy
- expected to meet performance targets
- expected to be better educated
- expected to be team managers and facilitators leading empowered staff, rather than autocrats.

Low barriers to entry

Another characteristic of a large segment of the hospitality, leisure and tourism sector is the ease with which individuals can own and operate their own business. There is no requirement for qualifications or professional memberships, so anyone may own and operate an establishment for any reason without management skills, experience or expertise.

Unsurprisingly until 1994, only 12 per cent of hospitality managers were qualified at the appropriate level in the UK (HCTC, 1994). Wood (1994) thinks this, together with relatively inexpensive start-up costs, helps explain the practice of hands-on management; noting that 70 per cent of all hotels are owner operated.

In sum, it is alleged that this combination of contextual factors affects a management style that is predominantly despotic and operationally focused. It suggests that managers operate at the mercy of uncontrollable variables which they seem unwilling to manipulate.

In independent small to medium-sized organizations this is a reasonable response because often establishments are undercapitalized due to limited resources. Thus, reactive 'fire fighting', thinking one one's feet, crisis management and other practices are understandable.

However, any self-respecting manager would probably disagree with the idea that they simply react, puppet-like, to the ebb and flow of the trading environment. It is more likely that these external characteristics provide constraints, with some being more difficult to manage than others. Indeed, to suggest otherwise would be to ignore key management decision-making processes.

Key point 12.6

Characteristics alleged to differentiate the hospitality, leisure and tourism sector from others include the nature of the product, management training, organizational structures, employee attitudes and the total reward system, and low barriers to entry.

Reflective practice

1 Having read the 'unique characteristics' section of this chapter, repeat the last Reflective practice exercise.

Conclusion

Management may be described as achieving organizational goals through others. It is complex and embraces activities which may be categorized according to a variety of non-exclusive arbitrary roles. The practical constraints of managing organizations clearly suggest that the original thesis proposed by early classicists was fanciful and unrealistic. However, some of their tenets are reasonable and help us to understand the job of manager. Thus, dimensions of planning, organizing, leading and controlling present themselves, but do so under situational, operational and contextual constraints.

Managers defined as either top, middle or first-line have been affected by recent changes; this is particularly so for middle managers. Due to imperatives of increased productivity and improved communication, these individuals must now be skilled in other areas such as team-building and membership and delegation of responsibility (empowering workers).

Service companies increasingly recognize that an effective way to establish and maintain competitive advantage is through their workers. In other words, they must be perceived as assets rather than costs. One way of doing this is through creating opportunities for innovation by encouraging intraprenuerism. According to Peters (1993) these measures are crucial given the unpredictability of future trading environments. Indeed, future managerial work will be influenced by a need to manage innovation and change, growing workforce diversity, globalization and concern with quality and continuous improvement.

Similarly, to take advantage of future dynamics, organizations must ensure swift responses to environmental shifts, concern themselves with quality and include employees in decision-making. They must also maintain a customer focus and, where possible, become smaller and more flexible.

Several of these recommended future organizational characteristics are already present in the hospitality, leisure and tourism sector. Some consider these factors unique and instrumental in creating a management style that is predominantly despotic and operationally focused. These factors include:

- training
- semi-skilled jobs and labour turnover
- employees and the total reward system
- flexible organizational structures
- management training and qualifications
- low barriers to entry.

Reflective practice

1 Identify a management job in practice and observe how the individual carries out their work. Using examples, comment on time spent by the manager undertaking hands-on work and planning, organizing, leading and controlling that of employees. Make an informal ten-minute presentation to the class of the findings.
2 Discuss your understanding of the term manager or management.
3 Critically analyse the statement: 'Managers do not actually do anything.'
4 Identify and explain some key issues impacting on the future practice of management and suggest organizational examples where these changes have already taken effect.
5 Compare and contrast the roles and activities between top and first-line managers for:
   (a) a large leisure centre
   (b) a small hospitality or tourism organization of your choice.

References

Adams, J. S. (1965). Inequity in social exchanges. In *Advances in Experimental Social Psychology* (L. Berkowitz, ed.) vol. 2, pp. 267–300, Academic Press.

Ajzen, I. and Fishbein, M. (1980). *Understanding Attitudes and Predicting Social Behaviour*. Prentice-Hall.

Aldefer, C. P. (1972). *Existence, Relatedness and Growth*. Collier Macmillan.

Alpander, G. (1991). Developing Manager's Ability to Empower Employees. *Journal of Management* **10**, 13–24.

Anderson, B. A., Povis, C. and Chappel, S. J. (2002). Coping strategies in the performance of emotional labour. Working Paper Abstracts Council for Australian University Tourism and Hospitality Education 2002, National Research Conference, Perth, CAUTHE.

Argenti, P. A. (1998). Strategic employee communications. *Human Resource Management*, **37** (3–4), 199–206.

Ashforth, B. E. and Tomiuk, M. A. (2000). Emotional labour and authenticity: views. In *Emotion in Organizations* (S. Fineman, ed.), Sage.

Ashness, D. and Lashley, C. (1995). Empowering service workers at Harvester Restaurants. *Personnel Review* **24** (8), 17–32.

Atkinson, J. (1985). *Uncertainty and manpower management*. Report no. 89. IMS.

Atkinson, J. and Meagre, N. (1986). Is flexibility a flash in the pan? *Personnel Management* **18** (9), 26–9.

Ball, R. M. (1988). *Seasonality in the UK Labour Market*. Avebury.

Ball, S. and Johnson, K. (2000). Humour in commercial hospitality settings. In *In Search of Hospitality: Theoretical Perspectives and Debates* (C. Lashley and A. Morrison, eds), Butterworth-Heinemann.

Bandura, A. (1977). Self-efficacy: Towards a unifying theory of behavioural change. *Psychological Review* **84**, 191–215.

Bandura, A. (1986). *Social foundations of thought and action: A social-cognitive view*. Prentice-Hall.

Barbee, C. and Bott, V. (1991). Customer treatment as a mirror of employee treatment. *Advanced Management Journal* **5** (27), 45–53.

Barry, T. (1993). Empowerment: The US Experience. *Empowerment in Organisations* **1** (1), 24–8.

Bartol, K., Martin, D., Tein, M. and Matthews, G. (2001). *Management: A Pacific Rim Focus*. 3rd edition. Irwin McGraw-Hill.

Bartunek, J. M. (1981). Why did you do that: attribution theory in organizations. *Business Horizons* September–October, 66–71.

Bateson, J. G. (1985). Perceived control and the service encounter. In *The Service Encounter* (J. A. Czepiel, M. R. Solomon and C. F. Superenant, eds), Lexington.

Baum, T. (1989). Managing hotels in Ireland: research and development for change. *International Journal of Hospitality Management* **8** (2), 131–44.

Bazzett, D. (1999). Communicating effectively. *IABC Communication World*, November, 3–5.

Belbin, R. M. (1993). *Team Roles at Work*. Butterworth-Heinemann.

Berlo, D. K. (1960). *The Process of Communication: An Introduction to Theory and Practice*. Holt, Rinehart and Winston.

Biddle, D. and Evenden, R. (1980). *The Human Aspects of Management*. Institute of Personnel Management.

Blake, J. J. and McCanse, A. A. (1991). *Leadership Dilemmas: grid solutions*. Gulf Publishing.

Blauner, R (1964). *Alienation and Freedom: The Factory Worker and his Industry*. University of Chicago Press.

Bolman, L. G. and Deal, T. E. (1997). *Reframing Organizations*. 2nd edition. Jossey-Bass.

Brownell, J., (1991). Middle managers: facing a communication challenge. *Cornell Hotel and Restaurant Association Quarterly*, February, 52–9.

Butler, R. W. (1980). The concept of a tourist area cycle of evolution: implications for management of resources. *Canadian Geographer* **24**, 5–12.

Byrne, D. (1986). *Working in Hotels and Catering*. LPU.

Cassell, J. (1996). The woman in the surgeon's body: understanding difference. *American Anthropologist* **98** (1), 41–53.

Cattel, R. B. (1973). Personality down. *Psychology Today* July, 40–6.

Cattel, R. B. and Kline, P. (1977). *The Scientific Analysis of Personality and Motivation*. Academic Press.

Chivers, T. S. (1971). Chefs and cooks. PhD thesis, University of London.

Clampitt, P. G. and Downs, C. W. (1993). Employee perceptions of communication and productivity: a field study. *Journal of Business Communication* **30** (1), 5–27.

Comen, T. (1989). Making Quality Assurance Work for You. *Cornell Hotel and Restaurant Quarterly* November, 23–9.

Conger, J. A. (1989). Leadership: The Art of Empowering Others. *Academy of Management Executive* February, 17–24.

Conger, J. A. and Kanungo, R. B. (1988). The Empowerment Process: Integrating theory and practice. *Academy of Management Review* **13**, 471–82.

Cooper, C. L. and Lewis, S. (1989). *How to Manage your Career, Family and Life*. Kogan Page.

Cooper, R. and Sawaf, A. (1997). *Executive EQ*. Orion Business.

Cotton, J. L. (1993). *Employee Involvement*. Sage.

Crompton, R. and Jones, M. (1984). *White Collar Proletariat*. Macmillan.

Cunningham, I. and Hyman, J. (1999). The poverty of empowerment a critical case study. *Personnel Review* **28** (3), 222–41.

Dalen, E. (1989). Research into values and trends in Norway. *Tourism Management* **10** (3), 183–86.

Deal, T. E. and Kennedy, A. (1982). *Corporate Cultures*. Addison-Wesley.

Demming, W. (1986). *Out of the Crisis*. Cambridge University Press.

Department for Education and Employment (DfEE) (1999). *The Leisure Sector. Skills Task Force Research Paper 6*. DfEE.

Department for Education and Employment (DfEE) (2000). *Employer Skill Survey: Case Study Hospitality Sector*. DfEE.

Dickens, L. (1997). Gender, race and employment inequalities in Britain: inadequate strategies and the role of industrial relations actors. *Industrial Relations Journal* **28** (4), 282–90.

Doeringer, P. B and Piore, M. J. (1971). *Internal Labour Markets and Manpower Analysis*. Heath Lexington Books.

Doherty, L., Guerrier, Y., Jameson, S., Lashley, C. and Lockwood, A. (2001). *Getting Ahead: Graduate Careers in Hospitality Management*. Higher Education Funding Council, England.

Eaglen, A. and Lashley, C. (2001). *Benefits and Costs Analysis: The Impact of Training on Hospitality Business Performance*. Leeds Metropolitan University.

Eaglen, A., Lashley, C. and Thomas, R. (1999). *Benefits and Costs Analysis: The Impact of Training on Business Performance*. Leeds Metropolitan University.

Elliot, T. (1969). *Food Service Management*. New University Education.

Ellis, S. and Dick, P. (2000). *Introduction to Organisation Behaviour*. McGraw-Hill.

Eysenck, H. J. (1960). *The Structure of Human Personality*. Methuen.

Fayol, H. (1949). *General and Industrial Management*. Pitman.

Festinger, L. (1957). *A Theory of Cognitive Dissonance*. Stanford University Press.

Fiedler, F. E. (1967). *A Theory of Leadership Effectiveness*. McGraw-Hill.

Fineman, S. (ed.) (1993). *Emotion in Organizations*. Sage.

Fineman, S. (2000a). Emotional arenas revisited. In *Emotion in Organizations* (S. Fineman, ed.), 2nd edition, Sage.

Fineman, S. (2000b). Commodifying the emotionally intelligent. In *Emotion in Organizations* (S. Fineman, ed.), 2nd edition, Sage.

Fox, A. (1973). Industrial relations: social critique of pluralist ideology. In *Man and Organisations* (E. J. Child, ed.) Allen and Unwin.

Fox, A. (1974). *Beyond Contract: Work, Power and Trust Relations*. Faber & Faber.

Francis, A. (1995). The structure of organizations. In *Personnel Management: A Comprehensive Guide to Theory and Practice in Britain* (K. Sissons, ed.), Blackwell.

Frone, M. R. and Major, B. (1988). Communication quality and job satisfaction among managerial nurses. *Group and Organizational Studies* **13** (3), 332–47.

Galbraith, J. (1973). *Designing Complex Organisations*. Addison-Wesley.

Gerloff, E. A., Muir, N. K and Bodensteiner, W. D. (1991). Three components of perceived environmental uncertainty: an exploratory analysis of the effects of aggregation. *Journal of Management*, December, 749–68.

Gilbert, D. and Guerrier, Y. (1997). UK hospitality managers past and present. *Service Industries Journal* **17**, 115–32.

Gilsdorf, J. W. (1998). Organizational rules on communicating: how employees are – and are not – learning the ropes. *Journal of Business Communication* **35** (2), 173–201.

Ginzberg, E., Ginsburg. S., Axelrad, S. and Herma, J. L. (1951). *Occupational Choice*. Columbia University Press.

Givens, B. K. (2002). *Teaching to the Brain's Natural Learning System*. Association of Supervisory and Curriculum Development.

Go, F., Monachello, M. L. and Baum, T. (1996). *Human Resource Management in the Hospitality Industry*. Wiley.

Goldthorpe, J. H., Lockwood, D., Bechhofer, F. and Platt, J. (1968). *The Affluent Worker: Industrial Attitudes and Behaviour*. Cambridge University Press.

Goleman, D. (1998). *Working with Emotional Intelligence*. Bloomsbury.

Graicunas, V. A. (1937). Relationship in organisation. *Papers on the Science of Administration*, University of Colombia.

Gregory, K. (1983). Native view paradigms: multiple cultures and culture conflicts in organizations. *Administrative Science Quarterly* **28** (3), 359–76.

Greiner, L. (1972). Evolution and revolution as organisations grow. *Harvard Business review* **50**, 37–46.

Guerrier, Y. (1987). Hotel managers' careers and their impact on hotels in Britain. *International Journal of Hospitality* Management **6** (3), 121–30.

Guerrier, Y. (1999). *Organizational Behaviour in Hotels and Restaurants: An International Perspective*. Wiley.

Guerrier, Y. and Adib, A. (2000). Working in the hospitality industry. In *In Search of Hospitality: Theoretical Perspectives and Debates* (C. Lashley and A. Morrison, eds), Butterworth-Heinmann.

Guerrier, Y. and Lockwood, A. (1989). Core and peripheral workers in hotel operations. *Personnel Review* **18** (1), 9–15.

Hackman, J. R and Lawler, E. E. III (1971). Employee reactions to job characteristics. *Journal of Applied Psychology Monograph*, No. 55, 259–86.

Hackman, J. R. and Oldham, G. R. (1974). *Motivation through the Design of Work: Test of a Theory*. Yale University Press.

Hackman, J. R. and Oldham, G. R (1980). *Work Design*. Addison-Wesley.

Handy, C. (1984). *The Future of Work*. Blackwell.

Handy, C. (1993). *Understanding Organizations*. 4th edition. Penguin.

Harcourt, J., Richardson, V. and Wattier, J. (1991). A national study of middle managers' assessment of organizational communication quality. *Journal of Business Communication* **28** (4), 348–63.

Harlos, K. P., and Pinder, C. C., (2000). Emotions and injustice in the workplace. In *Emotion in Organizations* (S. Fineman, ed.), 2nd edition, Sage.

Harrison (1972). How to describe your organization. *Harvard Business Review* **50**, May–June, 119–28.

Harvey, D. F. and Brown, D. R. (1996). *An Experiential Approach to Organizational Development*. 5th edition. Prentice-Hall.

Hatch, M. J. (1997). *Organisational Theory, Modern Symbolic and Postmodern Perspectives*. Oxford University Press.

HCTB (1988). *New Employment Forecasts – Hotel and Catering Industry*. HCTB.

HCTC (1994). *Catering and hospitality industry key facts and figures*. Research report. HCTC.

Heider, F. (1953). *The Psychology of Interpersonal Relations*. Wiley.

Herriott, P. and Pemberton, C. (1995). *Competitive Advantage Through Diversity: organizational learning through difference*. Sage.

Hertzberg, F., Mausner, B. and Snyderman, B. B. (1959). *The Motivation to Work*. Wiley.

Heskett, S. H., Sasser, W. E. and Hart, C. W. L. (1990). *Service Breakthroughs: Changing the Rules of the Game*. Free Press.

Hisrich, R. D. and Peters, M. P. (1998). *Entrepreneurship*. 4th edition. Irwin McGraw-Hill.

Hochschild, A. R. (1983). *The Managed Heart: Commercialization of Human Feeling*. University of California Press.

Hochschild, A. R. (1993). Preface. In *Emotion in Organizations* (S. Fineman, ed.), Sage.

Hofstede, G. (1980). *Culture's Consequences: International Differences in Work-Related Values*. Sage.

Holland, J. (1966). *The Psychology of Vocational Choice – A Theory of Personality Types and Model Environments*. Ginn and Co.

Holland, J. (1985). *Making Vocational Choices: A Theory of Vocational Personalities and Working Environments*. 2nd edition. Prentice-Hall.

Honey, M. and Mumford, D. (1986). *Manual of Learning Styles*. BBC Books.

Hospitality Training Foundation (HtF) (2002). *Labour Market Review 2002 for the Hospitality Industry*. HtF.

Huczynski, A. and Buchanan, D. (1985). *Organizational Behaviour: an introductory text*. Pearson Education.

Huczynski, A. and Buchanan, D. (2001). *Organizational Behaviour: an introductory text*. Pearson Education.

Huyton, J. and Ingold, A. (1995). The cultural implications of TQM – the case of the Ritz-Carlton Hotel, Hong Kong. In *Services Management: New Directions, New Perspectives* (R. Teare and C. Armistead, eds), Cassell.

ILO (2001). *Hotel, Catering and Tourism Sector*. Paris: International Labour Office.

Ingold, A., McMahon-Beattie, V. and Yeoman, I. (eds) (1999). *Yield Management Strategies for the Service Industries*. 2nd edition. Continuum.

Ivey, A. E., Ivey, M. B. and Simek-Downing, L. (1987). *Counselling and Psychotherapy: Integrating Skills, Theory and Practice*. Prentice-Hall.

Jameson, M. J. (1987). Hotel shop stewards: the implications of their activities for the development of industrial relations in hotels. MPhil thesis, Huddersfield Polytechnic.

Johlke, M. C. and Duhan, D. F. (2000). Supervisor communication practices and service employee job outcomes. *Journal of Service Research* **3** (2), 154–65.

Johns, N., Chan, A. and Yeung, H. (2002). The impact of Chinese culture upon service predisposition. Unpublished data.

Johnson, K. (1980). Staff turnover in hotels. *Hospitality*, 28–36.

Johnson, P. R. (1993). Empowerment in the Global Economy. *Empowerment in Organisations* **1** (1), 13–18.

Johnson, R. and Redmond, D. (1999). *The Art of Empowerment: the profit and pain of employee involvement*. Financial Times Management.

Johnston, R. (1989). Developing competitive strategies in the service sector. In *Management in Service Industries* (P. Jones, ed.), ch. 7, Pitman.

Joiner, T. (2001). The influence of national culture and organizational culture alignment on job stress and performance: evidence from Greece. *Journal of Managerial Psychology* **16** (3), 229–42.

Jones, E. E. and Gerrard, H. B. (1967). *Foundations of Social Psychology*. Wiley.

Jones, P. and Lockwood, A. (1989). *The Management of Hotel Operations: An Innovative Approach to the Study of Hotel Management*. Cassell.

Jung, C. G. (1968). *Analytical Psychology: Its theory and Practice*. Routledge and Kegan Paul.

Kacmar, K. M. (1997). Further validation of the perception of politics scale (POPS): a multiple sample investigation. *Journal of Management* **23**, 627–58.

Kandampully, J. (2002). *Services Management: The New Paradigm in Hospitality.* Hospitality Press.

Kandampully, J., Mok, C. and Sparks, B. (2001). *Service Quality Management in Hospitality, Tourism and Leisure.* Haworth Hospitality Press.

Kandola, R. and Fullerton, J. (1998). *Diversity in Action: Managing the Mosaic.* IPD.

Karmel, B. (ed.) (1980). *Point and Counterpoint in Organisations?* Dryden.

Kats, D. and Kahn, R. L. (1966). *The Social Psychology of Organisations.* Wiley.

Kelley, H. H. (1973). The process of causal attribution. *American Psychologist* February, 107–28.

Kelly, J. and Kelly, C. (1990). Them and us: social psychology and the new industrial relations. *British Journal of Industrial Relations* **29** (1), 24–37.

Kikoski, J. F. (1993). Effective communication in the intranational workplace: models for public sector managers. *Professional and Organisational Development* Spring, 84–95.

Kolb, D. (1985). *Experiential Learning: Experience as the Source of Learning and Development.* Prentice-Hall.

Kotter, J. P. (1982). What effective general managers really do. *Harvard Business Review* **60** (6), 156–67.

Labich, K. (1995). Winners in the air wars. *Fortune* 11 May, 68–79.

Lashley, C. (1985). Why women don't become chefs. Unpublished thesis, University of Warwick.

Lashley, C. (1995). Towards an Understanding of Employee Empowerment in Hospitality Services. *International Journal of Contemporary Hospitality Management* **7** (1), 27–32.

Lashley, C. (1997). *Empowering Service Excellence: Beyond the Quick Fix.* Cassell.

Lashley, C. (1999). Employee Empowerment in Services: a framework for analysis. *Personnel Review* **28** (3), 169–91.

Lashley, C. (2000a). Empowerment Through Involvement: a case study of TGI Friday's restaurants. *Personnel Review* **29** (5/6), 791–815.

Lashley, C. (2000b). *Hospitality Retail Management: a unit manager's guide.* Butterworth-Heinemann.

Lashley, C. (2000c). Empowered franchisees? In *Franchising Hospitality Services* (C. Lashley and A. Morrison, eds) Butterworth-Heinemann.

Lashley, C. (2001). *Empowerment: HR Strategies for Service Excellence.* Butterworth-Heinemann.

Lashley, C. and Rowson, W. (2000). Wasted millions: staff turnover in licensed retail organisations. In *Ninth Annual Hospitality Research Conference Proceedings* (A. Williams, ed.), University of Huddersfield.

Lashley, C. and Shaw, M. (2002). Student Learning Styles: variations and change. European Learning Styles Network Conference Proceedings, University of Ghent.

Lashley, C., Thomas, R. and Rowson, B. (2002). *Employment Practices and Skill Shortages in Greater Manchester's Tourism Sector.* Leeds Metropolitan University.

Lawler, E. E. (1973). *Motivation in Work Organizations.* Brooks/Cole.

LCAT (1990). *Recruitment Challenges: Tackling the Labour Squeeze in Tourism and Leisure.* NEDC.

Lee-Ross, D. (1996). A study of work motivation amongst seasonal hotel workers in the UK. PhD thesis, Anglia Polytechnic University.

Lee-Ross, D. (1998). Comment: Australia and the small to medium-sized hotel sector. *International Journal of Contemporary Hospitality Management* **10** (5), 177–79.

Lee-Ross, D. (2000). Development of the service predisposition instrument. *Journal of Managerial Psychology* **15** (2), 148–57.

Lee-Ross, D. (2001). A comparison of hospitality and healthcare service predispositions. Working Paper Abstracts Council for Australian University Tourism and Hospitality Education 2001 National Research Conference, Canberra, CAUTHE.

Legge, K. (1995). *Human Resource Management: Rhetorics and Realities*. Macmillan Business.

Leidner, R. (1993). *Fast Food, Fast Talk: Service Work and the Routinization of Everyday Life*. University of California Press.

Leinster, C. (1985). Playing the tipping game. *Fortune Magazine* **112** (11), 139–40.

Levitt, T. (1972). Production-line approach to service. *Harvard Business Review* September–October.

Locke, E. A. (1968). Towards a theory of task motivation and incentives. *Organizational Behaviour and Human Performance* **3**, 157–89.

Lockwood, A. (1996). Empowerment: the key to service quality – an operations perspective. In *Conference Papers – Fifth Annual Hospitality Research Conference*. Nottingham Trent University, Nottingham.

Lovell, G. (2001). Can a hotel entrance be an event? Working Paper Abstracts Council for Australian University Tourism and Hospitality Education 2001 National Research Conference, Canberra, CAUTHE.

Lucas, R. (1995). *Managing Employee Relations in the Hotel and Catering Industry*. Cassell.

Maghurn, J. P. (1984). *A Manual of Staff Management for the Hotel and Catering Industry*. HCTB.

Mann, S. (1998). *Psychology Goes to Work*. Purple House.

Mann, S. (1999). *Hiding What We Feel, Faking What We Don't: Understanding the Role of Emotions at Work*. Element.

Marchington, M., Goodman, J., Wilkinson, A. and Ackers, P. (1992). *New Developments in Employee Involvement*. Department of Employment, Research Series No 2, HMSO.

Marrett, C. B., Hage, J. and Aiken, M. (1975). Communication and satisfaction in organisations. *Human Relations* **28** (7), 611–26.

Mars, G. and Mitchell, P. (1976). *Room for Reform*: A Case Study on Industrial Relations in the Hotel Industry. Open University Press.

Mars, G. and Nicod, M. (1984). *The World of Waiters*. Allen and Unwin.

Mars, G., Bryant, P. and Mitchell, P. (1979). *Manpower Problems in the Hotel and Catering Industry*. Saxon House.

Maslow, A. (1954). *Motivation and Personality*. Harper and Row.

Mayfield, R. M., Mayfield, M. R. and Kopf, J. (1998). The effects leadership motivating language on subordinate performance and satisfaction. *Human Resource Management* **37** (3–4), 235–48.

McClelland, D. C. (1961). *The Achieving Society*. Van Nostrand Reinhold.

McClelland, D. C. (1975). *Power: The inner experience*. Irvington Press.

McGregor, A. and Sproull, A. (1992). Employers and the flexible workforce. *Employment Gazette* **100** (5), 225–34.

McShane, S. and Travaglione, T. (2003). *Organisational Behaviour on the Pacific Rim*. McGraw-Hill Irwin.

Miller, N. E. and Dollard, J. C. (1955). *Personality and Psychotherapy*. McGraw-Hill.

Mintzberg, H. (1973). *The Nature of Managerial Work*. Harper and Row.

Morgan, G. (1986). *Images of Organization*. Sage.

Morgan, G. (1988). *Riding the Waves of Change: Developing Managerial Competencies for a Turbulent World*. Sage.

Morgan, G. (1997). *Images of Organisations*. Sage.

Muchinsky, P. M. (1977). Organization communication: relation to organizational climate and job satisfaction. *Academy of Management Journal* **20** (4), 592–607.

Mullins, L. (1999). *Management and Organizational Behaviour*. Pitman Financial Times.

Mullins, L. (2002). *Management and Organizational Behaviour*. Pitman Financial Times.

Mullins, L. J. (1996). *Management and Organisational Behaviour*. 4th edition. Pitman.

Mullins, L. M. (1992). *Hospitality Management: A Human Resources Approach*. Pitman.

Nailon, P. (1982). Theory in hospitality management. *International Journal of Hospitality Management* **1**, 135–43.

Naisbitt. J. (1993). *Megatrends, Het Spektrum,* Wijnegem.

Orpen, C. (1997). The interactive effects of communication quality and job involvement on managerial satisfaction and work motivation. *Journal of Psychology* **13** (1), 519–22.

Passport to the Sun (2002). Lifestyle Channel, Austar. Broadcast 13 November at 3 p.m.

Pavlov, I. (1927). *Conditioned Reflexes*. Oxford University Press.

Perrow, C. (1967). A framework for the comparative analysis of organizations. *American Sociological Review* April, 194–208.

Peters, T. J. (1993). Thriving on chaos. *Working Woman* September, 29.

Peters, T. J. and Waterman, R. H. (1982). *In Search of Excellence*. Harper and Row.

Pheng, L. S. and Yuquan, S. (2002). An exploratory study of Hofstede's cross-cultural dimensions in construction projects. *Management Decision* **40** (1), 7–16.

Poole, M. (1986). *Towards A New Industrial Democracy: workers participation in industry*. Routledge and Keegan Paul.

Porter, L. W. and Lawler, E. E. (1968). *Managerial Attitudes and Performance*. Irwin.

Potterfield, T. A. (1999). *The Business of Empowerment: democracy and ideology in the workplace*. Quorum.

Prais, S. J., Jarvis, V. and Wagner, K. (1989). Productivity and vocational skills in services in Britain and Germany: hotels. National Institute of Economic and Social Research, London, pp. 151–71.

Putnam, L. L., and Mumby, D. K. (1993). Organizations, emotions and the myth of rationality. In *Emotion in Organizations* (S. Fineman, ed.), 2nd edition, Sage.

Ridley, S. (1995). Towards a new business culture for tourism and hospitality organisations. *International Journal of Contemporary Hospitality Management* **7** (7), 36–43.

Ritchie, J. R. B. (1991). Global tourism policy issues: an agenda for the 1990s. *World Travel and Tourism Review* **1**, 152.

Ritzer, G. (1993). *The McDonaldization of Society*. Pine Forge Press.

Robbins, S. F. (1998). *Organisational Behaviour; Concepts, Controversies, Applications*. 8th edition, Prentice-Hall.

Robbins, S. F. (2001). *Organisational Behaviour*. 9th edition. Prentice-Hall.

Robbins, S. P. and Hunsaker, P. L. (1996). *Training in Interpersonal Skills: TIPS for Managing People at Work*. 2nd edition. Prentice-Hall.

Robbins, S. P., Bergman, R., Stagg, I. and Coulter, M. (2000). *Management*. 2nd edition. Prentice-Hall.

Rodwell, J. J., Kienzie, R. and Shadur, M. A. (1998). The relationships among work-related perceptions, employee attitudes and employee performance: the integral role of communication. *Human Resource Management* **37** (3–4), 277–93.

Roper, A., Brookes, M. and Hampton, A. (1997). The multi-cultural management of international hotel groups. *International Journal of Hospitality Management* **16** (2), 147–59.

Rosenberg, M. J. and Hovland, C. I. (1960). Cognitive, affective and behavioral components of attitudes. In *Attitude Organization and Change* (C. I. Hovland and M. J. Rosenberg, eds), pp. 1–14, Yale University Press.

Salaman, G. (1974). *Community and Occupation*. Cambridge University Press.

Salaman, G. (1979). *Work Organisations: resistance and control*. Longman.

Sanchez, P. (1999). How to craft successful employee communication in the information age. *Communication World* August–September, 9–15.

Sandelands, L. E. and Boudens, C. J. (2000). Feelings at work. In *Emotion in Organizations* (S. Fineman, ed.), 2nd edition, Sage.

Sanzgiri, J. and Gottlieb, J. Z. (1992). Philosophic and pragmatic influences on the practice of organizational development 1950–2000. *Organizational Dynamics* Autumn, 57–69.

Schein, E. H. (1985). *Organizational Culture and Leadership*. Jossey-Bass.

Schmenner, R. W. (1995). *Service Operations Management*. Prentice-Hall.

Senge, P. M. (1990). *The Fifth Discipline: The Art and Practices of the Learning Organisaton*. Currency Doubleday.

Shamir, B. (1975). A study of working environments and attitudes to work of employees in a number of British hotels. PhD thesis, London School of Economics.

Shannon, C. E. and Weaver, W. (1949/1963). *The Mathematical Theory of Communication*. University of Illinois Press.

Sheppard, D. (1989). Organisations power and sexuality: the image and self image of women managers. In *The Sexuality of Organizations* (J. Herren, D. Sheppard, P. Tancred-Sherrif, P. and G. Burrell, eds), Sage.

Sherif, M. (1936). *The Psychology of Group Norms*. Harper and Row.

Simms, J., Hales, C. and Riley, M. (1988). Examination of the concept of internal labour markets in UK hotels. *Tourism Management*, 3–12.

Sisson, K. (1994). Personnel management paradigms, practice and prospects. In *Personnel Management* (K. Sisson, ed.), pp. 3–50, 2nd edition, Blackwell.

Skinner, B. F. (1953). *Science and Human Behaviour*. Macmillan.

Sparks, B. and Bradley, G. (1997). Antecedents and consequences of perceived service provider effort in the hospitality industry. *Hospitality Research Journal* **20** (3), 17–34.

Sparrowe, R. T. (1994). Empowerment in the Hospitality Industry: an Exploration of Antecedents and Outcomes. *Hospitality Research Journal* **17** (3).

Stewart, R. (1982). *Choices for the Manager*. McGraw-Hill.

Stewart, R. (1983). Managerial behaviour: how research has changed the traditional picture. In *Perspectives on Management: A Multidisciplinary Analysis* (M. J. Earl, ed.), pp. 96–97, Oxford University Press.

Stewart, T. A. (1993). Welcome to the revolution. *Fortune* 13 December, 66.

Tannebaum, R. and Schmidt, W. H. (1973). How to Choose a Leadership Pattern. *Harvard Business Review* May/June, 162–80.

Taylor, D. (1983). Taking over. *Catering Times* December, 38.

Taylor, F. W. (1947). *Scientific Management*. Harper and Row.

Thomas, K. W. and Velthouse, B. A. (1990). Cognitive Elements of Empowerment; an interpretive model of intrinsic task motivation. *Academy of Management Review* **15**, 666–81.

Thompson, J. D. (1967). *Organisations in Action*. McGraw-Hill.

Thompson, P. and McHugh, D. (1995). *Work Organisations: a critical introduction*. Macmillan Business.

Thomson, K. (1998). *Emotional Capital*. Capstone.

Tribe, J. (1995). *The Economics of Leisure and Tourism: Environments, Markets and Impacts*. Butterworth-Heinemann.

Trompenaars, F. (1993). *Riding the Waves of Culture*. Brealey.

Turner, A. N. and Lawrence, P. R. (1965). *Industrial Jobs and the Worker*. Harvard Graduate School of Business Administration.

Van Maanen, J. and Barley, S. R. (1992). *Research in Organisational Behaviour* **6**, 287–365.

Van Oudtshoorn, M. and Thomas, L. (1993). A Management Synopsis of Empowerment. *Empowerment in Organisations* **1** (1).

Vroom, V. H. (1964). *Work and Motivation*. John Wiley.

Wahab, S. and Cooper, C. (2001). *Tourism in the Age of Globalization*. Routledge.

Wasserman, V., Rafaeli, A. and Kluger, A. N. (2000). Aesthetic symbols as emotional cues. In *Emotion in Organizations* (S. Fineman, ed.), 2nd edition, Sage.

Weaver, D. and Opperman, M. (2000). *Tourism Management*. Wiley.

Weaver, T. (1988). Theory M: motivating with money. *Cornell Hotel and Restaurant Administration Quarterly* November, 11–17.

Weber, M. (1947). *The Theory of Social and Economic Organisation*. Free Press.

Welford, R. and Prescott, K. (1994). *European Business: An Issue-Based Approach*. 2nd edition. Pitman.

Whyte, W. F. (1948). *Human Relations in the Restaurant Industry*. McGraw-Hill.

Williams, C. (1998). The state of quality management in six leisure related research sites. *TQM Magazine* **10** (2), 95–103.

Windmuller, J. P. (1987). *Collective bargaining in industrial market economies: an appraisal*. ILO.

Witt, C. A and Witt, S. F (1989). Why productivity in the hotel sector is so low. **1** (2), 28–34.

Wood, R. C. (1992). *Working in Hotels and Catering*. Routledge.

Wood, R. C. (1994). *Organisational Behaviour for Hospitality Management*. Butterworth-Heinemann.

Woodward, J. (1958). *Management and Technology*. HMSO.

Woodward, J. (1965). *Industrial Organization: Theory and Practice*. Oxford University Press.

Index

Hospitality, Leisure & Tourism Series